The Tragic End of
the Bronze Age

An original theory unraveling a monumental human catastrophe and the agonizing reemergence from it that made us what we are today.

The Tragic End of the Bronze Age

A Virus Makes History

Tom Slattery

Writers Club Press
San Jose New York Lincoln Shanghai

The Tragic End of the Bronze Age
A Virus Makes History

All Rights Reserved © 2000 by Matthew Thomas Slattery, III

No part of this book may be reproduced or transmitted in any form or by any means, graphic, electronic, or mechanical, including photocopying, recording, taping, or by any information storage or retrieval system, without the permission in writing from the publisher.

Writers Club Press
an imprint of iUniverse.com, Inc.

For information address:
iUniverse.com, Inc.
5220 S 16th, Ste. 200
Lincoln, NE 68512
www.iuniverse.com

First Draft, titled "Tin, Variola, and Iron,"
Copyright 1992 by Matthew Thomas Slattery; III

Matthew Thomas Slattery; III(Tom Slattery)
396 Oak Cliff Ct Bay Village, Ohio 44140-2964
telephone (440) 871-3415
tslat@worldnet.att.net

ISBN: 0-595-12146-2

Printed in the United States of America

To all those who suffered and died from smallpox, ancient and modern

Contents

List of Figures vii
Edited Author's Preface from 1992 xi
Added to Author's Preface/1997 xv
Chapter One 1
   An Unparalleled Catastrophe *3*
Chapter Two 15
   Egypt Before the Catastrophe *17*
Chapter Three 33
   Bible Support Elements *35*
Chapter Four 71
   Late Bronze–age Background *73*
Chapter Five 93
   Biblical Joseph and Haran, and "Neo–hyksos" *95*
Chapter Six 127
   Greek Seepages Across the Barrier of the Dark Ages *129*
Chapter Seven 167
   Tin, the Petroleum of the Late Bronze Age *169*
Chapter Eight 199
   After the Smallpox Epidemic and Disruption of the Tin Trade *201*
Appendix—Other Added Bits 219
Text Notes 233
Index 237

List of Figures

Frontispiece: Map of Ancient Egypt prior to the catastrophe.

Rough Chronology: 2100 BC to 400 BC, xviii

Figure 1, Pyramids at Giza, 14

Figure 2, Map of Nile Delta, Land of Goshen, 32

Figure 3. Simplified cartouches of Tuthmosis and Rameses, 39

Figure 4, Map of Sinai, with Edom, Moab, and Midian, 69

Figure 5, Tomb Model Egyptian Soldiers, 69

Figure 6, Map of Late (Tin) Bronze-age Empires, 92

Figure 7, Amenhotep III, 125

Figure 8, Nefertiti, 125

Figure 9, Akhnaten (Amenhotep IV), 126

Figure 10, Sun Temple Obelisk, Heliopolis, 164

Figure 11, Sphinx at Thebes, 165

Figure 12, Map of Old World showing known tin depositis, 165

Figure 13, Closer map of central Asian tin ore, 166

Figure 14, Map of portages between North Sea and Black Sea , 197

Figure 15 "Ozymandias," Usermaatre Rameses II, 198

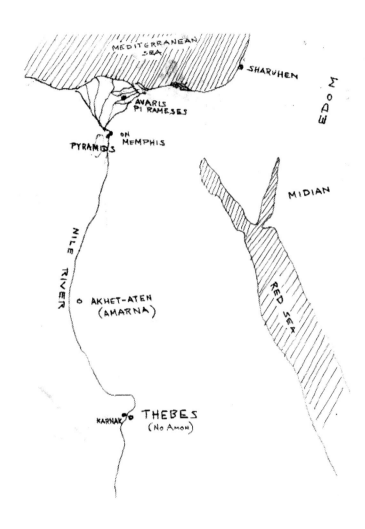

Frontispiece: Map of Ancient Egypt before the Catastrophe.

Edited Author's Preface from 1992

I call this an experiment in history. It falls short of a history, as such.

My notes and references are limited to a minimum necessary. I originally planned to have none at all, but occasional unusual information and hypotheses required explanations or references

The majority of books and periodicals mentioned in *The Tragic End of the Bronze Age* are cross-referenced on computer screens at main libraries, and these can now be instantly accessed on the Internet. The traditional scholarly system of noting publisher, publication date, and city in which published seemed antiquated, especially for a popular history book. Experts will know the material and know where to find information, and the rest of us only need to feel comfort that the facts are accurate and supportable.

Over and above notes, further experiment seemed necessary along another line, historical generalism. History books on this particular ancient time, which still must draw from the science of archaeology, are excruciatingly specialized.

Perhaps because I had no focused academic specialty, I rummaged-up items of general interest that specialized scholars may have overlooked. In addition, I created a wide general framework in which to place them. Conjecture around these seems to offer a new picture of the Late Bronze Age and how, when our collective psyche emerged from this period, we came to think and feel the way we do today.

The Tragic End of the Bronze Age came about by accident. In the fall of 1987, just before the stock market crashed, I found myself in the unemployment line. With an unemployment check coming in, and no employment likely, I began to hang around local libraries.

The history sections were the least used and therefore the quietest and least disturbing. I rummaged through the time of the Trojan War and the Exodus. Over the weeks, I became aware that something had happened, something had destroyed ancient civilizations rather suddenly, and Classical and Biblical writers seemed to have been attempting to preserve and recover from remnant oral traditions something of a greatness that had been and was now lost—to them in their time, apparently forever.

I kept looking into it. One thing bothered me. Books covering the Late Bronze Age were very segregated by both scholarship discipline and geographical area. There were, for instance, books on the stone age, the bronze age, the iron age, and then these tended to be divided by region, Europe, Mesopotamia, Egypt, East Asia, etc.

Then there were scholarly works on the Judeo-Christian Bible. When covering historical background, they were focused in the area we know as ancient Canaan. Separate from these were scholarly works on Classical and pre-Classical Greece and Crete. Archaeologists tended to become further segregated. There were books on Mesopotamia, further divided into Sumer, Babylonia, Assyria, and other local ancient civilizations. There were books on ancient Egypt, but these largely ignored Egypt's complex relationships with other proto-nations in the area.

Intensely scholarly works were mixed in with popular books. The latter advanced adventurous theories while the former thoughtfully explicated ancient remnants.

It seemed to me that by the 1990s enough had been gathered and evaluated to move from a localized discovery-phase of archaeology to more generalized historical overviews. Ancient languages had been deciphered. Documents had been widely translated. The science of linguistics had been enhanced with computers to trace movements. Advances in chemistry and nuclear physics permitted precise dating as well as tracing of material in archeological artifacts back to original mineral deposits.

Radiocarbon dating techniques used mass spectrometers to reach back farther and with more accuracy. Other dating systems had been established with wide scholarly acceptance. If, this far back in history, precise dates were not possible, general timeframes were now known and accepted.

What I most longed to find in those down-and-out but mentally stimulating days in the library was a thoughtful historical overview of what we call the Late Bronze Age and the Iron Age, even by an amateur. But none turned up.

While rummaging, I kept finding things, things that no one else—possibly for lack of a need for a generalized overview—had yet questioned.

For instance, while researching for my screenplay adaptation of Mary Shelley's *The Last Man*, I came across a popular book on ancient mummies that had a good clear photograph of the unfortunate pharaoh Rameses V—a picture worth well over a thousand words and offering a dramatic new theory on the last days of the Bronze Age.

Even while suspecting I had hit upon something, so uneducated and unfamiliar was I with the whole field that I had to look up when he had reigned. When I did, it fit exactly with a forming hypothesis, and as a result, I believe I discovered something significant and exciting about what happened to our ancestors and why we are the way we are.

It had been there, cryptically, in the ancient histories, in the ancient poetic literature, and in the foundation documents of our present three great Western religions. No one had seen it. It explained why great civilized empires had fallen, why strategic mineral access over which great wars had been fought mattered no more, why great fortresses to protect vital trade routes and great monuments to no-longer-worshiped gods lay in ruins.

By early 1991, I had accumulated a drawer full of notes and preliminary written sketches. I decided to write it up for you interested readers.

One final word: we have all inherited a universally used present-day secular calendar. It once had a religious foundation, but is now simply the worldwide means of marking time. BC in this book therefore means *B*efore *C*alendar, avoiding the clumsiness of BCE, and if AD is utilized two or three times, it is to clarify on which side of this time scale we are talking.

July 11, 1992
Tom Slattery
Bay Village, Ohio

Added to Author's Preface/1997

Five years went by. The earlier text, hastily written under abominable writing conditions, contained errors. I had made it up into small desktop-published books and handed them around. I have some regrets at having jumped the gun.

I sit here at the same, now five-year-old, computer in the same unheated former porch-area window hastening to get the writing done and printed out before winter, when it gets too uncomfortable in here.

The Tragic End of the Bronze Age was never meant to be, and still is not, a scholarly work. The minimal notations are meant more for reference-interest and clarification than support. Scholars who know the material should be familiar with it. Average readers may find the references useful for further reading.

The ancient historical facts are, to the best of my knowledge, as accurate as history has left us with them. My speculations and assertions around them are common-sense reasoning. The resulting conclusions and implications may sometimes run contrary to accepted understandings, but this was purposeful and should be interesting and thought provoking to scholars and history buffs alike, even where they may sometimes disagree.

October 27, 1997
Tom Slattery
Bay Village, Ohio

chronology

years BC

Around 2120 BC, "Thebes" (No-Amen) replaces Memphis (Hikaptah) as capital of Egypt. ⇒

2000 ⇒		1900	⇒	1800
3rd dynasty of Ur conquered & Pharaoh Sesostris I & Arsenic-Bronze Age	Achaean-Minoan Aegean culture-invasion-merger	Amenemhet III builds "Labyrinth" at Fayyum, Egypt & Sesostris III expands empire		Hammurabi makes laws in Babylon

1700	⇒	1600	⇒	1500
Hyksos pharaoh "Salitis" (Mae-ibu-re Sheshi) builds capital, **Avaris**	Hittite Empire begins in Turkey	Aryan invasions & Tin-Bronze-Age begins.	Aegean volcano-island Thera explodes	**Avaris** falls, New Kingdom Egypt begins

1400	⇒	1300		1200
Thutmosis IV "marries" a Mitani princess, son, Amenhotep III "marries" Mitanni princess Tiya, son⇒	Amenhotep IV marries Nefertiti changes name to **Akhnaten**, builds city of Akhet-aten	Smenkhakhare, Tutankhamen, Ai & Horemheb destroys Akhet-aten, revives Amen-Re religion	Seti I battles Hittites. **Rameses II** battles Hittites, peace treaty "signed."	**Rameses III** Sea Peoples war. Troy? Exodus? Rameses V dies of smallpox.

1100	⇒	1000	⇒	900
Old World civilizations vanish rapidly. Rameses XI, the last of the Rameses.	Joshua conquers, then "Judges," Saul, and David in Israel.	Solomon builds temple, marries Egyptian princess.		Iron technology in use Homer writes down oral ballads. "Old Testament" begins to be put in writing.

800	⇒	700	⇒	600
Heyday of new Assyrian Empire. Egypt recovers temporarily.		Saite (restored almost-Egyptian) Dynasty in Egypt.		Nebuchadnezzar, rules new Babylonian Empire, Solomon's temple destroyed.

⇒ Aeschylus (525-456 BC), Sophocles (495-406 BC), and Euripides (484-407 BC) write dramas about ancient "mythical Greek" Thebes, and Argos.

Rough Chronology: 2100 BC to 400 BC.

Chapter One

An Unparalleled Catastrophe

In the twelfth and eleventh centuries BC, centered within a single generation between 1150 and 1130 BC, an unparalleled catastrophe struck. There was an enormous decline in population. Empires suddenly collapsed. Whole nations and cultures abruptly ceased to exist.

Throughout the Old World, governments evaporated. Economies collapsed. Mighty military machines vanished.

Where arts and music had flourished, skills and traditions died. Where trade and commerce had prospered, the legal and business structures virtually concluded final transactions and fell forever silent. Written languages faded and disappeared.

Cherished religions slipped into oblivion to be replaced by new ones. Civilized societies came crashing to an end and were replaced by more severe survival governances.

It sounds like the stuff of science fiction—the familiar nuclear war aftermath—and in a way it was. But fiction it was not. Three thousand years ago it actually happened to our remote ancestors, and the world fell into its longest and deepest dark age, lasting as much as seven or eight hundred years.

In the chaos and turbulence following the catastrophe, oral tradition superseded written documentation. We are now left only with vague fragments to point to its cause.

Written records in new languages gradually reemerged over the long centuries, but by then all that remained for poets, dramatists, historians, and religious writers—from whom we must obtain most of our present information—were oral ballads and folk tales. What really had happened had slipped away, and the best of minds could only speculate—as we continue today.

But while the cause and historical specifics were lost, the unparalleled catastrophe left profound lasting effects on thought and belief—on how we think, what we believe, and as a result what we are today.

At virtually the same time as the onset of the catastrophe, Moses fled Egypt and initiated the basis of Western monotheism. A little to the north, the fortress Troy fell at or just prior to the onset of the catastrophe, the story of its heroic defense and eventual capture by clever military ruse forming the bases of a wide swath of Classical Greek and Roman literature centuries later, thus having some influence on the literary and scholarly bases of Western thought through the subsequent ages.

Most of the great ancient Greek dramatic works of Aeschylus, Sophocles, Euripides, and Aristophanes, written in the sixth century BC, are set suggestively just prior to the time of the twelfth century BC catastrophe, and some of the earliest surviving ancient Greek writings of Homer and to some extent Hesiod, composed in the ninth century BC, refer back, as with a certain nostalgic yearning, to the final years of this seemingly greater age, as if to preserve something mysterious but important across the boundary between the ancient and the emerging modern world.

It would greatly serve our understanding of ourselves if we would closely examine what happened, carefully but creatively utilizing the fragmented remnants that have somehow survived three millennia.

Let's begin with a quick general survey of known historical facts.

Between 1150 BC and 1050 BC, all the great bronze-age civilizations of the Western World came crashing to an end. Some vanished forever. Others retained recognizable continuity with the past, but revival took place only after centuries of the world's longest dark age.

The Hittite Empire completely disappeared, and the Hittites themselves slipped shortly into oblivion along with their language and culture. The Achaean and Danaan Greeks of Homer's ballads all but totally vanished, along with the whole Mycenaean-era Greek civilization.

Not only did the Egyptian New Kingdom suddenly come to an end, Egypt itself slid into sharp decline and came under a series of foreign dominations lasting three thousand years until 1952, when Egypt declared itself a republic and negotiated the withdrawal of the last British colonial military forces to at long last regain its independence. What we popularly call Ancient Egypt, the proud mighty imperial bronze-age nation of hieroglyphics, pyramids and great temples, collapsed, eventually into monumental desert wreckage. Nineteenth century English poet Percy Bysshe Shelley symbolically captured how we still feel in his poem about the broken statue of a haughty New Kingdom Egyptian monarch, *Ozymandias* (the pharaoh Rameses II) and what remained of all he had ruled, lived for, and stood for:

> ...Round the decay
> Of that colossal wreck, boundless and bare
> The lone and level sands stretch far away.

Similar to Egypt, in Mesopotamia civilizations collapsed, and Babylonia and Assyria reemerged as something different. Canaanite culture and language became extinct except in forms preserved in Hebrew culture and language. In Europe shortly after 1200 BC, the bronze-age Tumulus Culture was replaced by the interim Urnfield Culture which cremated its dead, which was in turn superseded after two or three centuries by the early iron-age Hallstatt Culture, sometimes called, with a touch of euphemism, the Celtic Empire. And elsewhere Old World nations and cultures vanished. Even in far-away China, the Shang Dynasty civilization collapsed and disappeared forever.

In short, all over the known and literate world cities and civilizations vanished into mounds of earth awaiting rediscovery by modern archaeologists. Their ancient languages slipped away until modern scholars learned again to read them.

A catastrophe like this would certainly have been accompanied by the most thorough economic collapse the world has ever known, and that seems to have been the case. One of its visible manifestations was a disruption of trade in strategic minerals, especially rare and vital tin for making bronze, which brought an end to the Bronze Age.

In the centuries following the catastrophe a psychological fallout was deposited that left in minds an envious awe of the scattered monumental wrecks of ancient bronze-age civilizations and a resignation that the glory and lush living of the past had permanently slipped from human grasp. Accompanying it, a new view emerged that not only the anciently accepted personal judgment day awaited each human when his or her time was up, but that a shadow of Armageddon and apocalypse now hung over the human race as a whole.

Centuries after the catastrophe, when new literate iron-age societies began to coalesce into nations and empires, this awe and resignation began to be transcribed from surviving oral liturgies, secular and religious oral ballads, and folk tales. By then objective first-person accounts of bronze-age civilization had disappeared, and the new scribes and scriptures could only access remnants retained in altered artistic forms.

By the time of Homer, Hesiod, and the early writers of the Bible, three to four centuries after the catastrophe, the writer-preservationists, who were then living amid rampant warlordism and in survival economies during final phases of recovery, could no longer even begin to grasp the human achievement and magnitude of civilization in the distant history of their past. They wrote down and preserved what they could, but they appear to have understood the great ancients largely in terms of their own contemporary petty feudalistic societies.

Where four centuries earlier there had been bureaucracies, schools, written laws, recorded business transactions, documented court decisions, labor trained and organized to build magnificent temples, and high levels of art and culture, there remained only wrecked monuments and balladic oral histories. Where there had once been government, trade, growing expectations, and large disciplined standing armies, there had evolved generally crude warlordism ruling over societies suffering at existence levels.

For centuries people gazed on the monumental ruins and fictions emerged to explain away their awe and amazement. Increasingly remote progeny, who groped to understand these products of educated human minds and organized trained labor, concocted and passed on tales of superhuman forces, and left future generations ignorant of ancient human effort and knowledge.

Until new Assyrian, Babylonian, Greek, Jewish, and Persian imperial governments and civilizations began to emerge from the social and economic chaos four to six centuries after the catastrophe, there was no context from which even the best of minds could draw to fully appreciate that mere human beings just like themselves had accomplished the ruined remnants of remarkable things. And even then one can imagine it was difficult for them to see how civilizations ranging from centuries to millennia into the ancient past could have been more sophisticated, and in most ways more advanced, than the ones they were in the processes of painfully constructing far down the river of time.

It is easy to see, then, how perceptive minds like Hesiod came to believe that humanity had successively degenerated from superior noble forms. Strikingly the reverse of our present scientific comprehension of improving hominid forms and subsequent progress in human societies, technologies, and values, Hesiod—who like Homer lived 300 years after the catastrophe and drew from contemporary views—perceived the world as having declined from an age of golden men to an age of silver men, then an age of bronze men, then briefly recovering into an age of heroes, and then finally, in his time, having again declined to an age of grimy groveling iron men.[1]

Interestingly, in "The Five Ages," Hesiod seems to preserve a remnant of then held historical knowledge in placing his age of Homeric heroes at the end of his bronze age and prior to his iron age. Also, his placement of iron men as the last in the series, as if degenerated further, may betray the slow progress and sorry state of iron technology development up to his time, a widely utilized but less desirable metal than bronze in 800 BC.

The three centuries between the time of the catastrophe and the time of Homer and Hesiod were themselves unique in recorded human history. Unlike all other catastrophes that affected human progress following the end of the last ice age, the catastrophe of the twelfth century BC stands out alone as having virtually destroyed civilization itself—destroyed it as opposed to setting it back some as did the collapse of the Roman and Han Chinese empires a millennium-and-a-half later. During the intervening ten generations the civilized structures of the past had all but slipped away except for monumental ruins and growingly garnished folk tales and oral ballads from which the likes of Hesiod and Homer would draw their knowledge and inspiration.

A high-end number reflecting the magnitude of the population decimation devastation is noted by William R. Biers in the beginning of "The Dark Ages," the fourth chapter of his widely used textbook *The Archeology of Greece*. There he states that the population of Mycenaean-era Greece declined as much as 75 percent during the disaster that destroyed the civilization of Homer's heroes. If this estimated loss of three-fourths of population is extrapolated to other areas known to have been in contact with the Mycenaean-era Greeks, the scope of this great tragedy is without question unparalleled in history.

Certainly there is ample evidence, and therefore wide agreement among historians and archaeologists, that somewhere between 1200 BC and 1000 BC, and centering on about 1150 BC, a disaster accompanied by an enormous drop in population occurred throughout the Old World.

If it was not quite that mind-boggling seventy-five percent depopulation, it was still a staggering percent, and a huge number of people suddenly died off in a population decimation catastrophe apparently far worse than anything known to have preceded or followed it in human history, including the famous Black Death in Europe almost 2500 years later.

But what caused it? What could have caused this catastrophic sudden drop in population that perhaps triples the tragedy of the one-fourth decline in medieval Europe's Black Death? There is one powerful remaining clue after thirty centuries, one evidentiary "smoking gun" on which to build a whole new picture of the end of the Bronze Age, the beginning of the Iron Age, and the framework of our modern world.

In about 1141 BC, after a brief reign of three years, the pharaoh Rameses V died and was properly mummified. Fortunately his mummy still exists because on the mummified epidermis is the "smoking gun" pointing to the culprit in the great catastrophe. Rameses V's mummified body is covered with what are almost certainly mummified smallpox vesicles.

A good photograph showing these skin eruptions, along with a qualified diagnosis of smallpox, can be seen in *Mummies, Disease, and Ancient Cultures*, edited by Aidan and Eve Cockburn, Cambridge University Press, 1980.

In 1911 the British archeologist Sir M. A. Ruffer found the lesions on the mummy of Rameses V to be consistent morphologically and histologically with smallpox. He co-authored a paper, "An Eruption Resembling That of Variola in the Skin of a Mummy of the Twentieth Dynasty (1200-1100 BC)".[2] While presenting a good case for the lesions being those of smallpox, Ruffer, with admirable nineteenth century British scientific objectivity and reserve, cautiously called it "probable existence of small-pox."

Few diseases cause skin eruptions that closely mimic smallpox. It appears that this unlucky pharaoh died of whatever disease caused the skin eruptions, and very few diseases other than smallpox with this type of skin eruption are fatal at that stage of the disease.

The remarkably catastrophic drop in population coincided with the time of Rameses V's death. So while Ruffer may have been professionally cautious, it not only seems reasonable to assume that Rameses V died of smallpox, but to assume that there was a great smallpox epidemic raging at the time of his death. This circumstantial evidence would at least appear acceptable for the sake of an argument to open an inquiry.

Exactly when or where the epidemic struck first may never be known. Precise dates this far back in history are hard to pin down. In his careful analyses of ancient Mycenaean, Canaanite, and other related pottery, the Swedish pottery expert Arne Furumark establishes a pottery period, with a notation comment on a possibly related "catastrophe zone," beginning in 1125 BC[3]. The date is close to the date of the apparent smallpox death of the pharaoh Rameses V in 1141 BC, and the date of the pharaoh's death fits nicely into the "catastrophe zone" concept as a whole.

Possibly, then, the most devastating effects of the epidemic were focused in the span of about one generation just past the middle of the twelfth century BC. The scenario cannot have been greatly different from what happened in modern times when smallpox struck the Aztec Empire and adjacent Native Mexican nations during the conquest of Mexico. There, as we can assume was the case in the ancient Old World, the native population had no resistance to the disease, and as soon as Cortez and his European army brought it ashore, people began dying like flies.

This very image, in fact, is recorded by in *History of the Indians of New Spain*, by Motolinia—pen name of Fray Torobio—who arrived in Mexico during the Conquest. Written in 1541, exactly twenty years after Cortez accepted the surrender of the Aztec Emperor, it paints a gruesome picture we can easily extrapolate back to an earlier time in the Old World. To quote the 1950 translation by Elizabeth Foster:

> "For as the Indians did not know the remedy for the disease and were very much in the habit of bathing frequently, whether well or ill, and continued to do so even

when suffering from smallpox, they died in heaps, like bedbugs. Many others died of starvation, because, as they were taken sick at once, they could not care for each other, nor was there anyone to give them bread or anything else. In many places it happened that everyone in a house died, and, as it was impossible to bury the great number of dead, they pulled down the houses over them in order to check the stench that rose from the dead bodies so that their homes became their tombs. This disease was called by the Indians 'the great leprosy' because victims were so covered with pustules that they looked like lepers."[4]

California State University professor Francis F. Berdan notes in his book *The Aztecs* the effect of new European diseases. Fifty years after the Conquest, the Native Mexican population was one-half to one-third its preconquest size. In view of the above observation by Motolinia, it seems safe to assume that most of the deaths had been caused by the *variola* (smallpox) virus. In this book Berdan includes an illustration taken from the *Florentine Codex*, drawn from life shortly after the Conquest, graphically shows Native Mexicans suffering and dying from smallpox. It was a terrible tragedy and obviously caused a variety of people to record it.

Tragic though it was, these records from recent historical times give us a glimpse of what probably happened when smallpox first struck in the Old World—most likely in the twelfth century BC. In Mexico a great empire and surrounding nations with magnificent temples, good roads and communications, governmental structures, and written language on a paper-like material, suddenly collapsed—not so much from European weapons as from European disease. In an eerie haunting replay of an earlier mass-tragedy in the Old World, a pre-iron-age civilization with pyramids and hieroglyphic written language was suddenly stuck by the *variola* virus and half to two-thirds of the population died off within a generation.

But there is a very big difference to remember. When smallpox struck in the ancient Old World two-and-a-half millennia earlier, there was no new civilization to immediately replace and restructure the old. Civilization just fell apart and did not return for centuries.

To more fully grasp the impact, imagine something like that happening today. While we have AIDS among us now, about the only imaginable modern parallel to the ancient smallpox catastrophe would be a hypothetical limited nuclear war with a sudden three-fourths loss of population and the destruction of our complex social, economic, educational, and governmental structures. One year there is civilization, ease of living, and quality of life; the next there is barbarism and struggle for survival.

Back when Moses, Rameses III, and Agamemnon were young, just prior to the catastrophe, there was civilization. Suddenly something terrible happened and survivors would never see civilization return in their lifetimes—nor would their children and progeny after them for centuries. Educated survivors may have been able to steal moments from the dull grind of survival to quietly think and reflect, but the social context of respect for time and ease in which to think and create had evaporated. Every individual was suddenly out for himself and herself, with little time for anything else but survival necessities.

Those who grew food in their own gardens and guarded it against marauders were most likely those who survived. Those who fled into the wilderness or desert and lived off of the land also had better chances than those who remained among infected populations.

Those who stole from the dead very likely caught the virus, which remained infectious on garments, walls, implements, and bodies themselves for up to two months. Those who stole from the sick caught the disease because not only physical contact but airborne sneezes and breaths spread it. The best strategy against infection would probably have been to take a few healthy friends, servants, and family members out away from everyone else, plant a few crops, live off the land, and stay isolated.

Across the Middle East and Eastern Mediterranean great cities and formidable fortresses were abandoned and left to rot or sometimes burned to the ground. Where burial had been the norm in funeral practices, cremation often replaced it. It is as if survivors—if only because they were survivors—minimized potential contact with infected areas and infected corpses.

Egypt, the most magnificent civilization that had ever existed until the catastrophe, must have suffered terribly, a great tragedy worthy of great poetic drama and religious message. Fragments alluding to its glory and collapse can still be found in the first five books of the Bible, and several strong hints pointing to a smallpox epidemic would also seem to have survived centuries of oral tradition, poetic license, and religious-political redaction of later texts. But before warily extracting these strong hints from this ancient text meant for religious teaching rather than preservation of historical fact, a chapter sketching ancient imperial Egypt and creatively assembling fragments of the surviving text and thoughtful speculation is necessary in order to understand the context.

Tangled in the Egyptian historical backdrop against which the latter parts of Genesis and then Exodus were played out are other powerfully dramatic stories, some of which may have found their way into the Western literary background. Therefore before investigating some intriguing allusions to an apparent smallpox epidemic in Exodus, Joshua, and other related biblical books, we should pause and skim through what has been learned to date about this fascinating five-century period in Egyptian history, from the Hyksos occupation of northern Egypt, through their subsequent defeat and expulsion into Canaan a century later, and the resultant New Kingdom Egyptian empire that lasted four hundred years until the great population decimation catastrophe.

Figure 1: Pyramids at Giza, designed and built by humans, not gods or space aliens.

Chapter Two

Egypt Before the Catastrophe

When the catastrophe struck, Egypt was the greatest civilization yet to exist in the world, the focal point of wealth, power, the arts, education, and technology. One only has to look at items found in tombs to see that upper class Egyptians lived as well as anyone would live until virtually our own time. They had modern-looking chairs on which to sit and modern-appearing beds to on which to sleep. Women wore sleek stylish clothes and jewelry, dabbed on scents from glass perfume bottles, and put on almost modern facial makeup. At banquets they were entertained by musicians who played in concert, and modern research has shown that the eight-tone Western scale was the basis of their music.

The mighty, well organized, and highly trained Egyptian army fought not only with whole regiments of armored chariots and infantry using bronze swords but had divisions of archers using laminated bows that could shoot arrows through metal armor. The country could not only field armies numbering in the tens of thousands but also logistically supply these armies in distant foreign wars.

The great ancient ruined Egyptian structures speak across the millennia for themselves. To construct them required organized labor, engineering knowledge, architectural plans, and sound healthy economies, all of which in turn betray extensive organized educational institutions. By the time ancient Egypt came suddenly and grindingly to a halt with the collapse of the New Kingdom at the end of the twelfth century BC, educational and religious institutions would probably have been steadily growing and developing for over twenty centuries. For a grasp of the length of time, recall that our present most widely used calendar begins only twenty centuries ago.

When it collapsed, the New Kingdom Egyptian Empire period itself was entering its fifth century. By comparison, the United States as a nation goes back only two centuries. A thousand years before day one in our calendar, a great tragedy struck. Two thousand years of continuous ancient Egyptian national history and five centuries of New Kingdom Egyptian history came to a sudden end.

Right in the middle of its long ancient history, Egyptian civilization built the great pyramids—eight to ten centuries prior to the catastrophe. As remarkable as these are, they do not stand as solitary monuments. Nowhere else in the world, even to this day, is there such a plethora of impressive temples, sculptures, and monuments scattered throughout an ancient or modern national countryside as you find in Egypt.

The great temples that amaze tourists far up the Nile at Karnak and Luxor—the latter still the largest and among the most beautiful religious edifices in the world—were last modified just fifty years before the catastrophe struck. When the man who had ordered these last modifications, the pharaoh Rameses II, died in about 1225 BC, Egypt was confidently the technological and cultural center of the ancient world, an almost modern nation with a military-backed political-economic empire second to none and with a government operating not unlike those of large nations in very recent history.

Early in the long reign of this last of the truly great pre-catastrophe pharaohs, a simmering power struggle with the Hittite Empire over territorial hegemony erupted into a real war that culminated in a great battle between the Hittite Empire and the Egyptian Empire and all of their minor allies at a place called Kadesh in what is now Syria. Two well organized and logistically well supplied armies, perhaps totaling between them a hundred thousand soldiers, fought each other to a draw with bronze weapons and military chariots. While the great gory battle produced no victor, it did result in the world's first known written peace treaty, and both of the virtually identical Hittite and Egyptian texts have survived to our time.

The battle in particular and the war in general show the level which sophistication in military training, tactics, logistics, and organization had reached. The peace treaty itself betrays a level of sophistication in diplomacy, written word usage, and translation services, and it cannot help but conjure up modern scenes of government representatives sitting around conference tables to hack out the details of a treaty.

Within a century, however, all this civilized sophistication came crashing to an end, and not many pharaohs later Egyptians and everyone else in the Old World were groveling for survival. About these last pre-catastrophe pharaohs there is some minor disagreement concerning succession, but the important thing to note is the short span of time. Basically Merneptah succeeded Rameses II and reigned about ten years, Seti II (Seth II) reigned another ten years. For a few years there was turmoil, and then came the last significant ancient Egyptian pharaoh, Rameses III, followed by two more of little note whom no one remembers for anything in particular, Rameses IV and V.

Last Significant New Kingdom Egyptian Pharaohs

Usermaetre Rameses II	—	c.1279–1212 BC
Baenre Merneptah	—	c.1212–1201 BC
Userkhephrure Seti II	—	c.1201–1195 BC
(insignificant ,or debatable due to turmoil, 6 to 10 years)		
Usermaetre Meryamon Rameses III	—	c.1185–1153 BC
Heqamaetre Rameses IV	—	c.1153–1146 BC
Usermaetre Rameses V (smallpox?)	—	c.1146–1141 BC

Altogether, from the death of Rameses II at the very peak of Egyptian power and civilization until the apparent tragic death by smallpox of Rameses V, there were only a little over fifty years. A child born into the greatness surrounding the reign of Rameses II and surviving a mere two or three decades until the reign of Rameses V would have been overwhelmed by the devastating decline.

A child we know as Moses was certainly born very close to this time, and in the next chapter we will examine some intriguing apparent links in the Exodus account to a smallpox epidemic. Moses and those knew and accepted him as their leader would seem to have lived before and during, and survived the catastrophe.

Moses may have been living, possibly growing into adulthood, maybe already middle aged, during the two decades of Merneptah's and Seti II's reigns. But somewhere in this period of time he was beginning to play his enormously influential role in history. It is in this time, just before or after Seti and Merneptah, that the early events of the Book of Exodus appear to have taken place.

Importantly here though, only a comparatively few years elapsed between the great war between the powerful and almost modern Egyptian and Hittite empires and the end of those empires and civilization itself. A little over twenty years went by between the death of Rameses II and the beginning of the reign of Rameses III, the last of the genuinely great ancient Egyptian pharaohs. Less than a dozen more years quickly slipped by between the end of the reign of Rameses III and the death, quite apparently from smallpox, of Rameses V in 1141 BC. It was apparently during this 30-to-40-year span of time between Rameses II and Rameses V that Moses led a small band of people then and now known as Hebrews out of the Nile Delta and into the Sinai as a first step toward occupying Canaan.

This span of time also includes the Trojan War, which archaeologists and historians generally agree probably took place roughly around 1200 BC. In his book *In Search of the Trojan War*, Michael Wood notes that the "Parian Chronicle Marble" (now among the Arundel Marbles at Oxford. Early dates are lost from damage in the civil war between Cromwell and Royalists, but a copy of it was fortunately made by John Selden, preserving dates back to the 14th century BC) gives a precise but dubious date for the fall of Troy, June 5, 1209 BC. The classical date for the fall of Troy is 1194 BC. If not precisely known, the timeframe of the legendary war is known to archaeologists to be within a few years of the beginning of the reign of Rameses III (c 1185-1153 BC), who either succeeded Seti II or came a few years later after some turmoil or another unrenowned pharaoh.

Rameses III was the last of the great pharaohs. Under him, the last great battle of imperial Egypt took place. The Sea Peoples had been raiding Mediterranean coastal cities, spreading havoc and disrupting trade. Under Rameses III the Sea Peoples were defeated on both land and sea as they attempted to enter the Nile Delta and northern Egypt, and graphic scenes of the great battles can still be seen on Rameses III's funeral temple at Medenet Habu. The scenes show the ships, the uniforms, the nationalities, and the weapons, and these must have been almost identical to those seen in the Trojan War and by the mythical Ulysses in his subsequent adventures. It has been suggested that the real man the mythical Ulysses represented was, in fact, one of these Sea Peoples raiders.

Some archaeologists conjecture that raiding Sea Peoples caused the downfall of all these ancient empires, but thoughtful questions sorely test this hypothesis. Could the great Greek fortresses of Mycenae, Tiryns, Gla and others have fallen to Viking-like Sea Peoples? Consider how long it took the well organized naval and military strength of Achaean Greek nations to bring down the great fortress of Troy—and then, as the story goes, only by ruse. The Sea Peoples may have helped to spread disease, but their raids seem unlikely to have caused the sudden collapse of bronze-age civilization.

Moreover, could the Sea Peoples have abandoned their ships and marched inland to the Hittite capital and then gone on for weeks to reach the Assyrian and Babylonian empires after fighting that battle? Even when the Sea Peoples had the advantage of their warships, they were soundly defeated in the Nile Delta by the Egyptians, who did not have great fortresses there and used a simple trick of stretching nets across rivers and canals to trap Sea Peoples' ships.

The same questions can be asked of other, and likely related, great migrations thought by some to have occurred during this increasingly chaotic time. Could Dorians or any other nomadic or migrating peoples have brought down great fortresses and virtually all of the old empires? It seems equally unlikely. It is more likely that they were epidemic survivors later drawn into a population and power vacuum caused by the probable smallpox catastrophe.

Even if they had represented an organized national or multi-national force, the Sea Peoples would surely seem to have suffered a disastrous and decisive defeat in northern Egypt, and this would have terminated their adventures against organized civilized nations and empires.

As the Sea Peoples were being defeated in the Nile Delta, the tragic smallpox epidemic may already have begun its rapid furious spread through the civilized nations of the Late Bronze Age. Thoughtful reflection and consideration of the known tenacity and terrible infectiousness of the variola virus would single it out as the culprit. The virus remains potentially active on clothing and other materials for up to two months, and over and above physical contact with infected bodies and material goods, it can be spread by a breath or a sneeze from an infected person. That combined with the known widespread interdependent trade networks of the late bronze age and perhaps opportunistic land and sea raids toward the end of the era appears to have brought the bronze age to a sudden horrible end. Even the careful government bureaucracy of Egypt, which planned for natural disasters and attempted to minimize calamity in its empire and even in the lands of its trading partners, could have had little time to study and counter the effects of the epidemic.

It was no slow progressing insidious AIDS epidemic. As it did 2500 years later in Mexico and the New World, it could only have spread sudden death like wildfire.

While early in his reign, Rameses III led the successful campaign against the Sea Peoples, late in his reign he had to deal with an assassination attempt by his own high government officials and may even have been assassinated. Could this have been due to social unrest caused by the havoc of a spreading catastrophic smallpox epidemic? Less than a decade later, his grandson Rameses V died of smallpox. The three pharaohs, Rameses III, IV, and V, would have been better able to isolate themselves than the average Egyptian if an epidemic had been raging through the land, and if they did, only the first two of them managed to do it successfully.

Following the assassination of or assassination attempt on Rameses III, Egypt still retained the vestiges of civilization. The last half of a papyrus scroll summarizing an inquiry into the crime and conspiracy—that has to remind readers in our time of the Warren Commission—still exists. A panel was appointed. Witnesses were called. Judgments were handed down. Some officials who had been appointed to the panel were later found guilty and also suffered harsh ancient Egyptian punishment.

Assassinated or not, when Rameses III died circa 1153 BC, not only Egyptian civilization but civilization in the general sense was teetering on the edge of its greatest disaster. Whether successful or not, the mere assassination attempt on this pharaoh, who was not only revered with deep religious conviction as the living God on earth but probably also admired for having led the victory over the Sea Peoples, shows a serious rent in the Egyptian social fabric.

Rameses III's son may have isolated himself from the epidemic, but his grandson (or perhaps other son) could not. In the few years between the death of Rameses III circa 1153 BC, and the death of Rameses V circa 1141 BC, there must have been spreading social havoc and institutional breakdown. If anything near the 75 percent drop in population estimated to have happened in Greece also occurred in Egypt, or even the one-half to two-thirds drop that occurred in post-Conquest Mexico, it would certainly have meant total economic collapse and social chaos. And if not total, certainly considerable social and economic collapse did occur, and Egypt never recovered.

The political and social landscape in Imperial Egypt in the years prior to the catastrophe and the Exodus is in itself fascinating and has some bearing on subsequent events. Somewhere between a few years or a few decades before the collapse, Moses led a small band of persecuted people out of Egypt and into the Sinai. The word for these people which has come down to us even from that ancient time is Hebrew (*ibri* or *apiru*, and close similarities in ancient Egyptian and its contemporary area languages), but it seems to have represented more a social class than an ethnic group—perhaps an international social class of skilled laborers or commodities traders, with hints of the latter in Genesis. It may also have been a word for a group of condemned political-religious dissidents, possibly a widely used reference to those who had plotted against the state or secretly spread the subversive ideas of heretical religions.

Thoughtful conjecture points to at least one large and formerly powerful, and then later condemned, social class who believed in an outlawed religion. About a century before the Exodus there had been the "Aten heresy" of the pharaoh Akhnaten, who changed his name from Amenhotep IV to advance his cause of proto-monotheism. After about two decades of possibly fanatic government-enforced worship of the new monotheistic sun-disk god, the Aten, the old religion centered on the Theban god Amon-Re was restored. The Aten priests and their devout followers seem to have gradually found themselves becoming outcasts as the Egyptian government and ousted Amon-Re religious institutionalists moved cautiously to reinstate the Amon-Re religion. But they appear to have become outlaws after the pharaoh Horemheb came to the throne five or ten years after the downfall or death of Akhnaten.

After obvious political and religious turmoil during the short reigns of Akhnaten's apparent youthful nephews, Smenkhakhare and Tutankhamon, and his father-in-law, the pharaoh Ay, Horemheb, a military general who married into the royal family, apparently brutally put down the Aten religion. Its shrines and temples were reduced to rubble with bronze sledgehammers, as was Akhnaten's new capital city of Akhet-Aten.

One can easily imagine that people guilty of political and religious heresy were regarded as criminals and treated as such. This would, of course, not only include the Aten proto-monotheists but all other religious and political deviations formerly, but no longer, tolerated in imperial Egypt.

If Atenists, subject foreigners, remnants of the Hyksos, and others suddenly felt the heavy hand of the conservative official Egyptian religious state, it must not have been much different than situation described in Exodus.

The Hebrews in the land of Goshen (as Ahmed Osman points out, *gsm* in ancient Egyptian language, a real, identifiable place in the Nile Delta, the present town of Faqus. Conjecture may also be made that Faqus still retains a hint of one of the two ancient syllables, "qus," and if so could conceivably be a corruption of P-Gsm, "The Goshen" indicating a later assertion of a place of historical importance) may have been made up of a number of these officially despised and oppressed groups.

Three or four centuries before Moses led his people into the Sinai, the Hyksos, who had been foreign rulers of northern Egypt for hundreds of years and appear to have become thoroughly Egyptianized, were overthrown by an Egyptian pharaoh named Ahmose from the southern Egyptian capital that we know by its Hellenistic name of Thebes and in ancient Egypt was called Nut Amen or Ne Amen (City of Amen, hence the city called No, or No Amon, in Nahum 3:8 of Biblical text).

For all but a few years of the four centuries from the defeat of the Hyksos in about 1550 BC until a few years after the catastrophe of the mid-twelfth century BC and the death evidently by smallpox of the pharaoh Rameses V in 1141 BC, Thebes would remain the nominal capital of a united Egypt under the numerous and often outstanding pharaohs of the 18th, 19th, and 20th dynasties of Egypt's most aggressive imperial period known as the New Kingdom.

The century of Hyksos rule in the north of Egypt was clearly an embarrassment to nationalist religious Egyptians. It was the only time until after the great catastrophe of the twelfth century BC that foreigners with foreign gods ruled a large part of Egypt.

For their part, the Hyksos appear to have either tried to soften occupied Egyptian animosities or tried to emulate superior Egyptian culture and civilization. Among other things, they became "pharaohs" and added Egyptian reign names to their own foreign names, so much so that their century of rule in northern Egypt is historically called the 15th and sometimes additionally 16th dynasties.

If they were Canaanite, they were also rather clearly Minoan-Mycenaean-Mediterranean, as all coastal Canaanites then may have been. Livia Morgan and other experts say fragments of wall paintings found in a late Hyksos palace of Avaris are unmistakably Minoan in character[5].

The present accepted meaning of Hyksos is that it comes from a Greek garbling of the Egyptian words *hka-ha-swt*, "people under foreign rulers," but ancient Egyptian historian Manetho's similar sounding term for "Shepherd Kings" may not have been completely wrong. Plays on words tickled ancient fancies more than in our time, and after their defeat, the Hyksos may well have been ridiculed by word play. This probably does not explain some occasional remnant references in Genesis and other Biblical books to shepherds, but it conceivably might.

The Hyksos century fell between four and five hundred years prior to the great population decimation catastrophe. The Hyksos arrived in northern Egypt at the beginning of the era of chariot warfare and the coincidence cannot be discounted. But chariot warfare would appear to have been made possible by the invention of the bronze alloy made from tin-copper, which replaced the earlier and more brittle bronze alloy arsenic-copper and ushered in the Late Bronze Age. So the Hyksos arrived in northern Egypt along with an appetite for the new strategic metal tin-bronze, and may have been, among other things, traders, dealers, and specialists in it.

The Hyksos need mention here because the same Biblical text material used as support for the smallpox epidemic hypothesis sometimes seems tenuously and cryptically linked to the Hyksos occupation of northern Egypt.

One of the Hyksos pharaohs has a strikingly Old Testament-like name, Merwosere Ya'cob-el (alternatively phonetic "Ya'cob-har," circa 1645 to 1635 BC). If nothing else, it shows a historical name "Jacob" in use roughly contemporary with the time that the Biblical Jacob would have lived, give or take a century or two. Some have gone further to suggest that the Hyksos pharaoh may actually have been the Biblical Jacob.

If there may be any historical basis for this presently insupportable speculation, it may be worth additionally pointing out a vague possibility that this pharaoh's Egyptian-language prenomen, or reign name, meaning strong-is-the-love-of-Re, "Merwosere," could lend itself to phonetic-based transliteration of meaningless foreign words across one or more languages, but at very least across Egyptian into proto-Hebrew Canaanite West Semitic, to become something sounding fascinatingly similar to "Israel."

To pursue this wild speculation one step further, might we dare raise a possibility of "Abraham" having been derived from the Egyptian prenomen of the previous Hyksos pharaoh, "Maaibre" or "Mayebre" (Seeing is the heart of Re) Sheshi?

In *Egypt, Canaan, and Israel in Ancient Times*, Donald B. Redford cleverly demonstrates how a longer list of gentlemen called Hyksos can be shortened to six actual Hyksos pharaohs and other *hka-ha-swt* (persons under foreign rulers) who merely appear to have supported the struggle or coup that brought the Hyksos pharaohs to power. He compares his list with that of the circa 300 BC Egyptian historian Manetho, who lived during the early Macedonian-Greek occupation of Egypt and wrote in Greek, thus whose Hyksos names are Hellenized and otherwise distorted by time. Manetho's listing was for centuries the only tangible evidence for the existence of the Hyksos.

The Historical Fifteenth Dynasty & Manetho's Hyksos

1. M³ᵉ-ib-r' Sheshy = Salitis
2. Mr-wsr-r' Ya'kob-har = Bnon/Pachan
3. Swsr.n-r' Khyan = Iannas
4. {—} Yansas-X = Assis
5. Three names of Apophis = Apophis
6. {—} H³mwdi = ———

These six reigns equal a century between 1650 and 1549 BC. (Note that not only does the last name of the second Hyksos pharaoh resemble "Jacob," but also his first name almost seems to have elements that might later become "Israel.")

adapted from list in *Egypt, Canaan, and Israel in Ancient Times*, by Robert B. Redford.

The Hyksos seem to have used little if any military force to obtain control over northern Egyptian territory. It appears from Redford's convincing proposal that the "persons under foreign rulers" had already been in northern Egypt for some time, almost certainly as Mediterranean traders with a retinue of managerial, skilled, and commercially educated people and thus nuclei of commercial power centers unto themselves. The seizure of control may originally have been to restore a local level of law and order amid an Egyptian political collapse, but once having done so the Hyksos found power too tempting and extrication too difficult. The chief executive officers appear to have appointed themselves a "pharaoh" in the Egyptian style, and this effectively established a northern dynasty that ruled for a century until it was militarily defeated and chased out by an Egyptian army into Canaan and perhaps beyond.

In *Black Athena, Volume II*, Martin Bernal compares the Hyksos to modern multi-national corporate executives. He also makes a convincing case that the Hyksos not only came out of what we call Canaan, but that they were involved in founding the Minoan and Mycenaean Greek civilizations as we know them. It would appear that these Hyksos were at least oriented toward Canaanite-Minoan trading civilizations, and their capital we know by its Hellenized name Avaris—derived from its ancient Egyptian name *Hwt Waret*, now called Tel-Ed-Dab'a, a partially excavated ruins in the northeast corner of the Nile Delta—is clearly situated as a Mediterranean trading city. Moreover, the New Kingdom imperial phase of Egyptian history, begun with the conquest of the Hyksos by Ahmose, suspiciously follows the destruction of Minoan and coastal Canaanite civilization as if due to the aftermath of the explosion of the volcanic island of Thera in the Aegean Sea, its resulting tidal wave, and possible global climate change from the ash cloud.

The conquest of the Hyksos capital Avaris by the pharaoh Ahmose may have been taking opportunistic advantage of the physical destruction and resulting political and economic chaos caused by the volcanic explosion and tidal wave. While Bernal now dates the Thera explosion about a century earlier, it is conceivable that Avaris could have been an important symbolic holdout of a deteriorating trading maritime empire, and it may have taken opposing political, economic, and military forces many decades to combine and overcome a complex political-military balancing act of the last Hyksos pharaohs. One is reminded of the long holdout of the last city of ancient Rome, Constantinople, until the Turkish Sultan Mohammed II finally stormed the city shortly before Columbus arrived in the New World. Thus it is possible that the Hyksos may have dwindled gradually, like other examples in history, until opportunistic pharaohs from Thebes finally toppled the last holdout, the fortified Mediterranean city of Avaris.

But there are some notes scrawled on the back of the Rhind Mathematical Papyrus that preserve a Hyksos view of and shed some light on the advance of Egyptian armies on their doomed capital of Avaris, and these notes not only show a militarily quick advance but a strategy aimed at cutting off land supply routes from Canaan, as if those were the only ones left after a massive Mediterranean catastrophe had destroyed ships and shipping.

With a date that would be early July it notes the Egyptian advance from the south to Heliopolis (in Egyptian On or Anu, on the eastern outskirts of modern Cairo).

With a date that would be mid-October it notes that the Egyptian forces captured the fortress of Sile, also called Tjaru (about twenty-five miles directly south of the modern city of Suez and guarding the edge of the Sinai), as if moving strategically to cut off overland support from Canaan to the Hyksos capital due to military intelligence that sea supply lines—ships and docks—had been destroyed by a catastrophe.[6]

Then apparently began the successful siege of Avaris itself, at least in part an Egyptian river-navy equivalent of a Marine Corps campaign and blockade preserved in writing by one of the marines, Ahmose-si-abina, years later in life to become the Egyptian equivalent of an admiral and buried in a small but significant tomb at his home town of El-Kab, near Aswan.

Something would appear to have suddenly upset the balance of power along the Nile and as a result the Hyksos seem to have been rather quickly defeated.

But if the Hyksos may have been militarily conquered, they may not have been entirely or permanently vanquished or vanished from the northern Egyptian political and economic scene.

Goshen (*gsm*) is not far from Avaris, the Hyksos capital city. Since the Hyksos apparently represented leadership of trading peoples, and since the conquering Egyptians clearly can be seen as a religion-oriented centralized government bureaucracy under a strong monarch, it is easy to see that trading and technical class people formerly allied with or led by the Hyksos may have supplied needed skills and trading contacts and worked their way back into power in Egypt.

In his book *Stranger in the Valley of the Kings*, Ahmed Osman makes a very good case that the Egyptian "vizier" (a borrowed modern Turkish word meaning a prime minister with judicial authority) under Tuthmosis

IV, a man with a foreign name of Yuya, was the Biblical Joseph in Genesis. If Joseph were not that particular real historical Egyptian prime minister, the biblical Joseph story in Genesis has at least been found to have historical authenticity in that he and other nonethnic-Egyptians did become Egyptian prime ministers during the empire.

Whether Prime Minister Yuya was Joseph or not, he and possibly others may well have had Hyksos ancestors. Yuya, the real power in Egypt, succeeded in having his daughter, Tiya, married to his boss' son, who became the pharaoh Amenhotep III. Their son, originally Amenhotep IV, changed his name to Akhnaten as he grew increasingly fanatic about his proto-monotheistic sun-worship, the new state religion.

Akhnaten, then, may well have been the grandson of the Biblical Joseph, and in this light the Aten heresy may well have been an attempt to establish proto-Hebrew religion in Egypt. At least one of Akhnaten's surviving Aten prayers bears strong resemblance to one of the Biblical Psalms. (See both in the section following last chapter of this book for comparison.)

Curiously, hundreds of years after the Hyksos had been overthrown, the mighty imperial pharaoh Rameses II erected a stele celebrating the 400th anniversary of the founding of Avaris at his new capital of Pi-Rameses, built on or very near the site of the Hyksos capital of Avaris. One is led to suspect either a strong earlier Hyksos link to the great Egyptian pharaoh, or that this powerful imperial monarch felt compelled to placate remnant Hyksos economic and political power in Canaan and the Egyptian Delta.

Figure 2: Nile Delta, Land of Goshen. 400 years after the founding of the Hyksos capital of Avaris, Rameses II built his capital of Pi–Rameses a stone's throw from it.

Chapter Three

Bible Support Elements

In Canaan, long under imperial Egyptian control, the city of Shechem—with apparent ties to Abraham, Jacob, and Joseph, and the "Hivites" (with an aspirated first syllable hinting improbable but not impossible similarity to the one in Egyptian language for Hyksos, *hka-ha-swt*)—had been known to the Egyptians by that name (*skmm*) since the city was defeated in a conquest of the area by the pharaoh Sesostris II, possibly about the same time as the events described in Genesis 14. Biblical place names like this can often be found in ancient Egyptian and Mideast records.

From the time of Sesostris II on, not only Shechem, but also Canaan (*Kinahhu* in Hurrian; *Ki-na-ah-num* in Mari; possibly *Ki-na-hi* in the Egyptian Amarna letters; and *Kahnanah* in Egyptian itself) as a whole was largely under Egyptian control[7].

Yet if Canaan was so firmly and for so long part of imperial Egypt—for 800 years from about 1900 BC until the great catastrophe circa 1100 BC—to the extent of possibly having supplied Egypt with leadership up to the level of prime minister, why is the Biblical text have Moses leading his people *out of Egypt* to settle eventually in Canaan? Though colonial, separate, and distinct, Canaan had been, by the time of Moses at the end of the Egyptian New Kingdom period, *within* Imperial Egyptian jurisdiction for centuries!

A catastrophic smallpox epidemic may shed some light on the misapprehension and offers some conjecture toward resolving the biblical contradiction with ancient history. But first we should look at the man

Moses, the prime mover and key player in the powerfully moving historical Exodus drama.

There may or may not be myth in the Biblical biography of Moses, and it must be noted that even an absolutely literal interpretation of the text is not at odds with historical evidence if one believes in miracles. But if one is to utilize a religious text as a historical document, it needs to be de-miracle-ized. For in attributing causes for historical acts and events we must be able to apply tests from knowledge and perception of physical and human nature and be skeptical of supernatural miracles and additionally critical of questionable events that seem invented or borrowed to enhance narrative and promote belief.

The story of the birth, abandonment, discovery, and adoption of the baby Moses by a person of the Egyptian royal household offers a case in point.

Some fourteen centuries before Moses fled Egypt with his band of followers, there was a Mesopotamian monarch named Sharru-kin, more popularly known as Sargon I or Sargon of Agade (Akkad), who certainly conquered and united the lands between the Tigris and Euphrates rivers and may have conquered as far as the Mediterranean island of Cyprus. His exploits left lasting legends in the ancient Mideast, and one of those legends is strikingly similar to a story about Moses.

On clay tablets numbered KK. 3401, 4470 in the British Museum, translated and published by Sir Ernest Alfred Thompson Wallis Budge, in *Babylonian Life and History*, we see "The Legend of the Birth of Sargon of Agade."

> Sargon, the mighty King of Agade, am I. My mother was of humble estate, I knew not my father. The brother of my father (or paternal uncle) was a dweller in the mountains (a forester?). My city is Azupirani, which lies on the banks of the Euphrates. My humble mother conceived me, she brought me forth in secret. She laid me in a basket (made) of reeds, she smeared my door with bitumin, she committed

me to the river which did not submerge me. The river carried me to Akki, a man who watered the fields. Akki, the man who watered the fields...lifted me out of the basket. Akki, the man who watered the fields, brought me up as his own son. Akki, the man who watered the fields, made me his gardener. Whilst I was a gardener the goddess Ishtar fell in love with me. And for...-four years I ruled the kingdom.

Sargon I of Akkad (Agade) in Mesopotamia died in 2582 BC, and Moses would probably have been born no earlier than about 1200 BC in Egypt, one thousand three hundred years later. Sargon remained a hero in Mesopotamia for 2000 years, six hundred years past the lifetime of Moses. It was clearly a treasured tale, and there was ample opportunity for borrowing.

Beginning with this apparent Mesopotamian borrowing of the story of the baby found floating in a basket among the reeds, the Biblical text sometimes appears to intentionally minimize the fact that Moses was not only a cultural Egyptian but treated as—if not in fact actually by birth—a member of the Egyptian royal family. If it were indeed borrowed from the Sargon story, the apparent biographical fabrication in the Moses story suggests that ancient oral story tellers and subsequent writers were attempting to hand down what they, and possibly Moses himself, felt was an overriding religious and political consideration. The Moses story repeatedly attempts to minimize his Egyptian national identity, Egyptian royal upbringing, and Egyptian upper class education and privileges to represent him as just one of the common people, a common man for all people across national and ethnic boundaries. If these were conscious efforts, they worked—probably beyond the wildest dreams of those who made them.

The promotional efforts would have been good politics when he was alive—especially if it were at a time when nations and empires, including the Egyptian Empire, were collapsing—and good religious infusion ever after, as we can see. But Moses *was*, at very least, an adopted royal Egyptian family member, and if the story of being found in the rushes was, as seems, a borrowing, he was probably a legitimate child of the royal household. He is pointedly called "the Egyptian" with a definite article elsewhere in the Bible, as if to indicate his ethnicity and nationality.

As a result of being in the royal household, he was probably given the kind of good education expected for a member of the royal family—who would be given, at very least, a post in the government bureaucracy or colonial administration. Later Biblical text trivialization of his royal class upbringing suggests that religious historical preservationists and writers, perhaps Moses himself, made calculated decisions to create a non-national, non-ethnic religion for all humanity, a large break with local gods and state religions that had prevailed up until that time—but a break not unprecedented in official Egyptian religion, as seen in the heretic pharaoh Akhnaton's hymns, probably written not long before the Exodus.

The name Moses is clearly Egyptian, a shortened form of a number of New Kingdom pharaohs' names. Many Egyptian monarchs have "Moses" in their names, Tuthmosis, for instance, which means "fashioned or created by the god Thoth" (the god of wisdom), which is a way of saying "son of the god Thoth." The famous Biblical name Rameses (in Egyptian, Re-moses) "means fashioned or created by" the sun god, Re, and likewise is a way of saying "son of the sun god Re."

So "moses" in ancient Egyptian names effectively means "son of" in about the same way as "Mc" or "Mac" means "son of" in modern Irish and Scotch Gaelic names. One may even speculate—although there is absolutely no evidence to support it—that the familiar Biblical name "Moses" may have been meant to convey an affectionate nickname in much the same way that Mac, which means "son of" in Gaelic, is often used as a nickname today.

Moses probably had a longer name, something like Ahmoses, Tuthmosis, or Rameses (which could also be translated "Ra-moses"). It is charming to think that he deliberately dropped longer, royal-sounding parts of his name to be part of the common people he led—a "just call me Mac" way of reaching out. A commonizing humanistic, socialistic, fatalistic strain seems to reverberate through the unwritten subtext in the Torah, but "just call me Mac" is offered only as something for admirers of the man to ponder, and there is no supporting evidence for it.

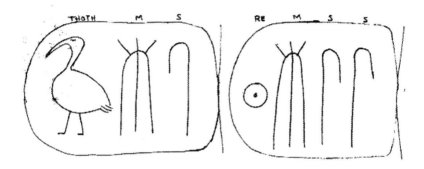

Figure 3 Simplified cartouches of Tuthmosis (left) and Rameses (right), showing "Moses" in both of their names.

If Moses, as tradition has it, actually did write the original draft of the Torah, the first five books of the Bible, he almost certainly would have written it in Egyptian-language hieratic script. The Hebrew alphabet was not invented until some three or four hundred years after his lifetime.

Thus combinations of translation, preservation by oral renditions, later transcriptions, and political and religious editing—some undoubtedly to justify dynastic transitions during the Jewish kingdom phases—would appear to leave us with a vital core to verify by scientific and historical reasoning. And this kind of reasoning would also have the shortening of a longer Egyptian name into "Moses" due to Hebrew speaker-and-listener difficulties with long foreign words and names, either in translation or during the three or four hundred years of largely oral preservation elapsing between the lifetime of Moses and the invention of a Hebrew-language alphabet.

As readers of the Biblical text know, although Moses was clearly destined for better things in life, he killed an Egyptian and had to flee Egypt as a result. He headed out across the northern Sinai and ended up in a country presumably "just over the border" from Egyptian imperial control called Midian. Midian was the land on the eastern side of the Gulf of Aqaba in what is now northern Saudi Arabia. The booklet of Vancouver's Expo '86, "The Great Pharaoh Ramses II" cites digs by Dr. Rothenberg in the "free-craftsmen" copper-mining community of Timna, just north of modern Eilat-Aqaba, in what he calls "the country of Midian." But this may have been on the border, and not deep in Midian itself. (Also interesting in the same paragraph is Rothenberg's discovery of a golden bronze image of a serpent in their temple to the Egyptian goddess Hathor, reminding one of a later episode in the Moses story).

Since Moses appears almost certainly to have been an educated member of the Egyptian royal family, he would have been aware of the peace treaty between Egypt and the Hittite Empire and that it included an extradition clause. Even if, at that time, the Hittites had gone into their sharp decline, the treaty still existed, and it might have been fatal to go through miles of Egyptian colonial territory in Canaan to arrive in Hittite territory, only to be given a police escort back to Egypt and handed over to Egyptian authorities for trial.

So Moses headed out toward Midian, where he met Jethro's daughter, Zipporah, at a watering place and went on to marry her. And here we may see a first tenuous hint that the biblical text could contain remnant material referring to a smallpox epidemic, text material that grows increasingly unambiguous and convincing as it continues.

One might ask, in beginning to consider a catastrophic smallpox epidemic, why Zipporah had trouble watering her animals. Sheep would mingle with sheep, but cattle might be shy or spooked by sheep. And if Jethro had owned a cattle ranch, Moses may have become infected with cowpox.

Millennia later, in 1795 AD, an English physician named Edward Jenner listened to folk tales that cowpox infecting milk maids prevented smallpox. He inoculated several people with scrapings from cowpox and later boldly inoculated them with smallpox. Cowpox prevented the dread ancient disease, and Jenner had not only invented the modern smallpox vaccine but had invented a preventative method for a wide range of other diseases.

Even if the animals at the well with Zipporah were not cattle and did not have cowpox, Jethro may well have had cows on his ranch, and young Moses could well have become infected with cowpox there or in the cattle-raising country of the Nile Delta from where he had just fled. But this is only the wildest conjecture and mentioned here as a possibility only because Biblical text vaguely hints that both Moses and his brother Aaron may have had immunity to the deadly disease.

The fact is that Moses went from royal to rural and enormously influenced history, more than he ever could have by remaining at the center of royal Egyptian power. The first few generations of oral historians may have been aware that this influence also grew from his acquired immunity to smallpox due to cowpox infection. A few generations after the epidemic was over the crucial detail may have become meaningless—especially in comparison with the profound religious enlightenment of his enhanced influence as a direct result of abandonment of royal political power—and perhaps the fragment of the episode at the well was preserved for its poetic and story value.

A first allusion that could be construed to imply smallpox comes in Exodus, chapter four, when a miracle is described that hints at symbolic representation of a cowpox infection. While it is called "leprosy" here, other places in the Biblical text refer to "leprosy" when a smallpox infection would fit the description and context. In this first instance, Moses shows the pharaoh a "leprosy" on his hand that is quickly cured—as if a remnant meaning that a smallpox-appearing rash or blistering prevents the usually fatal disease.

Egypt suffers a series of plagues—interesting in itself, especially Exodus 9:9 and 9:10 where Moses, Aaron, cattle, and "dermatitis breaking out into boils" are brought together in the text as if misconstrued or mistranslated centuries later when Hebrew script was invented.

This may be stretching meanings too far, but since Moses and his contemporaries would not have known modern immunology and thus what was happening, even the best preserved record could hardly show more than a strange sequence of events and coincidences. It would seem fair to venture guess that Moses may have been naturally "vaccinated" in Midian, and it would seem natural that he would be visited there by his brother, Aaron, who might also have acquired immunity to the dread disease this way.

Although there is no name "Aaron" found so far in Egyptian language, Aaron would have been either native Egyptian or Egyptianized-immigrant like his brother Moses, and the name seems Egyptian rather than Hebrew—tantalizingly close to the name Aanen, who was a brother of the influential Egyptian woman, Tiya, chief wife of the pharaoh Amenhotep III and daughter of the prime minister Yuya, who may be the biblical Joseph. Tiya was also mother of the heretic pharaoh Akhnaten. Her brother, Aanen, was high priest at the holy sun temple at On—its ruins now in the northeast suburbs of Cairo in the in the eastern Nile Delta, not far from Goshen—a place where much later in the New Testament, Mary and a later Joseph make a point of visiting during the flight to Egypt episode.

But while these possible remnant references to smallpox-cowpox may be stretching ancient text, later in the Biblical text descriptions of smallpox appear less doubtful and ambiguous.

Everyone knows the story. A series of "plagues" struck. These would appear to indicate a preserved folk memory of a minor El Niño-like climate change or an extremely "bad" normal year. At first glance it appears to begin with an unusual and probably worse than normal flood-caused redness to the normal Nile flooding in September-October.

Quite possibly it was not the normal annual inundation, which originates in Equatorial Africa, but flooding caused by abnormal heavy rainstorms across the northern desert caused by the minor climate change. These could have caused flash flooding in the barren gullies of red desert earth that can be seen surrounding the Nile today. In the Delta, people would have been unaware of what had taken place up to a thousand miles to the south and would have been mystified at the Nile turning red like blood.

Whatever the cause of the flooding, it in turn could have caused an overpopulation of frogs as it receded, it is described in steps that appear to continue through the year.

The rotting carcasses of the excessive population of frogs would have spawned more than normal populations of varieties unpleasant carnivorous insects.

The bad but by no means unusual hail that ruined barley and flax, but not emmer or late winter wheat, indicates that it fell within a few days after sowing and perhaps after sprouting that had not yet grown to lengths that could be destroyed by hail, possibly an attempt to preserve a precise time in ancient times when planting dates were carefully prescribed by astronomer-clergy and fairly well known, but popular calendars were lacking.

The excessive rainfall that had forced the worse than usual flooding could have created temporary vegetation conditions in the desert that allowed for the survival of unusually large numbers of newly hatched *Shistocerca gregaria* locust nymphs, and a more than usually hot and dry summer would have provoked and aided swarming of these grain consuming and destroying insects.

Following the abnormal desert rainfall, an unusually hot and dry summer, coupled with a temporary destabilization of climate and wind patterns could have caused unusually large combinations of brush fires and dust storms that brought a remembered darkness sweeping across the northern Nile Valley.

But as the plagues progressed, the pharaoh, or at least the Egyptian government, is shown to have grown increasingly impressed and would have been at least concerned, like any reasonable government, but still refused Moses' request for his cult followers' religious observances and civil liberation.

Whether these apparent climate-change-caused nine "plagues" took place during the twelve-or-so months just prior to the Exodus or were in folk memory as having happened around that time give or take some years may turn out some day to be important, but is not crucially so here.

Thus far the listed "plagues" would seem to show natural causes and explanations, and devastating and remarkable as they may have been, they would seem to have been within the bounds of experience. The tenth and last one, however, is a one-time occurrence clearly outside the normal experience of governments and people and thus with no real experience available for later comparison may not have been preserved well over generations, and with possible emphasis for purposes of religious lesson has come down to us in its present Biblical text form as apparently having had even more unexplainable and thus supernatural causes.

But if the first nine "plagues" can be explained by natural occurrences, might the tenth one-time one also have a natural explanation? Could the awful and devastating one-time "plague" that has come down to us as only having taken first-born lives have originally referred to the world's first smallpox epidemic that so wholesale took human lives no matter in what order they were born, then have become slightly garbled in telling and translations? Possibly it is a remnant of a garbled analogy, the analogy itself eventually having been lost?

There seems to have been an attempt to present a natural chronological order to the first nine "plagues" that would limit them to within a single year. Whether this would mean a continuous series of months right up to the original Passover—for whatever historical or ceremonial reasons a lunar-calendar approximation of the Spring Equinox—or whether there may have been a time gap until the next and profoundly different "plague" is unclear.

The "plagues" would not seem to be a composite of significant newsworthy events that had taken place over a number of years and had been reassembled in that order to enhance story because the list fails to mention other newsworthy disasters like earthquakes in that earthquake-prone part of the world, storms other than hail, and so on, that would have been remembered over years and made more dramatic story material. So it looks fascinatingly like the newsworthy events called "plagues" may have happened pretty much in the order described and may reflect a minor El Niño-type climate change.

But in support of a minor climate change hypothesis, the evidently increased rainfall suggested by the "plagues" might have made later living off the land in the Sinai just barely possible due to increased wild grain growth.

There is, of course, no way to tell now if something may have been intended to preserve a sense of time and an awful and important historical event unless something specific would be discovered by archaeologists or historians. It seems marginally possible that an effort like a global ancient tree-ring dating project could pinpoint a year in about the twelfth century BC when this minor climate change occurred, or that some chronology technology not yet invented might some day be able to pinpoint it.

But barring the insupportable conjecture of the "plagues" being caused by a real minor climate change and occurring within a year, the whole event package seems to chronologically correspond, at least roughly, to the great population decimation catastrophe that destroyed civilization at the end of the bronze age, and it is all the more intriguing when one examines subsequent events in the Biblical text. And if it might turn out to be the case, it could date the Exodus in the mid-twelfth century BC.

If, in addition to all the other troubles, a new mysterious deadly epidemic had been beginning to sweep across the Nile Delta, there would have been few options for people who sought to save their lives. One of them would have been to shutter themselves up in their houses. Another would have been to resort to prayer or magic spells. But the most practical and the one that might genuinely have saved lives would have been to flee into the desert with enough food and utensils to survive in the harsh elements for a while.

One might even speculate wildly that the "passover" markings on residences were a deception meant to buy time. Neighbors could have been told the apparent ritual markings were magical to prevent the dread epidemic when in fact they were simply identification so agents could quickly rouse and organize prepared cult members for a dash to the desert before authorities could stop them, at least stop them as an organized group.

But there is probably no way to tell from the surviving Biblical text. There may have been other reasons for the flight into the desert, certainly religious persecution being one of them.

There had also clearly been labor difficulties that might modernly be called a labor dispute. Hardships caused by a minor climate change to both laborers and the Egyptian government and its contractors could plausibly have exacerbated these difficulties and raised the stakes to a confrontation. The actual population decimation catastrophe may have struck later.

Moses, who had apparently approached the Egyptian government, and possibly the pharaoh himself at the then eastern Nile Delta capital of Pi-Rameses, felt compelled to lead the laborers and their families, the Israelites, through the eastern Delta of Imperial Egypt and into increasingly harsh desert conditions.

They had prepared for it by gathering equipment and baking unleavened bread wafers, likely a well known Egyptian army ration, already by then used in centuries of imperial Egyptian military campaigns to the north and east where food had to keep for a week during the crossing of the hot barren Sinai. It would have been well known by then that leavened bread would mold and rot in a few days. It hints at careful preparation for a prolonged stay in the desert.

The biblical record of the flight into the desert appears to be a reasonably accurate preserved account of a real historical event and thus may allow us to use it and related biblical text material to support a theory of an ancient smallpox epidemic.

The Israelites went across a saltwater marsh known as the Sea of Reeds (mistranslated and still tenaciously but wrongly held to be the Red Sea), possibly at the southern end of what is now the Suez Canal, or possibly pre-Suez-Canal Lake Timsah or The Bitter Lakes between the Red Sea and the Mediterranean, or possibly the fringes of one or the other Mediterranean Sea bays known as Lake Menzaleh and Lake Sirbonis. But no one knows for sure.

The Sea of Reeds, as a saltwater marsh affected by tidal surges, or as a dry inland lake with a dried crust that would bear foot traffic but not heavy military chariots, seems to have accidentally or deliberately trapped the heavily armed and weighted-down army of the pharaoh, and if it were a tidal flats area, the Egyptian military force could easily have been caught by an incoming high tide halfway across while the outcasts and heretics they pursued had already reached the other side.

Succoth was probably the Egyptian fortress of Tjeku, a one-day march from the palace of Rameses at Pi-Rameses. Etham means "a wall" and a military barrier wall is known to have been about where the modern Suez Canal is, so the Wilderness of Etham would probably be out past the wall and thus on the present east side of the Suez Canal.

Pi-hahiroth is probably an Egyptian temple, *pr Hthr*, temple of Hathor, wife of the god Horus.

Migdol indicates a military watchtower or small watchtower fortress. Baal-zephon is known from archeology to be about 27 miles southwest of modern Port Said.

Places like the bitter spring of Marah (meaning "bitter" in Hebrew) have been plausibly located as a spring modernly called 'Ain Hawarah, a spring just south of the Wadi Amarah.

Elim is probably the modern Wadi Gharandel, near the plain of el-Marah, a convenient large campsite.

Moses may have been heading for Midian again. But things happened. At Rephidim Moses was forced into a battle with the Amalek, also unknown and unidentified except that in Numbers 24:20 you have

"Amalek was the first of all the nations," apparently indicating a powerful nation among "the nations" and thus not a lone small desert band. Rephidim is an unknown place but with a prefix "re" which if Egyptian-derived could mean a mouth of a river, canal, or bay, hence Rephidim could be patch of land at a river, canal, or bay mouth or a land of a people there with this name, or maybe a mouth where two-or-more rivers, canals, or bay inlets join. It might mean a Mediterranean coastal location, and thus the Amalek could be one of the raiding Sea Peoples that Rameses III successfully fought and are likely represented in Western literature in the *Iliad* and *Odyssey*, part of the Minoan-Mycenaean-Canaanite sea and land trading "nations," possibly going back to Hyksos days.

In the absence of historical evidence one can speculate forever on these things, and the best use of that may be as a cure for insomnia. But one is free to wonder. Could Amalek be the last Mycenaean-era refuge of Amyklar—more an anachronism or even a pointed cynical joke than a mistake or misnomer for a Mycenaean civilization that was among the first of nations when Moses left Egypt but had succumbed to the smallpox epidemic even before Moses headed for Edom? Amyklai and outposts possibly founded by fleeing refugees on Cyprus continued for some time after the Mycenaean (Achaean) civilization crumbled. It may have been, therefore, that Moses was in the northern part of the Sinai along the Mediterranean coast and might have come into contact with remnants of the Sea Peoples raiding down the Levant.

Moses and his followers were in the Sinai for some unknown amount of time, apparently for years. It is written that they stayed at the desert oasis of Kadesh for forty years, but forty is one of those nice round numbers that shows up often in the Bible. Over and above these forty years, there was additional time spent wandering around the Sinai. All that can be said is that they were in the Sinai for some years, probably most of that at the oasis of Kadesh Barnea, now called Ain Kadis, about five miles south of the present Israeli-Egyptian border.

In the desert they became discouraged. Some died, including Miriam, Moses' sister, who more unambiguously than Aaron seems to have had an Egyptian name altered in years of oral rendition and translated copyings. Miriam is rather clearly a rendering of the common Egyptian name Merit-Amen, "Beloved of Amen," (the chief god of New Kingdom Egypt).

And with a few brief biblical passages on Miriam we may see the only remaining first-hand account of a devastating epidemic that destroyed civilization for centuries. The terse report in Numbers 20:1-7 of Miriam's death, apparently at a new encampment in the scrub brush desert wasteland possibly near present Ain Kadis (Kadesh Barnea) near the Israel-Egypt border in the Sinai, "and Miriam died there, and was buried there," is preceded eight chapters earlier by a brief religion-oriented anecdote that could conceivably have originally been derived from a longer heartbreaking account telling of devotion to a beloved sister and risk-taking amid the terrors of the new incurable and usually fatal disease of smallpox out in the vast hopelessness of the harsh and miserable desert.

It is less important that recriminations are reported in Numbers Chapter 12 to have been heard about Moses marrying a foreign wife because that would be part of an all too human normal reaction to the awful situation and its wholesale despair. What is interesting and could shed light on what may have been a lost profoundly tragic real life story is the emergence of Aaron and his sister Miriam, formerly Egyptian royalty or at least upper class Egyptian, from a "tabernacle," likely a lowly makeshift desert tent that served as both an abode for the leadership and an administrative and religious center with a dividing fabric partition—a wool tent not unlike those used by Bedouin tribes even today.

What we see after the "cloud" departed the tabernacle—as if a common desert mini-tornado dervish blew by with a gust of wind—is that Miriam is suddenly seen "leprous, white as snow." If one believes in supernatural intervention, then one can accept on faith that leprosy, which would normally take years or decades to manifest itself this way, suddenly and massively afflicted Miriam.

But in embarking on attempts to use the Biblical text for historical clues, we must seek plausible and therefore natural explanations. And here we may see a precious preserved remnant of a real event. If it is not "leprosy," then what?

When speaking of the non-immune native Mexican population's appearances when infected by smallpox a two-and-a-half millennia later, the Spanish friar Motolinia noted in his history, as mentioned earlier: "This disease was called by the Indians 'the great leprosy' because victims were so covered with pustules that they looked like lepers."

Motolinia, who spoke the Aztec language called Nahuat, has recorded here the "Indians" of Mexico describing a disease with which they were not familiar, smallpox, in terms of a disease with which they were, leprosy, apparently brought across Bering Straits to the New World with Amerindian migrations at the end of the last Ice Age. Would it have been any different 1500 years earlier if a new disease called smallpox struck all across the Old World?

The apparent preserved fragment in Numbers 12 describes Miriam as if she had suddenly been seen in a later stage of a smallpox, several days to a week following infection, when drying blisters, medically called vesicles and called pustules by Motolinia, have grown into a solid mass covering the whole body and depriving it of normal skin color, thus effectively appearing white. Aaron and Moses seem repeatedly through the text to have acquired immunity to smallpox either by unintentional cowpox "vaccination" or by possibly having survived smallpox itself. But Merit-amen, Miriam, probably a palace-protected royal Egyptian woman, may not have shared the immunity.

If she had come down with the dread and generally fatal disease, it would be plausible that Aaron could not bear seeing his august royal sister, who had already endured much anguishing privation, banished—as would probably have been the strictly enforced rule for the survival of the others—to the hot parched days and miserable cold nights of the desert outside the encampment. Royal Miriam, suffering miserable agony and known by experience to probably be dying in the desert far from civilization and anything familiar, would have evoked such sympathy in her brothers that they would have taken a great risk and hidden her condition from the others.

But something happened. Perhaps the "pillar of cloud" blew off the flimsy makeshift tent cover. Perhaps people were asking questions anyway, or overheard the family argument and exchanged recriminations through the sound-transparent tent fabric. Perhaps a combination of both.

Exodus families who had fled homes and comfort in civilized Egypt would have been forcibly divided and beloved family members would have been left to die alone in the desert for the sake of survival of the others. And suddenly Aaron was found to be hiding infected Miriam. What would have been the effect?

Even through all the three millennia that the story has been handed down, Moses is shown clearly to have been in agony over the only choice left to him. The cult leader, whose leadership must already have been shaky in the terrible hopeless desert amid a devastating epidemic, was left with one choice, banish his sister, like so many of the others must have been, to the harsh desert. And his words of anguish betray familiarity with progress of the disease smallpox. Miriam's dry white blisters would scab over and scabs would peel off to expose the raw underflesh.

"Heal her now, O God, I beseech thee," he surely may have shouted out into the desert in pre-Coptic Egyptian or proto-Hebrew Semitic.

And Aaron asks his cult-leader brother Moses on behalf of his very ill sister Miriam, "Let her not be as one dead, of whom the flesh is half consumed when he comes out of his mother's womb." The fragment of description seems the very image of a late stage of smallpox, with its blisters, called vesicles, typically bursting almost simultaneously over the whole body to expose raw skin which would then take some additional time to scab over, the whole body appearing raw and bloody, the best comparison for the ancients who had never experienced this disease being: like a baby freshly emerged from a womb, tender new flesh covered with placental blood. We may thus have inherited a remnant text fragment not only from the height of the world's initial smallpox epidemic that was sweeping away civilization, but at a precise and recognizable stage of the disease where Miriam was fighting for her life.

In other words, Aaron seems to ask his brother not to banish Miriam to the desert to die with raw flesh exposed in the hot sun and cold nights. But Moses apparently had to. And the text has Miriam banished to the desert for an often used round number of seven days, which may or may not be the precise number but undoubtedly reflects a number of days. And while the encampment waited before moving on to another encampment somewhere in the scrub desert of Paran, Miriam apparently recovered and survived, but possibly had been terribly weakened by the disease and the days out in the desert. She apparently died not long after.

We may thus be seeing in Numbers 12 perhaps the only surviving first-hand account, a mere one of the multi-millions of awful agonizing human tragedies that took place within a very few years around the middle of the twelfth century BC.

If, as it would appear, Miriam had come down with smallpox, the cult under the leadership of Moses must have come upon others in the desert in order to become infected. It would seem highly unlikely that they would not have met anyone over what must have been by then weeks or months. And it would appear by inference that the cult already had experienced the epidemic by then and stringent anguishing countermeasures and quarantine rules applied to all members.

The two brief sentences which describe Miriam's appearance and what she was clearly expected to next look like while trying to survive in the harsh desert seem to preserve descriptions of the poor woman as she appeared in later stages of smallpox.

But what almost immediately follows would seem to indicate that the "spies" sent out to bring back intelligence on Canaan brought back with them smallpox in addition. The present text of Numbers may not have been preserved in precise chronological order, or Miriam may not have had smallpox but a mimicking skin disease and hence survived and this was noted, or the men returning from Canaan a little further along in the text did indeed come back infected with smallpox and this provoked massive anger because, after their knowledge of all the draconian measures which had been anguishingly applied to keep members of the Exodus group from becoming infected, they could let themselves become so massively infected in Canaan.

But in the larger chronological framework the two brief Miriam accounts in Numbers 12 and Numbers 20 fall right into a textual timeframe of what would seem a remnant preservation in Numbers of a smallpox epidemic then sweeping civilization from the planet, showing up again in Numbers 14. It is, in other words, about where it should be even if it may or may not have been juggled slightly during the centuries between the events, and then the early recording of them in writing, and then the finalizing of the present order of the text.

What seems important is not the possible minor discrepancies, but that only here in Numbers 12 and 14, supported by fragments of Biblical text relating the Exodus through the conquest of Canaan, does there seem to be a hint of a preserved record of probably the greatest catastrophe to strike the human race since it launched into the present phase that we call civilization. However imperfect it may be as a historical source, it is all that we are left to draw from now. And there does seem to be something there.

Whatever skin disease infected Miriam, if she did not die of it—or from being too physically and immunologically weakened as a result of it—the rigors of desert encampment life led to this upper class Egyptian woman's untimely death. The descriptions of her appearance and expected appearance along with the historical chronological context make it possible that she was yet another victim, among untold millions, of the smallpox epidemic. Unlike Aaron, she probably did not visit Moses in Midian and perhaps as a result may not have acquired one kind of immunity or another.

The isolated desert oasis of Kadesh Barnea (Ain Kadis) where they appear to have set up camp has been visited by a number of Biblical and archeological scholars in recent times. It has been photographed and studied, and even under better climate conditions could have supported only in the range of a few thousand people. Even the few nearby oases could not have added support to many more. The same would, of course be true of oases in northern Arabia where some theorize the Hebrews (*ibri, apiru,* etc.) may have set up camp. It is difficult to see, then, how a small band of people could emerge from these oases to conquer the fortified city-states under the protection of imperial Egypt unless another factor is included.

The other factor is, of course, the great smallpox epidemic. And it appears to have been raging just prior to and during the stay at Kadesh Barnea or other isolated desert oases—appears to have been raging not only in Egypt but in the Egyptian colony of Canaan. Isolated out in the desert, the Hebrews may have been safe from it for a while, and in addition, if we creatively consider some remnants of history saved in Exodus, Leviticus, and Numbers, Moses would appear to have instituted strict isolation and quarantine regimens.

While still wandering the Sinai in the Wilderness of Paran and the Wilderness of Zin, Moses sent out intelligence-gathering and raiding parties into Canaan. Both aspects of these expeditions were important. The desert oasis probably provided minimal bare existence and supplies from the good farmland to the north must have been welcome. But the smallpox epidemic may have been closely tracked. Moses hardly needed real intelligence about Canaan itself, long an Egyptian colony and long said, by Egyptians (and long prior to the Bible) to be the "land of milk and honey" (or, noted by some, an allusion to "wine and pleasure"). What Moses would have wanted intelligence on was the course of the smallpox epidemic then raging in Canaan.

Amid the text of Numbers 13 relating raids north, obviously for survival foods, there is a prideful note that Hebron was built seven years before Zoan—Avaris, the Hyksos capital. We can only wonder at this mysterious linking of the Hyksos and Canaanite cities. Could it have been a later insertion arguing that Hebron (where modern tradition has—and may even then have had—the patriarchs and their wives, Abraham, Isaac, Jacob, Sarah, Rebecca, and Leah buried in the cave of Machpelah) had already been there for centuries when remnants of the defeated Egyptian Hyksos dynasty fled Avaris into Canaan and therefore could not have been founded by them?

Whatever its original intention, it is now just a curious insertion or assertion into the drama of spies and strategic planning.

The surrounding text, however, offers possible support for a smallpox epidemic beginning to consume Canaan at this time. In Chapter 13 of Numbers, spies are sent out and the gist of their report on returning is that Canaan is still strong. But immediately following in Chapter 14, their return causes a near rebellion, apparently not so much from the bad news that Canaan is still too strong to take militarily, but from what would seem to be smallpox brought back by the raiders and spies. Joshua and Caleb and those who followed them north into Canaan "and searched the land, rent their clothes" on return.

Isn't Moses being a bit unreasonable with his spooks and raiders, asking them to tear up their clothing? Familiar with rebelliousness under pressure from unfulfilled expectations and intolerable living conditions, later oral storytellers and then redactors anxious to supply teaching text for the rigors of Mesopotamian captivity may have altered things no longer understood. But in Leviticus 13 we see the suggestion of a preserved remnant—a possible explanation for this strange demand: "One who suffers from (the mysterious malignant skin disease called *tsara'at*) shall wear his clothes torn."

This may have been a directive to prevent reuse of the infected clothing, which would have spread the infection. At that time, especially to a small band isolated in the desert, clothing was far more valuable than anyone can imagine it now. Hard human labor went into the obtaining the raw material, animal or vegetable fiber. More went into hand spinning, hand weaving, and hand sewing. Since the average person did not know the dangers of smallpox-infected clothing, that which clothed a corpse must have presented a great temptation.

In addition to the clothing-tearing demand by Moses, we see that the angry Old Testament Deity threatens to "smite them with pestilence." Toward the end of the chapter we see, "And the men, which Moses sent out to search the land, who returned, and made all the congregation to murmur against him, by bringing slander upon the land." Then we see that, "Those men that did bring up the evil report upon the land, died by the plague." Could it be that the problem was not so much the evil report as the introduction of the evil smallpox epidemic? Doesn't it appear as if there is a preserved remnant of the horror here, perhaps something once very important but lost to later oral reciters and then to even later redactors?

It appears that some from these raiding and intelligence-gathering parties brought the smallpox virus back with them. Spies, after all, would have to mingle with the local population.

Only Caleb and Joshua seem to have survived. Biblical remnants show Canaan had not yet been thoroughly decimated by the "plague." The raiding party brought retaliation by a strong force of Amalekites and Canaanites. But the garment-tearing and mention of a "plague" shows some care was taken by story authors and later redactors to record and preserve knowledge that the "plague" had already been introduced to the encampment and that the Amalekites and Canaanites did not bring it with them.

In Leviticus we see stronger suggestions that it was a smallpox virus infecting the followers of Moses and that he took measures to quarantine infected people. Chapter 13 of the English translation of the Torah by the Jewish Publication Society (1962) shows this best, although the traditional Bible versions are quite adequate.

"When a person has on the skin of his body a *swelling*, a *rash*, or a discoloration, and it develops into a scaly affection on the skin of his body, it shall be reported to Aaron the priest or to one of his sons, the priests."

In his 1979 *Commentary* to the JPS translation, Baruch A. Levine more closely examines some of the words used. "Swelling" (*se'et*) is more precisely a "local inflammation, boil, mole," a generic term for a variety of inflammations or protrusions.[8]

This does not appear to be leprosy, Hansen's disease caused by his *Mycobacterium leprae*, a long-term chronic infection that takes between two and fifteen years to incubate and manifests itself in large blotches of skin discoloration and ulcers. In addition, the word "rash" (used above: *saphahat*) is a "breaking out" of the skin. Chapter 13 of Leviticus goes on at length to describe and apparently to differentiate between various rash diseases, and while these are called leprosy, they would not seem to have referred to leprosy.

The symptomatology of *tsara 'at*, described in the beginning of Leviticus 13, alludes to hair turning white as if covered by pus, eruption beneath the skin, how it might appear similar to and behave like burned flesh, possibly meaning first a redness then blistering, and a unique word for tearing that would seem to refer to peeling of skin. *Tsara-at*'s progress is dramatically fast, like smallpox involving days, as opposed to years for leprosy.

The Biblical text word "leprosy" would appear to be a cover-all generic word for skin diseases, and these references to rashes, breaking-outs, swellings, localized inflammations, and scaly affections look very much like various stages of smallpox. It appears that Moses and Aaron had a problem with smallpox, and conscious, and apparently successful, attempts were made to isolate and quarantine infected people to combat the disease.

In Numbers 14:37 we see that: "Those men that did bring up the evil report upon the land, died by the plague." Caleb and Joshua seem to have survived the disease: "But Joshua, the son of Nun, and Caleb, the son of Jephuneh, which were of the men that went to search the land, lived still." And this may explain later events. Many of the small band in the desert, however, seem not to have survived the epidemic they and "the men who went to search the land" seem to have brought back.

Their "carcasses," as the King James version graphically puts it in Numbers 14, fell in the wilderness—very much what one might expect if smallpox suddenly struck a non-immune population and only half to a fourth survived too terrorized and in total disarray to bury those who had died of a mysterious, new, but obviously contagious disease. It must have been a very bad time indeed, their numbers reduced by smallpox and war with Canaanites and Amalekites, the harsh desert offering survivors no comfort.

After some years at Ain Kadis, or at least at some desert oasis, Moses led his followers not north into Canaan but east toward Midian, where he had earlier lived. It does make more geographical sense if this small band were living in northern Arabia and decided to move north, but it does not really matter here which desert oasis they had been at. What is important is that by then the smallpox epidemic situation in Canaan and adjacent areas—situation of population decline and subsequent sheer social, political, and economic chaos—seems to have become critical, and Moses, having reasonably good intelligence, knew it.

But if they headed for Midian from the Sinai even if they were destined for Canaan, they attempted to turn north when they reached the Gulf of Aqaba. There they were halted in their tracks. The government of Edom, just north of Midian and covering the eastern side of the rift valley between the Dead Sea and the Gulf of Aqaba, would not allow Moses and his followers to enter the country or at least would not allow them to use the main highway north through the center of it.

What might have been the reason, or more importantly, what might the story have been attempting to preserve for later generations? Was it just a later animosity toward Edom, or might there be an ancient remnant of something profoundly more important and preciously saved here?

This prohibition by the government of Edom could have been either defensive measures by a small country when others all around were beginning to be ravaged by the smallpox epidemic, or the Edom authorities had the rare foresight to quarantine the country against the epidemic as it spread rapidly toward them, adamantly allowing no one from the outside to enter. Either way, Edom was not so badly decimated that it could not offer resistance to Moses and his followers, and they were forced to take a different route north, apparently back roads through the hot harsh arid desert mountains to the east of Edom.

Many died. Aaron died. Perhaps significantly, Aaron's son Eleazar is given his clothes to wear. The prevailing view is that this represents a transfer of priestly authority, as seen in our present root word for disciple and discipline. But note that Aaron's garment is not torn up. We have seen tenuous hints that Aaron may have been immune to smallpox, and here would seem a tangential allusion that he did not die of smallpox but something else in the harsh desert mountains.

Apparently no one felt that his clothing was infected—or alternatively, none in the band were any longer dying of smallpox, possibly because they were now all survivors of the dread disease. We see here an indication that the quarantine strategies had been abandoned. The epidemic was still wreaking its havoc, but elsewhere.

After the Edom incident, however, the ravages of the epidemic apparently reduced military resistance to the migrating band. On reaching Moab, just north of Edom and covering the area east of the Dead Sea, Moses probably not only began to see the fulfillment of his destiny but the extent of the devastation that the epidemic had wrought.

As they descended from the east into a dry gully leading out of the arid mountains and approached the next significant location, Moab, immediately southwest of the modern city of Amman, Jordan, the harsh desert landscape gave way to marginal scrub brush grazing landscape and then genuinely agricultural countryside.

An apparent careful attempt to precisely preserve the route down through the valley appears in the text. They met hill people, given general ethnic identity of Amorites—people, it would seem, who had recently fled in terror from their comfortable habitats and villages to the semi-desert hills as the mysterious horrible disease spread through the land. In a skirmish that must have been caused by fear and desperation on both sides, the Hebrew band defeated them and killed their leader, Sihon.

And here we may be glimpsing the very moment that divided the end of the epidemic from the onset of post-epidemic chaos and the beginning of the longest dark age in human history. For when the band reaches the formerly populated agricultural plain east of the Jordan River we see something that stretches credibility unless we postulate a natural disaster.

How could the disease-and-hardship-decimated small band of Hebrews have taken even these apparently minor towns from the Amorites—including Heshbon of the recently slain Amorite leader Sihon—who significantly was not safely behind its walls when slain, but up in the hills as if having fled there? It would appear that these towns had been virtually abandoned—as if by people utterly terrified by wholesale, ugly, and frightening deaths from a disease they had never seen before, a disease against which there was no defense except flight: smallpox.

If anything like three-fourths of their populations were suddenly wiped out, it would easily explain how Moses and a small band of virtual nomads could so conquer this large area, which must have included at least some garrisons of military professionals and fortified cities before the epidemic struck.

And another tantalizing possibility dangles before us here. Like Canaan, Moab and Ammon had been Egyptian-influenced territory if not outright Egyptian colonial territory. Into the chaos—the social, political, and economic devastation—came Moses and others with good Egyptian educations, trained at government administration. Not only had a large portion of the population been wiped out, thus making resistance impossible, but the chaos could conceivably have made Moses—and probably some of his Egyptian-educated followers—welcome to stunned survivors wandering deserted streets and staring blankly amid the ruins of the political, social, and economic fabric. Representatives of the old Egyptian order, the good old days prior to the catastrophe, did indeed enter what appears to have been an epidemic-caused disaster area. Would they have been unwelcome?

Moses, as we know, died before he could enter Canaan itself. Joshua, however, would seem to have been an educated and trained former Egyptian military man, quite likely what we might now call a field-grade officer. As such, it would seem that he also would have been, amid the chaos, welcome to some as a symbol of the old order even if opposed by others as an unwanted conqueror.

As we cross the Jordan River to the West Bank with Joshua, a scenario consistent with an aftermath of a smallpox epidemic continues.

After Joshua crossed into Canaan proper, he seems to have met with only token resistance where he met any at all. It is possible that in addition to the smallpox epidemic, there had been the added calamity of a large earthquake. Some have speculated that an earthquake-caused landslide made possible a crossing of the Jordan and further weakened the already ruined walls of the fortress-city of Jericho. But whatever happened, very little resistance was met by Joshua and the others in Canaan in the initial stages of the conquest. Archeological digs have shown that towns like Jericho and Ai were simply occupied ancient ruins, and "Ai" even literally means "ruin." Militarily speaking, these would have been easy to take.

The occupation of sites known to have been ruins is as if terrified Canaanites had fled comfortable habitats and villages to the uninhabited rubble and partial walls of Jericho and Ai as the smallpox epidemic raged because even as ruins they offered some minimal shelter from exposure to the elements than living in the raw countryside. People fleeing in terror did not have camping equipment in those days, nor do many even today as we may recall from recent television images of terrified Kurds surviving on mountainsides between Iraq and Turkey.

Those who fled to the Canaanite ruins presumably would have been people who had not been infected. Joshua, as noted earlier, would appear to have survived the disease and therefore had immunity. Moreover, all who survived the ravages that left "carcasses" falling in the desert at Kadesh Barnea would have been immune. In general, then, one can guess that the forces surrounding the ruins of Jericho were immune and by then aware of their immunity, and the people holding out inside were not immune and continued to be terrified of people outside their community who could be carrying the contagion. But to the undoubtedly rag-tag and probably somewhat desperate forces with Joshua, the resisting forces in the ruins represented a potential military obstacle to occupation as the epidemic began to subside and depopulated land and abandoned property came up for grabs to anyone who could grab it.

The incident with the spies and the prostitute Rahab at Jericho fetches speculation back to the nature of the wooden horse at Troy. In the case of Troy, a mysterious "plague" had already set in among the Greek forces. Might the real purpose of the horse been to deliver smallpox within the fortress, a biological warfare ploy that could have become common by the time of Joshua and Jericho, a ploy used by Homer in his fictional version retrieved from bardic oral tradition? What might the immune spies of Joshua have taken into the fortified ruins of Jericho?

One can only wonder at the viciousness that followed the fall of Jericho. That kind of viciousness generally stems from a root of stark fear. Perhaps new followers of Joshua gathered from those who had fled inhabited sites on both sides of the Jordan River were not immune and it was feared that the dread disease was returning. The terrible punishment of Achan—for looting goods that some could have feared from awful experience to have harbored the mysterious contagion—may further reflect that.

From the ruins of Jericho, Joshua's probably motley band went on to capture Ai, by preserved place name as well as archeological evidence, also inhabited ruins. The next significant place name, Gibeon, reveals something telling. Joshua negotiated an apparent mutual defense pact with the strategic and fortified city of Gibeon—among other things a wine-making city that must have supplied upper class tables of the Egyptian Empire only a few years earlier. It is notably the first real city and not archaeologically known ruins mentioned in the Joshua text. It may be, at that point at least, that Joshua had not gathered adequate forces for laying siege to a fortified city, or there may have been ancient alliances and relationships harking back to the recently ended days of the Egyptian Empire in Canaan. But the second seems unlikely.

Joshua and those who had suffered terribly in the desert after fleeing Egypt with an Egyptian army after them, who had been hunted down by Canaanites in the Sinai, who had been denied refuge in Edom, and who had clearly lost many family members and friends in the trek through the harsh hot arid mountains of what is now the modern Kingdom of Jordan, not to mention evident decimation from the smallpox epidemic, would have to have been superhuman as individuals and as a group to have a great amount of charity and good will, especially amid a total social, economic, and government collapse, when they reached Gibeon. Most likely, then, they were a force too weak to take a fortified and disciplined city and at the same time a group of individuals by then too savaged by experience and unruly, and thus perhaps too frightening even if smallpox may not have been feared, to be allowed into the city to partake of its comforts and security and to join in its defense.

The battles of the ruins at Jericho and Ai may therefore have been typically exaggerated over the long oral—probably national heroic ballad as well as devotional—preservation until the material was committed to writing centuries later. One cannot help but be reminded of the exaggerated claims of European settlers in the Indian Wars in the Americas three millennia later—and indirectly related to the same cause, smallpox, which eradicated native American civilizations and again decimated native populations by between two-thirds and three-fourths just as it had done earlier in the Old World. The added post-conquest social regression to small independent survival farmsteads across Canaan, much like those found in colonial America, strikes an ironic parallelism in Biblical names like New Canaan, Connecticut, across North America.

The choice of Shiloh for the new temporary center of government may have been, as Robert G. Boling suggests in his Anchor Bible Series book *Joshua*, because it is a natural amphitheater for a mass democratic convention of victorious soldiers. But a possible Egyptian derivation of the name suggests that Joshua was more welcomed as a potential restorer of the old order than resisted as a conqueror. Shiloh has a meaning suggesting that it may have been a colonial Egyptian tax or tribute collection center and therefore a minor provincial outpost of Egyptian colonial government. If he had been an Egyptian-trained military officer, Joshua could have been warmly welcomed by surviving remnants of any Egyptian colonial government. As a result, he could have added educated, trained, and capable people to his following as he advanced through Moab, Ammon, and Canaan.

But alternatively, much of the resistance that Joshua not only met but seems to have sought may have been hardline conservative remnant epidemic survivors of the hated Egyptian colonial and religious administration. Who were these people who seem almost to have fled plague-ridden cities to hide among the "safe" ruins of Jericho and Ai? Might they have been Egyptian colonial administrators and their fat native Canaanite beneficiaries? It would have been an emotional temptation for formerly persecuted religious liberal innovators, and a politically astute move to gain following of surviving native "Canaanites."

Why put up a tent at Shiloh—a point deliberately made and preserved? With as much as—or even more than—three-fourths of the population dead, there should have been a wealth of unused buildings. It could, of course, have been a symbolic traditional tribal tent, recalling the Japanese Tokugawa-era *bakufu*, tent-government. But as we have seen, after their early—and continuing—experience with smallpox, strict isolation, quarantine, and other disease-prevention measures seem to have been put into effect and rigorously enforced. No one back then knew what a virus was, but they undoubtedly observed how the disease was spread. At very least they must have noticed that contact with diseased persons, corpses, and their clothing and things they had come into contact with spread the disease.

Clothing and housing must have presented problems. The temptation to acquire these must have been great. Given human nature, strict discipline probably was not enough. Measures had to be taken to insure that no one would be tempted to come into contact with infected material. We see in the Book of Joshua, 6:24, that he had Jericho burned to the ground. And there had to be severe punishment. Among the things unfortunate Achan looted from Jericho was a "goodly Babylonish garment," potentially a smallpox-infected garment, and maybe the taking of this was far more reason for condemning him to death by traditional stoning than the looted silver. Or maybe Achan was the only one to actually touch the forbidden loot. The collection and deposit of the loot may have been ordered done by the unfortunate inhabitants of Jericho themselves—before (and this would seem otherwise unnecessarily cruel) every man, woman, young, old and even oxen and sheep were put to death with the "edge of the sword." Fear of mysterious lethal smallpox had to be deep. Desperate measure had to be taken.

Following the capture and burning of Jericho, Joshua repeated it at the ruins called Ai (the very name meaning a ruin). After its capture, some kind of curiously controlled looting took place and then the habitation—perhaps a shantytown or tent-city—was put to the torch. In fact, it would almost seem that habitats all over the eastern Mediterranean were deliberately torched in desperate attempts to halt the spread of the disease. Do you see this additionally in cities like Pylos, Ioleus (Thessaly), Orchomenus, Thebes, Gla, Tiryns, Argos, and Mycenae in Greece or in northern Canaan, Ugarit (Ekeret in Egyptian), cities burned to the ground with much left intact? It seems unlikely, but it would make sense and recalls Motolinia's post-Conquest comment about houses being pulled down over Native Mexicans who had died in them of smallpox.

More ominously, might we see a remnant of knowledge of biological warfare in the stories of the fall of both Jericho and Troy? Recall that near the end of the Trojan War a "pestilence" struck the Greek camp, and as in the Bible we also see a remnant reference to a mysterious epidemic in the *Iliad*. What was carried into the bawdyhouse between the walls of Jericho? What was in the wooden horse left outside the gates of Troy? Smallpox-infected blankets or other items? It is a terrible accusation, but given both human nature and the similarity of the two contemporaneous stories, one has to wonder.

Forgetting ancient biological warfare possibilities, a fragment remains to pin down a fairly close chronological connection between the Trojan War and the conquest of a small part of Canaan by Joshua. In the Book of Joshua, 10:13, the sun and the moon are said to have stood still in the sky at the ancient city of Gibeon until the people and armies led by Joshua "avenged themselves upon their enemies." In his notes in *Joshua*, Boling notes[9], on page 283, that there was a solar eclipse on September 30, 1131 BC.

While Boling states that he is not persuaded by this explanation, it seems one of the best explanations of the otherwise physical impossibility that anyone has yet given. The awesome mysterious event of a total solar eclipse might have been understood by a less knowledgeable ancient person as: a day naturally dawning, a mysterious darkening into night somewhere in the middle of the day as the eclipse covered the sun, and then effectively another day beginning again after the eclipse was over. In other words, the impression would be two days happening in one day's time. Some distance away from the shadow of the total eclipse, the image of the partially eclipsed sun would have appeared and could have been reported as similar to a crescent moon.

Generations later, when the actual event could no longer be recalled by anyone alive, it is easy to see how it could have become garbled and then yet later misinterpreted, poetically altered, and miracle-ized into the sun standing still and then further altered from there to fit balladic poetic patterns and religious teaching necessities.

The year of the eclipse, 1131 BC, fits the approximate timeframe of other less precise chronological references to events recalling or confirming the Exodus from Egypt by Moses and the invasion of Canaan by Joshua. It also agrees very well with archeological evidence from the area. It is very tempting to seize on this date as a preserved relic of an actual date, September 30, 1131 BC, for the battle that took place near Gibeon and pursuit that went toward Beth-horon. If so, it would put Joshua's "invasion" of Canaan about sixty to seventy years after the famous Trojan War, possibly less. An imaginative mind could invent a hypothetical youngster who survived the smallpox epidemic and witnessed both, like an American might have seen the Civil War in his or her childhood and World War I in his or her extreme old age.

The oral renditions that became the Bible from Exodus through Samuel would seem then to represent a surviving textual reference to a world fallen from great complex imperial civilizations of the beginning of the twelfth century BC into the dark ages of illiteracy, warlordism, and frontier farmsteads in massively depopulated Canaan by the end of that century. That the Carthaginian general Hannibal also had the title *shofet* (judge) hints that the "judges" were military personalities if not outright warlords themselves. Carthage itself (corrupted from Phoenician-Canaanite *Karta Hadasha*, "New City") was founded by Canaanites circa 1100 BC, hinting at a possible fleeing from the smallpox epidemic.

The oral ballads recorded by Homer are a glimpse at a world that could raise a fleet of a thousand ships, but through the eyes of those who came after and could not really understand the great civilizations that had perished. After all, he preserved the oral tradition in writing only after it had been handed down for several hundred years from mouth to memory. And since, as Martin Bernal points out in *Black Athena, Volume II*, Carthaginians continued to consider themselves as Canaanites into Roman times, there are suggestions that the occupying Hebrews borrowed Canaanite titles and that Carthage (founded circa 1100 BC) may have been a refuge for Canaanites fleeing the disease or the invasions.

Later balladic entertainer-historians and religious instructors were increasingly less able to comprehend the greatness that left curious stories and almost unbelievable structures. By the time literacy returned, poetic form and religious instruction priorities had prevailed over historical fact for centuries.

In between the crashing end of ancient civilization and this cautious re-emergence of new literate civilization that Homer, Hesiod, and the earliest Biblical writers represent, there were centuries of dark ages. As generation succeeded generation, the greatness that had once been was lost. Later Greeks could look up at the walls of Mycenae and Tiryns and marvel, and to explain away what they saw, they invented fictions of the likes of Cyclopes to build them.

So great was the ancient Egyptian civilization that only in recent times could it be appreciated—and even in our time some have invented fictions to explain away the building of the pyramids and other marvelous monuments (by beings from outer space, etc.). So thorough was the catastrophe that caused its fall that its written language slowly slipped into oblivion and was only decoded enough to read less than two centuries ago.

A devastating smallpox epidemic might well explain some of the mysteries surrounding the sudden collapse of bronze-age civilizations and of the end of the very Bronze Age itself. Perhaps now we can read a great irony into Homer's epics and the Books of Genesis and Exodus. Great nations and their wasteful great wars, and heroes hacking at and killing one another for glory or vital national interests, had little to do with the course of history. A mysterious force apparently outside human control took the mighty as well as the meek, the victors as well as the vanquished.

By the time literate civilizations reemerged, both on the eastern Mediterranean coast and in Greece, a few writers only knew something valuable in the distant past had to be preserved from the ballads and oral histories. A rare strategic mineral, tin, once so vital to bronze-age economic and military power, was by then a comparatively useless decorative metal, and the meaning of ancient struggles to sequester control of it and deny it to others was lost on new ears.

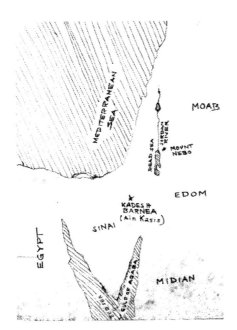

Figure 4: Map of Sinai showing Edom, Moab, and Midian.

Figure 5: Tomb model, Middle Kingdom period, trained Egyptian soldiers marching in step, carrying camouflage shields.

Chapter Four

Late Bronze-age Background

What was it like? No catastrophe of this magnitude has happened since, and it is genuinely difficult to imagine. Let us, therefore, pause for a moment and reflect before glimpsing pre-catastrophe ancients. Their daily routines were hardly much different from our own. Their fragile lives, civilized aspirations, and hopes for a better future were not unlike ours.

For all the attempted permanence of mummies and pyramids, they may have realized that everything changes and nothing lasts forever. Like us, they had to hope, however, that their individual lives had some positive effect and meaning, and additionally that their succeeding generations and increasingly long national history had some incrementally positive effect, just as we expect the long plodding evolution of life and humanity has some purpose, hoping—maybe beyond reasonable hope—that a small mysterious incremental something was gained by each of our lives over time, which we cravingly search for in history, archeology, paleontology, and cosmology.

But to be realistic—as the ancients would have been in reflective moments—if we allow ourselves a touch of painful honesty, maybe it *was* all for nothing and it all balances out to zero in a great hypothetical mathematical equation describing the universe. If so, at least we—just as they could—can look to progress in organizing ourselves into tenuous social structures that allow us degrees of safety and comfort, to cumulative technologies that enrich the quality of our lives, and out of these to social and intellectual climates where thought and art can seek the greater or lesser answers to what we are and why we are here. In short, both they and we would have been able to see life getting better for selves and posterity.

Consider, however, the sudden abrupt sinking feeling that must have followed the catastrophe. Picture the survivors of the apparent massive smallpox epidemic wandering around horrified, dazed, and stunned by it—throughout their lifetimes. They must have felt that human lives and human progress had all been for nothing when all over the known world their marvelous levels of civilization came crashing down and very few of their neighbors, friends, relatives, and children survived to even commiserate with.

Amid the chaos of complete commercial, social, economic, and political breakdown, the surviving members of that generation—the last to retain a direct memory of the civilized past—were probably too stunned and too concerned with survival necessities to seriously reflect on or record the disaster. The generations born after it heard incrementally less and less in growingly altered tales of what had really been. As the old reality disappeared from experience and then from memory, they struggled to make sense of monuments from great civilization increasingly disappearing into ruin and submerging under the blowing desert sands.

There are minor area and ethnic differences. In Mesopotamia new great empires would eventually spring up and replace buried and fabled old relics with their own, but in Egypt much later foreigners, who could not help but be impressed, added their own layers of civilized rubble and sometimes restored monumental ancient glory. Ancient Egypt, and especially the Egyptian New Kingdom Empire, had been so great, had gone back in history to something so ancient, and had been so enviously marvelous when the catastrophe struck that when it fell, it fell hard and irreparably into ruin.

The cause of the fall of not only Egypt but also the whole ancient civilized world is educated conjecture. A great population decimation catastrophe clearly took place and a massive initial smallpox epidemic would appear to be the agent.

But other than the mummy of Rameses V and hearsay by a missionary who claimed to have seen apparently now lost Chinese documents pointing toward the end of the Shang Dynasty, none of the ancient civilizations appear to have left tangible evidence or documents that point to a smallpox epidemic. It may be that few survivors were aware enough of the cause of the disaster to examine and record it, although this thought does not coincide with ancient compulsions to record such things. It is also possible that the problem is on our end of the time scale. With no hypothesis of a great smallpox epidemic out there, our modern archaeologists and historians simply were not searching for evidence to confirm or deny it.

Remaining text in this book will sometimes probe through extraneous items and ideas, the primary purpose being to lay out material for consideration to those who may be able to, one, grasp a yet unnoticed connection, two, provide a still ungrasped insight, or, three, be led onto a hitherto untraveled path of discovery. Both scholars and other interested persons may be led to retrospective reevaluations of archeological artifacts, ancient documents, and long held assumptions—resulting in a few morsels of new understandings.

It also presents background that may allow an average reader an understanding of the severity of the catastrophe and what precious little continuity survived across the collapse of civilization and the barrier of the long dark ages.

Widely scattered archeological items like the Hittite "Plague Prayer of Mursilis," presently dated circa 1325 BC, and thus a little too early for this particular epidemic, might nevertheless be reexamined. Plagues abounded in ancient times, and god-monarchs had religious duties to offer prayers and sacrifices to prevent and alleviate them. Apparently this particular plague went away leaving Hittite society intact or Mursilis would not have been so anxious to publicize his prayer.

But the text brings to mind that of the Spanish friar Motolinia when he describes the Aztec smallpox epidemic. So one may legitimately wonder whether some yet uninvented chronology technique, might allow archaeologists and historians to discover it was not too early, or maybe amended and reinvoked for the later catastrophe.

Mursilis's plague seems unusually horrible and disastrous. To quote Albrecht Goetze's translation of this plague prayer—part three, where the Hittite emperor apologizes to the Storm-god for diminution of proper worship: "The few people who were left to give sacrificial loaves and libations were dying too." Later it talks of a war with Egypt in which Egyptian prisoners were brought back: "When they moved the prisoners to Hatti (Hittite) land, these prisoners carried the plague into Hatti land. From that day on people have been dying in the Hatti land." It would seem a terribly infectious "plague," much like smallpox.

And there are other references to a plague from Ugarit and other places that while apparently also just a little early, may possibly, with some future chronology technology, turn out to be substantiating material.

There is one more Egyptian mummy, an apparently eighteenth dynasty female, with smallpox-like lesions. If the dating is correct, it would seem that the smallpox epidemic was beginning in Akhnaten's time, and this would then explain the earlier references to an unidentified "plague" in the Hittite Empire and Ugarit. But in view of the disaster following European introduction of the disease in the Americas, especially Mexico, a century-and-a-half-long smallpox epidemic with ancient civilization not only remaining intact but also fighting great wars boggles the mind.

The earlier "plagues" may just have been some of the usual deadly epidemics that struck crowded unsanitary ancient cities. But that still leaves the eighteenth dynasty mummy. Were the lesions on it caused by smallpox, or by some other skin disease? If they are smallpox lesions, might the *variola* virus that caused them have later opportunistically mutated to its modern form and become suddenly either more contagious or more lethal, or both, in the middle of the twelfth century BC? That real possibility should scare the daylights out of us moderns who have been dealing with the AIDS, *ebola*, and other viruses with similar potentials.

There are, as has been noted, suggestions of additional factors precipitating the disaster—a significant volcanic eruption or an unusually powerful El Niño event causing a temporary climate change that destroyed crops and resulted in widespread hunger and chaos-caused stress. These, we now know, would have reduced human immune systems. This in turn would have allowed more virulent mutations of the *variola* virus to spread, infect, and kill on a massive scale.

The key to whether this happened or whether the *variola* virus suddenly appeared on the mid-twelfth-century BC bronze-age scene in its present form, much as it did in Mexico in 1519 AD, is in the eighteenth dynasty mummy. But whatever it was, something surely did massively reduce population in the mid-twelfth century BC, and that something tantalizingly has all the appearances of an initial smallpox epidemic caused by a *variola* virus of modern virulence.

There are sometimes tempting second hand or third hand references that might bring to light the cause of the ancient scourge and could be more rigorously investigated in this retrospect. The Jewish historian Josephus (c 37 to 95 AD) in his resentful comments ("his lying stories," etc.) on the Egyptian priest Manetho's (c 250 BC) now lost history of ancient Egypt frets about what he takes to be, correctly or incorrectly, Manetho's account of the Exodus. There was apparently something similar to accounts in Exodus but running contrary to religious text, composed and finalized at least two thousand years ago and as familiar to him as to us, because Josephus virtually rages criticism of Manetho. The Egyptian historian-priest's account mentions disease.

We see in *Greek and Latin Authors on Jews and Judaism*[10] that Josephus says: "...he took the liberty of interpolating improbable tales in his desire to confuse with us (Jews) a crowd of Egyptians, who for leprosy or other maladies had been condemned, he says, to banishment from Egypt." Josephus goes on to talk about a wise seer named Osarseph assigned to work in stone quarries with "polluted people," and "people wasted with disease," apparently inferring that Manetho meant someone like Moses, and then contends to quote Manetho *verbatim*:

> When the men in the stone-quarries had suffered hardships for a considerable time, they begged the king (the pharaoh) to assign to them as a dwelling-place and a refuge the deserted city of the Shepherds (the Hyksos) Avaris, and he consented. According to religious tradition this city was from earliest times dedicated to Typhon. Occupying this city and using the region as a base for revolt, they appointed as their leader one of the priests of Heliopolis (On) called Osarseph, and took an oath of obedience to him in everything. First of all he made a law that they should neither worship the (Egyptian) gods nor refrain from any of the animals prescribed as especially sacred in Egypt, but should sacrifice and consume all alike, and that they should have intercourse with none save those of their own confederacy.

Exactly where Josephus ceases to directly quote Manetho is uncertain, but the text continues about a war between Osarseph's followers and the pharaoh that does vaguely suggest events in Exodus. Osarseph-Moses as leader of people with diseases condemned to work in stone quarries near the abandoned Hyksos capital of Avaris tantalizingly fits the smallpox epidemic scenario, but there is no direct reference to anything like smallpox, let alone anything identifiable as Moses or the Exodus, and the Josephus version of the Manetho history is well after the facts, third-handed, and hopelessly vague.

No ancient Egyptian papyrus equivalent of the Mexican *Florentine Codex* has yet been found. But it is not unreasonable to assume that there may never have been a written record of any kind let alone an unambiguous, careful, and exhaustive record. When the ancient bronze-age civilizations massively depopulated and collapsed, there was no virus-immune European population and superior level of technology to move into the vacuum and restructure or replace them. The whole known world just collapsed into chaos, and whole nations and empires crashed into oblivion.

The stunned survivors would have initially been busy hastily disposing of the massive numbers of corpses of relatives, neighbors, friends, and acquaintances. Then they would have been reduced to struggles for survival after the civilized structures for food production and distribution were destroyed. After some years of spending all their time and energy begging the surviving petty bureaucrats for means of sustenance, subsisting off of hastily planted gardens, garnering surviving livestock, and living off the wild land, they may have been weary and only grateful for having managed to exist through the terrible crisis.

There would surely have been little social demand or motivation for creating a record of something so awful that it could only have been a punishment from the ancient gods—who would best not be further offended by reminders. Whatever happened, we are left now looking back three millennia at a terrible catastrophe that surely took place, wondering why almost nothing survived to tell us what happened.

Without anything further to document or support the theory of an ancient smallpox epidemic, let us then catch a glimpse of the growth of a civilized past leading up to the tragic end of the bronze age and then follow fragments across the great dark age barrier to explore what may have been treasured, and as a result, remains to influence us in our time. And then following that, let us briefly glimpse at the causes and effects of the technological transition from the Bronze Age into the Iron Age.

Long in their distant past, twenty five centuries before the catastrophe, human beings had created genuine permanent civilization—interestingly in close proximity with reed marshes in both the Tigris-Euphrates and the Nile riverbanks and deltas.

One might wonder if reed ships like the Tigris of Thor Heyerdahl had plied the seas in widespread heavy trade at the brink of the coming of civilization, it might explain why the first civilizations appeared where there were plentiful reeds as well as mud and hot sun for sun-dried bricks to build cities and monuments[11]. Fertile and loose soils for easy planting, and long growing seasons were certainly prime factors. Long rivers as irrigation sources and transportation routes were also. Reed boats from large reed marshes would seem the easiest to construct and thus be the original modes of river-transportation. A quick glance at a world map of early civilizations shows that long rivers subject to regular and irregular flooding like the Tigris-Euphrates, Nile, Indus, and Hwang-ho were deciding factors in its beginnings.

Whatever its cause, civilization suddenly sprang up around 3500 BC. Within a very short period—as few as fifty years—human beings had constructed the first genuine permanent cities, the first substantial permanent agriculture, the first real metallurgy, the first wheeled carts, and the invention on which all of these depended, the first written languages and records.

By the time of the great population decimation catastrophe two-and-a-half millennia later, these first fragile literate civilizations had evolved into what we can understand in modern terms as not only great nations but also great empires. They had long known, and sometimes recorded, histories. Trade had become intense and widespread. An illustration of just how intense came with the discovery of a densely populated late bronze-age trading city on the presently barren small desert island of Pseira off the coast of eastern Crete. It can only have existed in an enormous volume of sea-going trade.

It is apparent that whole nations of specialized producers of this or that had grown to become dependent on one another for products or raw materials, or had become massive importers of food paid for by their export specialties. The known world at the end of the Late Bronze Age had become virtually as trade-oriented and complexly interdependent as our present world.

The possibility of supernational trading empires much like our present-day multi-national corporations is intriguing. Some seem to have firmly established themselves, and the Egyptian delta Hyksos (c 1650 to c 1550 BC)—called in Egyptian documents "people under foreign rulers"—might have been one of these. Martin Bernal (in a chapter subtitle in *Black Athena*) refers to them as a multi-national corporation. The real center of this "multi-national corporation" civilization, of which the Hyksos capital of Avaris may have been only an outpost, seems to have been far to the north in Crete, called Keftiu by the ancient Egyptians.

Surviving Minoan (Crete) art from Crete itself and from the exploded volcanic island time-capsule of Thera show levels in both skill and aesthetic appreciation that would seem more sensitive and sophisticated than even in Egypt itself. Minoan naval protection of sea-going trade has been compared to the Pax Britannica of our recent history. And it must, indeed, have been a time of relative peace in long troubled human history. Arts flourished, commerce flowed, and the scanty record of the eastern Mediterranean shows perhaps less major conflict than our own highly civilized time.

While foreign-dominated Hyksos trading wealth and apparently naval power held sway in northern Egypt, religious, political, and cultural conservatives struggled to maintain traditional values in southern Egypt from their capital city we know as Thebes. It is not difficult to imagine that the conservatives in the south looked on the physical and intellectual encroachment in the north with great anxiety. It was not only a threat to a long matrilineal succession of male god-kings we call pharaohs, it was a threat to religious orthodoxy and long established religious-political bureaucracies. The Egyptians holding out in Thebes must have bided their time and gnashed their teeth through the Hyksos century, scheming and planning to throw the upstart rascals out and praying to quash their threatening religious and political ideas.

Their chance may have come as if sent by the pantheon of ancient Egyptian deities themselves. The volcanic island of Thera (Santorini) exploded—old reckoning circa 1550 BC, but some feel to have been seventy-five years earlier around 1625 BC—in perhaps the largest focused seismic event in the whole of human history. The island, clearly once a center of Minoan Crete wealth and power in itself, blew itself off the face of the earth. Only a few fragments of it now remain, huddled around the still active caldera.

The explosion produced an enormous tidal wave (*tsunami*) that devastated shoreline trading towns along northern Crete. It must have been large enough and forceful enough to have washed over wharfs, warehouses, living quarters, and commercial buildings hugging the shores all over the eastern Mediterranean.

Some have speculated that this might have been the "flood" of Noah? That "flood," according to the biblical text, was only 15 Egyptian cubits in depth, about 24 feet (one royal-standard Egyptian cubit equals 52.3 cm). That would not even get to the foot of Mount Ararat. A wall of water 24 feet (7.5 meters) high caused by a *tsunami* would, however, devastate ancient shoreline communities and facilities.

But if the number 15 cubits also has a vague resemblance to some number taken down for reports by officials from high water marks, preserved while much of the context around it was not, it could also be a fragment of a recorded Nile flooding high water mark. The number itself may be accurate since apolitical numbers seem better suited for accurate preservation than weighted disputable propagandistic historical storylines. Until a theory of the explosion of Thera was put forth in the 1950s, many archaeologists felt these collective stories originated from an unusually large river valley flood.

In addition to the biblical story, the ancient Greeks, the ancient Mesopotamians, the ancient Egyptians, and many others had stories of a great "flood," but none would seem quite so specific about its depth. Fifteen cubits could be a typical annual large river flood level. Of course a dramatic larger-than-normal recorded flood—say 15 cubits over normal flooding—in itself could relate back to the volcanic explosion of the island of Thera. Rain-forming nuclei from volcanic ash and its additional solar-reflective-caused atmospheric cooling would have induced global increases in rainfall for months and even years subsequent to the event itself. Across the usually dry Mideast there must have been a lasting long period of unusually heavy rainfall and notable cold, enough for the biblical writers to use the "forty" number they reserved to convey not precisely known but fairly long periods of time.

But a hypothetical concentric tidal wave flowing from the volcanic blast at Thera and diminished to twenty-four feet as it struck the shores of Canaan and Egypt would better explain fragments of history in ancient stories. The annual flooding of the Nile was, after all, regular, predictable, and understood. From a combination of the great tidal wave and the unusual and unexpected river flooding, the sudden loss of food, goods, records, ships, structures, and skilled and educated human beings could only have had a devastating effect on fragile bronze-age economies.

A striking temporary global climate change surely accompanied the enormous dispersion of volcanic ash into the upper atmosphere, a "winter" through at least one summer in areas farther north, and this, in turn, surely destroyed at least one year of crops. So the multiple fabled great floods may have been caused by a real catastrophic event and in turn precipitated major historical events and would thus be important to understanding bronze-age history.

Probably causally related, but at least coincidentally, the great Aryan invasion of Persia, northern Mesopotamia, and eventually India began about the same time as the volcanic explosion of Thera. It must be noted that these Aryans had very little in common with the Nordic types promoted by the late unlamented Third Reich, and in fact, an offshoot of these Indian-Persian Aryans might even have coalesced into proto-Jewish peoples and tribes.

A sudden summer-turned-to-winter and the resultant obliteration of food for survival could have driven both nomadic and settled peoples, including the Aryans, south out of Russia and Siberia to areas where food may have been in good supply due not only to warmer but wetter weather. The "ar" in "Aryan" seems to have the same Indo-European root as our English "ore," hence "Aryan" is "Ore People." Intriguingly, the Aryan invasion virtually initiates the defined Late Bronze Age, where the superior tin-copper alloy of bronze replaced the inferior arsenic-copper alloy of bronze of the two earlier bronze ages.

The Aryans may have driven south, using new chariot warfare technology made possible by the new alloy, from lands in or joining one of the few known and rare tin-producing areas of the world—roughly the area around where modern Uzbekistan, Tadzhikastan, Khirghizistan, and Kazakhstan come together. Might these Aryans have utilized—possibly even invented—the superior new metal alloy for swords, chariot axles and hubs, horse-control hardware, and armor in their sweeping southward conquests?

One offshoot of this sweep, an Aryan people called the Mitanni (*Mtn* in Egyptian), pushed down into northern Mesopotamia and eastern Anatolia, and probably into what might be loosely defined as northern Canaan, settled there, and became deeply involved in Egyptian history. They established a kingdom the Egyptians called Naharin (Haran of Abraham, Isaac, and Jacob in the biblical text), between the Tigris and Euphrates Rivers reaching to the northeast Canaan border (the later province of Galilee, then known as Khurru, sounding like the Hurru, another name for the Mitanni).

On one hand these Mitanni may have been opportunistic participants in the Hyksos-Minoan collapse after the tidal-wave and weather-caused economic "recession" surely threw all affected governmental leadership into terrible domestic political crises and necessitating reduced defense expenditures even while forces were diverted to control social unrest. A "Great Depression" that would make our own seem pale by comparison surely followed the explosion and tidal wave, and any "Hyksos-Minoan economic empire" would have been an economic "basket case."

On the other hand it is marginally conceivable that the Mitanni—or their parent body, the larger great Aryan invasion—may have actually included these people the Egyptians called the Hyksos. If Bernal and others are correct about an earlier date for the explosion of Thera, the Hyksos invasion of northern Egypt would coincide with it.

In the former scenario, after the explosion of the volcanic island of Thera—how long after being the only thing really in question—Hyksos influence and power had sufficiently diminished to allow the southern Egyptian pharaoh and his army and navy eventual successful conquest.

In the latter scenario, the great climate and economic disruption caused by the powerful seismic event gradually subsided over about seventy-five years. Widely spread out horse-and-chariot-warfare Aryan military power slipped, not only relative to the new social stability and economic health returning to surrounding nations, but to their growing capacities to fight this new and very tin-bronze-dependent kind of war.

In this scenario the Aryan Mitanni invasion may have overthrown strongly disliked Egyptian colonial regimes or at least Egyptian influence in Canaan, gained or coerced Canaanite support, and continued on down into Egypt. Their permissiveness concerning trade and local religions and customs may have been much like the much later Mongols and gained them allies. If nothing else, Canaanite rulers had the wisdom to see where the new military power lay and allied themselves with the Mitanni. On later New Kingdom Egyptian records, Canaanite princes and kings did ally themselves with the Mitanni a number of times after the fall of Hyksos Egypt.

The Egyptian name for the Hyksos, the "People Under Foreign Rulers," implies a loose hegemony or alliance, and they would almost certainly have been in this alliance in conjunction with Mediterranean trading cities, part of a probable Minoan Crete trading empire. There was, then, a Hyksos-Minoan and a Hyksos-Canaanite connection. In addition, the Hyksos-Minoan-Canaanite connection existed at the time of the Aryan invasion and its Mitanni offshoot—either at the beginning of it or at the end of it, but contemporary with it. So, loosely at least, there is a Mitanni-Hyksos-Canaanite-Minoan connection—the last meaning the Minoan-era civilization reaching into Greece.

Whether the Hyksos were spurred by the Mitanni offshoot of the greater Aryan invasion, or backed by the Mitanni, or part of a Minoan "multi-national" trading conglomerate, or Canaanites pressured south by the Mitanni, or combinations of these—their rule in northern Egypt lasted a century. Around 1550 BC their Nile Delta capital of Avaris fell after a recorded siege to forces led by the southern pharaoh Ahmose.

Pursuing the fleeing Hyksos army, and probably navy, north, the Egyptian forces prevailed in a final major battle in southern Palestine, at a fortress called Sharuhen, now believed to be a ruin called Tel-el-Ajjul, virtually the present city of Gaza. The army pushed north from there, "mopping up" into Lebanon, which also had the effect of pulling the up-until-then provincial southern army (and probably also navy, for supply if nothing else) out of Egypt and giving the conservative Egyptian dynasty a taste for military imperialism. Ever after that, for four hundred years until the great population-consuming catastrophe brought it to an abrupt end, Egypt was an empire reaching far beyond its own territorial, linguistic, and cultural borders.

Following the defeat of the Egyptian Hyksos, the Mitanni to the north, who if they were not themselves part of the Hyksos Empire apparently allied themselves out of sympathy or military necessity with remnants of the Canaanite Hyksos. This alliance preoccupied and fought against the next two pharaohs, Amenhotep I and Tuthmosis I, the latter campaigning all the way to the far side of the Euphrates River, deep into Mitanni territory, where he erected a stele. Tuthmosis III (a long reigning monarch, 1504—1450 BC) fought one battle in Canaan, a record of which survives providing a glimpse at bronze-age military maneuvers, in which 924 chariots, 2041 horses, 200 suits of armor, and exactly 502 bows were captured, giving an idea of the size of these military confrontations.

The terrain may have been harder on the chariots than the battle was on the horses, because only 924 of the two-horse chariots were captured, but 2041 of horses were, an apparent excess of ninety-six pairs of horses and an extra horse.

The record of this single important, but not—like the great battle fought at the same place by Rameses II against the same enemy almost two centuries later—singularly outstanding battle, shows the size and scope of forces that bronze-age national governments could field, supply, and skillfully maneuver in battle. Some significant number of chariots would have been destroyed. Guessing forces opposing the Egyptian army to have entered the fray with 1200 chariots, and the Egyptians opposing them with close to an equal number, creates a scene like a Cecil B. DeMille spectacular with a battlefield total of two thousand to twenty-five hundred war chariots warring on a Canaan plain, not to mention a large unknown number of foot soldiers with bronze swords and spears and, from the record, a battalion of archers on each side, a total thousand men firing deadly arrows into the fray.

The strategic planning and tactical maneuvering of forces this size on a battlefield would test the skills of military generals even today.

In addition to repeatedly subduing rebellious Canaanite princes, in 1472 BC the next male pharaoh—following the world's first female monarch of significance who reigned in between—Tuthmosis III, again took on Aryan Mitanni of Naharin (Haran) itself. The land of the Mitanni remained an adversary and a problem, and his son, Amenhotep II, fought battles to maintain an Egyptian control of Canaan and regain Canaanite cities lost to Mitanni control.

However, in one of those quirks of international politics, like the British and French abandoning animosities and joining forces to oppose the Germans early in this century, Egypt and the land of the Mitanni reached a written-and-lost or just unwritten accord. A profound change began to assert itself, and cooperation replaced conflict. First Canaan and Syria—between Egypt and the Mitanni—became a *de facto* buffer zone and Canaan became an outright Egyptian colony. Then an unmistakable Mitanni and Canaanite presence began to be felt in internal Egyptian politics.

All the while, the Egyptians not only kept local Canaanite rulers tightly under their control, they established their own administrative centers in colonial Canaan at, among other unknown places, Jaffa, Beth Shean, and Gaza, as well as others in present Jordan and present Syria. To honor the god of their own southern Egyptian capital city of Thebes, Amon, they brought back booty and slaves, built huge beautiful religious temples, and founded and funded great religious institutions. Amon, combined with the sun god Re, as Amon-Re, replaced or had his name and attributes added to local gods like Baal and Astarte. Amon-Re became the sponsor-god of the new Egyptian empire, called by modern historians the New Kingdom.

But during this time the Canaanite and Mitanni and even, it would seem, Hyksos, power and influence in Imperial Egypt seem not to have totally succumbed to Egyptian military victories.

Not only did empire, as it always does, erode and corrode conservative and traditional values, remnants of Hyksos wealth, trade, skills, religion and culture seem to have seeped back into the Egyptian governmental-religious royal families and ruling circles. Seventy-five years after the fall of Avaris, the great granddaughter of the conquering pharaoh, a woman named Hatshepsut, became the first significant female political leader in history, reigning for about twenty years. Shortly thereafter, just over a century after Avaris fell, the inviolate rule of royal matrilineal succession that apparently permitted this "Queen" Hatshepsut to take the throne was violated with the "marriage" of her great grandson, Tuthmosis IV, to a foreign woman, Mutemwiya from, interestingly, Naharin (Haran), the Kingdom of the Mitanni.

In addition, Tuthmosis IV appointed a man with a clearly foreign name of Yuya, possibly the biblical text Joseph, and likely a Canaanite, to be his prime minister. One can only wonder if the population fretted about traditional values falling apart.

The next pharaoh, the son of Tuthmosis IV and Mutemwiya, an outstanding pharaoh named Amenhotep III, took the daughter, Tiya, of his father's prime minister, Yuya (Joseph?), as his chief wife and widely proclaimed their relationship with commemorative scarabs, the bronze-age Egyptian equivalent of commemorative coins.

Their son, the next pharaoh, Amenhotep IV, went even farther in defying Egyptian convention and scrapped the old-time religion of Amon-Re, replacing it with his own proto-monotheistic sun deity, the Aten. He changed his very reign name to Akhnaten to promote his radical new political-religious cause.

This act of virtual religious heresy finally seems to have broken the back of ethnocentric conservative Egyptian religious and social tolerance. But while the new state religion lasted only about two decades and essentially was scrapped for the old time religion of Amon-Re closely following the pharaoh Akhnaten's reign, it had been the official state religion, like it or not, for a generation.

And now, as we read this over three millennia after it was quashed in an orgy of return to the Amon-Re orthodoxy by a military general named Horemheb (who legitimized his rule by marrying into the royal family and is often compared to Generalissimo Franco), its "monotheism" may still be thriving in its evolved forms of Judaism, Christianity, and Islam. Whether or not there is this direct a connection, the "monotheistic" Aten-worship heresy, coming as it did not long before the Exodus, certainly must have provided some sparks of influence to what is now mainstream Western religion.

The Theban Amon-Re political-religious orthodoxy regained power under Horemheb, apparently accompanied by a welcome restoration of civil order. But one feels from modern experience that the restored old religion failed to prevail as totally as before. Once established, a religion like Akhnaten's "protestant" Aten-worship does not quickly vanish even under austere oppression. Moreover, as an official state religion, Aten-worship must have had a significant population percentage of Egyptian adherents—with additional adherents in Egyptian colonial territory and out in the larger sphere of Egyptian economic and cultural influence, especially of interest here in adjacent Canaan and in Mycenaean-era Greece. These would have been genuine believing adherents, over and above the ever present bogus ones and fawning political climbers going with the flow. With the restoration of the Amon-Re orthodoxy, the Aten-believers would have slipped underground and continued to practice their religion.

Way back from the defeat of the Hyksos in 1550 BC, and as the New Kingdom Empire grew to include widely diverse peoples, there would have been populations of non-Egyptian religions, undoubtedly often persecuted not only by the official religious state but by average ethnocentric Egyptians. But as defensive tight-knit communities they may have collectively grown into a sizable political-economic-social force that enabled, and perhaps encouraged, Akhnaten to pull off his religious coup shortly after being crowned in 1360 BC. After the final official overthrow of the Atenists, no later than 1328 BC, this new large population of religious outcasts would have joined the others, the difference being that almost all of the newcomers would have been ethnic Egyptians.

During times of official oppression there would have been seething underground unrest, and when this was lifted, there would have been a climate of vibrant exchanges of philosophies reaching into the upper levels of political and official religious society into which even the pharaohs would have been drawn.

A pharaoh took a reign-name of Seti (1296-1279 BC), the old Hyksos patron. And finally his successor, Rameses II, a redhead and therefore possibly only part ethnic Egyptian, erected a stele—carefully phrased to avoid using the actual words for Hyksos or their capital Avaris—honoring the founding of the Hyksos capital of Avaris four hundred years earlier. The mummy of the pharaoh Ahmose, who had defeated the Hyksos and initiated the New Kingdom Egyptian Empire three centuries earlier, may have turned over in his Theban tomb.

To review New Kingdom Egypt briefly, after the military defeat of the Hyksos, ancient Egypt took on all the trappings of a modern empire. In this four-century-long imperial context Egypt underwent some surprising political and even religious changes. First there was the world's first major female ruler. Then the matrilineal line of royal succession was violated. Then the next pharaoh married a commoner, the daughter of his foreign prime minister. Then the old state religion was dumped in favor of a new experimental proto-monotheism. While this was in itself overthrown in a return to religious orthodoxy after a generation, succeeding pharaohs took reign names with suggestions of foreign influence. Finally it all came to an end in a great catastrophe after five centuries—including the Hyksos century—of remarkable political, religious, gender-rule, and governmental experimentation. The catastrophe was so great that we are now left to guess what may have survived across the centuries of dark ages that followed it.

Recurring references to the Hyksos, and the hypothetical "neo-Hyksos" of the mid-New Kingdom Egyptian period may be because they were economically and politically tied to the Minoan-Mycenaean civilization to the north and the Hebrew-Canaanite civilization to the east. Fragments that managed to filter down across the dark ages were recorded centuries later in both Hebrew religious text and ancient Greek ballads, myths, and dramas. And of all the ancient world following the great catastrophe, these ancient Hebrew and Greek writings of living and breathing characters through which we may feel the ancient world have been the ones preserved and passed down to us reasonably intact to compare with reserved scientific modern archaeological discoveries.

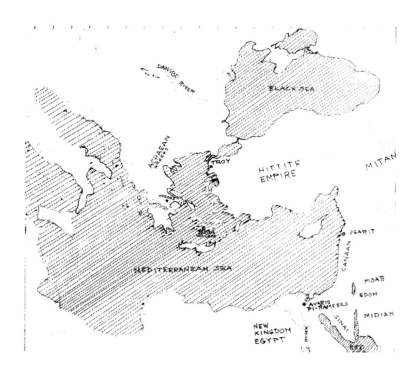

Figure 6: Map of Late (Tin) Bronze Age Empires.

Chapter Five

Biblical Joseph and Haran, and "Neo-hyksos"

Imperial Egyptian civilization had grown confident enough and secure enough to permit a female god-monarch to rule even if she had to be addressed as "king" because appropriate language had yet to be invented and there simply was no word for a female monarch. Ultimately it led to political reorganization and religious revolution, a tangential outgrowth of which has quite clearly lasted into our time.

The reign of this "Queen" Hatshepsut appears to have opened up a Pandora's box of Egyptian social, political, and religious experiments in toleration. Fragmented remnant memories of these courageous and outrageous experiments seem to have survived in our precious sacred and secular literature. It is as if they were in themselves precious to generations of ancients following the demise of civilization, who took pains to pass them on them on from generation to generation as oral and then written social and religious commentary.

"Queen" Hatshepsut, who may remind us of Queen Elizabeth I of England, was either succeeded by or overthrown by her son, Tuthmosis (Thoth-moses) III. He eventually allied himself with the Mitanni and involved Imperial Egypt in the first recorded war between great empires—between the Egyptian empire and the Hittite empire—which terminated in the first of eventually two great indecisive battles at Kadesh in modern Syria, at the limits of logistical reach of both empires. The location of this battlefield shows a need to maintain a direct border between the Mitanni kingdom and the Egyptian Empire, a common border to allow trade to flow freely between the two nations.

Tuthmosis III's son, Amenhotep II, continued the imperial war tradition but on a smaller scale. Among his recorded achievements is the capture of seven foreign kings, who were "sacrificed" to the god Amon and following that their bodies were hung upside down on the walls of Thebes—except for one, who was spared and sent south with the news of what happened to the others. How the message was taken, no one now knows. But Egyptian Empire went on, and Amenhotep II reigned for over a quarter of a century. When he died, circa 1400 BC, Egypt was secure and free to experiment with internal change.

With his son came what would appear to be the beginnings of some fragmentary foundations of modern Western culture and religion. As with the Hyksos—by then gone a hundred fifty years earlier—we may glimpse remnant rudiments of events and deeds that survived obliteration but not alteration across the barrier of the long dark ages.

Even today our concepts, beliefs, understandings, and even perceptions are modified by material surviving across the dark ages that sprang from two significant royal decisions. Tuthmosis IV became the first pharaoh to "marry" a non-Egyptian woman, a Mitanni princess named Mutemwiya. More importantly, while he only reigned for ten years, Tuthmosis appointed a non-Egyptian prime minister, Yuya, whose direct influence continued on into subsequent reigns and may continue in oblique and unique ways even to this day.

Clearly more than just a monarch-and-prime-minister symbiotic political arrangement, the evident power behind the throne of Tuthmosis IV for his reigning decade was his prime minister, Yuya, a man with, as Ahmed Osman demonstrates, a foreign name, whose mummy betrays features suggesting Indo-European genes.

The son of Tuthmosis IV and Mutemwiya, Amenhotep III, also looks strikingly non-Egyptian—some have even suggested Slavic or Far Eastern. Traditional Egyptian artists apparently had difficulty with this, and the many surviving renderings betray a certain amount of perplexity. To say the least, Amenhotep III looks different than the long line of inbred Egyptian pharaohs who went before him and this appears to have given the careful and skilled Egyptian sculptors and artists a little trouble.

He not only continued the deviation from traditional Egyptian norms his father had initiated, he added his own. Half-foreign himself and probably not happy with rampant Egyptian ethnocentricity, Amenhotep III "married" the daughter of his father's non-Egyptian prime minister Yuya. Her name was Tiya, and while only a brief oblique reference to her may be in the biblical text Genesis 45:8 when Joseph says he is "father to Pharaoh," possibly meaning father-in-law of the pharaoh Amenhotep III, and another use of the pharaoh's "house" (meaning wife) in Genesis 46:31, where Joseph "said unto his brethen, and unto his father's house," where "father" may be a reference to the pharaoh who, though technically his son-in-law, may have required an official address of "father." It would seem very unlikely and unnecessary for a person to be remembered for speaking to the four walls of a house itself, or even in a house itself. Unless Joseph's "house," or wife, had some terribly significant importance to story or history, she would have been, like so many women, ignored in the biblical text.

We are left to wonder then whether Joseph's daughter, conceivably the same person as prime minister Yuya's daughter and wife of the pharaoh Amenhotep III, might have once accompanied Joseph to and from Canaan. If so, this journey of prime minister Joseph-Yuya would probably on official government business rather than a tribal family visit, quite likely on royal Egyptian naval ship to colonial Canaan rather than days of difficult overland travel on Sinai desert roads. After the collapse of civilization, when the workings of great imperial governments could no longer be grasped, the story of this person, who was quite clearly an imperial Egyptian prime minister and said to be "governor over all the land of Egypt" (Genesis 45:26), took on a survival-economy tribalistic tone that could be understood in the telling.

Whether Tiya was the biblical Joseph's daughter or whether she was simply, as on the face of it, the daughter of the non-Egyptian prime minister Yuya and married to the half-Egyptian pharaoh Amenhotep III, her life and marriage would appear to have had a remarkable effect on our present ways of thinking, believing, and perceiving reality.

Like Amenhotep III apparently half-foreign herself, Tiya was skillfully captured by the Egyptian court artists as an attractive, intelligent, and very determined looking woman. Three thousand years later a glance at various renderings communicates a sharp clear mind determined to have her say in history, a well educated resolute half-foreign woman, the politically aware daughter of the powerful and respected former prime minister, and the influential chief wife of the pharaoh.

As a key player in the saga beginning with Tuthmosis IV, the marriage into Egyptian royalty and subsequent influential life of Tiya focuses on what almost seems to be a slowly accumulating neo-Hyksos resurgence, beginning less than fifty years after the defeat of Hyksos with the clear diminishing of Egyptian tradition that brought a female monarch, Hatshepsut, to power. A more noticeable further abandonment came a century after that when Amenhotep III married as his chief wife a half-foreign daughter of his apparently popular non-Egyptian and possibly "neo-Hyksos" prime minister. And the next pharaoh, very likely their child, Amenhotep IV, abandoned the old ways entirely and changed his reign name to Akhnaton when he established his "protestant monotheistic" Aten-belief as the official state religion.

If Tiya's father's position as Tuthmosis IV's prime minister and her own marriage to the pharaoh Amenhotep III meant a tenuous but growing reestablishment of Hyksos "multi-national corporation" influence and power in Egyptian affairs, she was certainly her father's political daughter. There is a suggestion that her efforts kept this "neo-Hyksos" control of Egyptian government going—even that her strident efforts created a backlash and brought its downfall.

This was no longer the secure isolated Egypt of the pyramids and the sphinx. The pyramids were old by then, the last of them almost a thousand years old. This was imperial Egypt, though militarily secure in its borders and isolated from world turmoil by desert and ocean, deeply and necessarily involved in "world" trade and "world" politics. Trade with the known world was brisk and vital. Imperial military adventures were becoming fairly commonplace. Not only goods and booty came into Egypt as a result, ideas did, religions did, and people did. In reverse, Egyptian goods and ideas went out into the world, and Egyptians also did.

Amenhotep III presided over a rare time of peace. He built monuments and temples all over Egypt and its colonies in the security and with the wealth that his father's and grandfather's conquests had provided. His firstborn son, probably carefully prepared to lead this wealthiest, most artistically and intellectually sophisticated, and most powerful nation on earth, apparently died only shortly before him when he was old and ill, possibly with cancer of the liver. It may have brought on a crisis, not so much for Egyptian succession to the throne as for the growing neo-Hyksos recovery of Egyptian political influence and power that the Yuya and Tiya father-and-daughter team appear to have represented.

Another son, who may not have been fully prepared to rule the wealthiest and most militarily powerful nation on earth, suddenly found himself heir to the Egyptian throne was crowned the pharaoh Amenhotep IV. He "married" a princess from his father's harem, called Nefertiti in Egyptian, meaning "Beautiful One Who Has Come," the name suggesting that she had come from elsewhere, speculation being from Mitanni.

She still impresses us as a strikingly beautiful and mysterious looking woman whose delicate feminine features stare out at us from renderings over three thousand years old. From being a minor "princess" in the royal harem—already, that is, a wife of Amenhotep III for about two or three years—she became his son Amenhotep IV's chief wife, the First Lady of the Land of Egypt in all modern respects, as had been with her mother-in-law Tiya.

In addition to the influence that both Yuya and Tiya had on the young new unprepared pharaoh, he now had a brilliant, well-educated, politically sophisticated, and extremely attractive young woman as his first lady. Suddenly and unexpectedly raised to being the all powerful and never questioned god-king, he may not have had much time to thoughtfully develop his own agenda. But you have to wonder at the agenda and political machinations of a "former" non-Egyptian prime minister in conjunction with his very determined daughter, the late pharaoh's chief wife and now queen mother, and the additional brilliant beautiful and apparently foreign woman who became his own chief wife.

To say the least, Amenhotep IV was an odd looking man with an elongated face, as with Amenhotep III apparently alien and difficult for traditional Egyptian artists to render with standardized pharaoh formats. They rendered him with an odd "laid-back" torso and thick wide hips and legs. His appearance and large belly have suggested disease to many, but it may have been his personal influence on artistic style and his political statement for imperial Egyptian "laid-back" life-style, campaigning for popularity by countering New Kingdom Egyptian imperial militarism begun by Ahmose.

Amenhotep IV, whether for personal or political reasons—the latter understandable in the context of a neo-Hyksos grab for politico-religious power—scrapped the old Theban religion of Amon-Re and put in its place a new official state religion, worship of the Aten (*itn*), the disk of the sun. The effort was vigorous. Workmen were sent to sites throughout Egypt to obliterate names and images of Amon-Re. Even tall stone obelisks were scaled to remove images from their tops.

While "Aten" is translated into solar disk, it would seem to mean something we moderns would call life-energy of the sun, or solar energy. But whatever it meant, it was so different and broke so sharply with the old religion of Egypt that nothing like it happened again until Constantine abandoned Roman state polytheism for the monotheism of Christianity a millennium later.

To drop the revered traditional god Amon-Re out of his royal name, he changed it to Akhnaten (Beloved of the Sun Disk). With that, the proto-monotheistic worship of the Aten became the Egyptian state religion. By the ninth year of his reign he had dropped all traditional references to older gods from his official cartouches to purify their religious expression with a virtual monotheistic Aten.

There had never been a religious revolution quite like it before. There had been inclusion of Canaanite deities in northern Egypt during the Hyksos occupation two centuries earlier, but this was expected with military and political takeovers.

There had never been an outright religious revolution, especially not in Egypt, and if these apparent motivating persons, Akhnaten, Tiya, Nefertiti, and possibly aging Yuya were a "neo-Hyksos" power elite, they were taking a big gamble in order to sidestep the influential conservative ethnic-Egyptian Amon-Re religious bureaucracy that virtually dictated Egyptian religious politics out of the capital city that was then called by their god's name, No Amon (*Niwt Imn*), the City of Amon, that we now call Thebes. On one hand the pharaoh was religiously believed to be the living god on Earth who could do no wrong and therefore could not be questioned for what he did. On the other, this was a new religion with a new god under whose authority the pharaoh was acting. The believers in the old-time religion would have been confused at best and most likely made doubtful and angrily offended.

There had been a touch of monotheism running through Egyptian polytheistic religion in that a single Creator God, Khnum, was recognized. But the Aten religion actually scrapped the Egyptian pantheon in favor of a single deity, the Aten. It was a the single important step that seems to have directly led to modern monotheism and the three great Western religions of today. The fact that at least one of the Biblical psalms, Psalm 104, shows considerable derivation from "The Hymn to the Aten," apparently composed by the pharaoh Akhnaten, cannot have been an accident.

The entrenched orthodox political-religious institutions of Amon-Re, like all established and powerful religions, seethed bitterly even if they dared not oppose the god-king. Orthodox opposition simmered and waited. Opposition in Thebes may have been so intense that Akhnaten was forced to build a new capital city for himself far to the north, a city called then Akhet-Aten (Horizon of the Aten), now referred to as Amarna from the modern Arabic name for the ruins, Tel el-Amarna.

If Akhnaten were influenced to promote this new and strange religion by his grandfather, mother, or wife—for political or whatever reasons—he became its most vigorous believer himself. He became, in fact, a fanatic, and one has to suspect, therefore, that it was all his idea in the first place. A surviving diplomatic message from the Assyrian emperor tells Akhnaten not to subject the Assyrian ambassador to standing out on the sun for hours. It may be okay for Egyptians, it says diplomatically, but too much sun is not good for Assyrians.

While the believers in the eclipsed institutions of the old time religion of Amon-Re seethed, Akhnaten promoted his new religion and ran his government in his "laid-back-California" way out of the new city of Akhet-Aten. The Egyptian Empire began to disintegrate. Desperate messages from allies to the north got perfunctory replies. Finally, the Mitanni kingdom we know as Haran was overrun by the Hittites and divided between them and the Assyrians. Probably not by coincidence, Nefertiti disappeared from the record at this time.

The heretical and evidently fanatical laid-back reign of Akhnaten lasted thirteen to fifteen years. More like Cromwell than Henry VIII, his religious-political revolution collapsed shortly after that. He may even have been blind from looking too long at his sun god and in his lifetime was deposed or voluntarily replaced by a very young son or nephew Smenkhakhare, who apparently reigned as pharaoh for two or three years and appears not to have been totally satisfied with the new religion.

Whatever happened that cut short the life and reign or co-regency of Smenkhakare, he was succeeded by his younger brother, Tutankh*aten* (the famous King Tut, for his fabulous tomb full of treasure). Possibly to ally himself with the powerful conservative forces of the Amon-Re religion, Tutankhaten changed his name to Tutankh*amon* apparently violently succeeded his brother, scrapped the proto-monotheistic Aten religion, and re-established the old familiar polytheistic Amon-Re pantheon as the official state gods.

When Tutankhamon died—with his mummy showing a massive head injury—Tiya's brother Ay, who had apparently been high priest at the politically and religiously powerful sun-temple of On, took the throne. Like "King Tut," the pharaoh Ay did not oppose the Theban religious orthodoxy of Amon-Re, but the Aten religion was allowed freedom of worship. It would appear that he was a compromise pharaoh, a member of the neo-Hyksos clique and not opposed by that political faction, but smart enough to side with the Amon-Re religious forces and if not acceptable at least not opposed, for the time being, by these establishment religious-political conservatives.

This last "Amarna" pharaoh, Ay, reigned for about five years—long enough, at least, to insure that construction was completed on Tutankhamon's fabulous tomb, that it was stuffed with treasure and artifacts and that it was sealed well enough to remain unviolated for three thousand years. Ay may have survived as pharaoh because he had been not only the irreproachable high priest of the Sun Temple at On, but the military general in charge of chariotry, the modern equivalent of a tank corps commander. If so, it would be easy to see why the Amon-Re priesthood held back from totally eradicating Atenism during his reign and why it was permitted to continue even if it was no longer the official state religion.

No mummies of the pharaohs Akhnaten or Ay have yet been found, and this may be due to the efforts of the next Egyptian monarch. Whether he was overthrown or not, after the pharaoh Ay came "General" Horemheb, an arch-conservative but administratively capable pharaoh who returned real "law and order" to Egyptian government after years of social and religious experiment, Mitanni and Canaanite sway of authority, laissez faire government, and political chaos. Horemheb (1328-1298 BC) had the remaining monuments to the Aten and the city of Akhet-Aten itself put to the bronze sledgehammers and put great effort into eradicating all traces of the heretic Akhnaten and his reign, ironically, by the act, preserving some of them, albeit in fragments painstakingly still being restored.

But while Horemheb tore down the physical and institutional structures of Atenism and the Amarna period, he could not, as with numerous other great social, political, and religious movements throughout history, destroy the memories and the spirit of them. It would clearly seem that while the conservatives dominated during this "return to normalcy," the opposition "party" now—to theorize from numerous later historical parallels—consisting of "neo-Hyksos" and allied world-trade "corporate" heads, religious progressives and ecumenicals, intellectuals, and educated and skilled technicians and managers, may have been subdued but could not be heavy-handedly eradicated.

The heady time of historical break-out from conservative Egyptian political and religious values—that we might speculate had a "neo-Hyksos" influence—had gone on for about seventy-five years, beginning around 1400 BC and lasting until about 1325 BC. Similar eras in our more recent history are remembered with fondness and some awe even after they succumbed to sobering reality and faded away. The Renaissance comes to mind, or perhaps more to the point the frivolity and abandonment of The Roaring Twenties and The Nineteen Sixties, eras remembered in themselves for something—usually for accompanying small advances in social, cultural, and artistic realizations. Might there have been something lingering in the back of the ancient mind that pointed to "The Abandoned Era of the Egyptian Capital," or whatever they may have called it—even perhaps with a morality play on the word "abandoned"?

Even as he was the instrument of restoration of order and old values, Horemheb was an intrinsic part of the fondly recalled era of exciting change, a dramatic opposite, the Great Depression against which the Roaring Twenties would be contrasted and the result for which they could be condemned. And this remnant dramatic kernel of a rare slice of history may have crossed the barrier of seven centuries of dark ages. Additional in preserving it may have been the turnover of the Sothic cycle in 1321 BC, an ancient Egyptian equivalent of a turnover from one millennium to another in our time, a time of hype, hysteria, and marking of an old and new era.

After Horemheb came a short-lived first Rameses, and then a pharaoh named Seti, a name clearly allied with Canaanite Baal-El worshippers in the eastern Nile delta and in Canaan and its trading affiliates. These pharaohs tellingly established their capitals in the Nile Delta not far from the old Hyksos capital of Avaris but remarkably far from Thebes, the City of Amon—perhaps as far as they could get.

After the first Seti came the second Rameses, who early in his reign fought the second great—and this time massive even by modern measures—battle between empires, again apparently to a draw, at Kadesh. If he did not ceremonially "sign," he at least philosophically signed onto, the world's first recorded peace treaty between great empires, a peace treaty with an extradition clause for criminals and other troublemakers.

Rameses II (1279-1212 BC) lived to about ninety-four years old and reigned for sixty-seven of those years. Canaan would have been under tight Egyptian control following the treaty with the Hittite empire, and the remaining long reign must have been a time of relative if not total peace in the Egyptian empire and Canaan in particular. Rameses II put national energies into building and rebuilding great temples and monuments and as a result left his name and likeness everywhere in Egypt. Among the things he did was make the last significant addition to Karnak and Luxor.

After him came a Merenptah (1212-1201 BC), then another Seti (1201-1195 BC) who reigned in a period of civil unrest where an alternative pharaoh called Amenmesse, a possible short-reigning female monarch, and two other pharaohs vied for power and sometimes reigned simultaneously (1200-1185 BC). Then came a whole series of pharaohs named Rameses through Rameses XI, who died in 1064 BC.

But the grand New Kingdom imperial period came to an end on April 18, 1153 BC with the death of Rameses III, the last great pharaoh Egypt would ever have, who had reigned for thirty-two years. Following him pharaohs exclusively reign-named Rameses ruled the shrinking empire and collapsing nation for almost a century, 1153-1064 BC, Rameses IV through Rameses XI, almost as if there may have been a hope that a great name could revive a glorious past.

But only twelve years into this long series of pharaohs with the same name, Rameses V (1146-1141 BC) seems rather clearly to have died of smallpox, and it would seem that he died in the midst of a massive smallpox epidemic that swept away bronze-age civilization.

If, after the death of Rameses III, there may have been hopes and opportunities for restoration of imperial Egyptian glory that had begun with the fall of Avaris and the defeat of the Hyksos four hundred years earlier, these surely died with Rameses V in 1141 BC, if they had not with Rameses III twelve years earlier.

Ancient bronze-age Egypt had been great and would be no more. But even across the barrier of long dark ages, bronze-age Egypt seems to have had an influence on history and culture. During its four hundred years, the New Kingdom Egyptian Empire was *the* power, glory, and cultural influence of the known world, and even after the devastation that followed, some of this had made its impressions.

But these impressions have been filtered for us through oral lore and myth, and only in recent times have lost facts recovered by scholars and archaeologists come to light for comparison with what had survived in this way. Even the name of the ancient bronze-age nation itself did not survive. "Egypt," as noted earlier, is a Greek-derived name from a later time, a corruption of the name of the city of Memphis, Hikaptah. This became "Aegyptos" because like us the Greeks seem to have had terrible difficulties at hearing and pronouncing Egyptian and other foreign names.

To the ancient Egyptians Egypt was "Taawy," which might be pronounced Tarwy, literally "Two Lands"—of Upper and Lower Egypt, going back to the unifying conquest of the north by the southern pharaoh Narmer at the dawn of Egypt's history in about 3050 BC.

"Tarwy," it must be noted, has a curious sound similarity to the Homeric "Troad" and "Troas" that we call Troy, and one can wonder if there may be a real connection. Also interesting is the fact that the Hebrew word for Egypt simply translates word meanings and incorporates the concept, Mizraim (Two Lands), as if directly and respectfully translated far back in Egyptian history.

Pharaoh, the word we get through the Bible, was a New Kingdom Egyptian term. It apparently referred to the office and institution rather than the monarch since *per-o* in Egyptian means "Great House" in something of the same way we speak of the American presidency as "the White House" (as in: "The White House announced this morning...").

We see the word pharaoh in the biblical text because there are significant links between the history of the Hebrew-speaking people and New Kingdom Egypt. The patriarch Abraham may have entered Hyksos Egypt from the land of the Mitanni (Haran), but Joseph—whether he was Yuya or not—was clearly part of New Kingdom Egypt and an apparent neo-Hyksos partial restoration.

In the time of Yuya-who-may-be-Joseph, a new liberal spirit, or more likely the "neo-Hyksos" power-grab and its consequences, began with Tuthmosis IV and his taking a Mitanni foreign woman as his heir-providing primary wife. Moreover, he appointed a foreigner as his prime minister, Yuya of the family of Akhmim. One can only speculate now at the reasons for this.

The Mitanni lived in the land the Egyptians called Naharin (*Nhryn*), also called Hurru or Hurrian, sometimes Subarru, and we see them as Haran and the Horites in the biblical text. Their country bordered on the northeastern end of Imperial Egypt, where the Egyptian pseudo-colony of Canaan apparently touched it.

The land route up through Canaan went next through Mitanni. But most important to the Egyptian government would have been the geographical fact that to reach the northeastern foothills of the Tien Shan (Tyan Shan) mountains of central Asia from the eastern Mediterranean, one would have to pass through Mitanni, an Aryan nation with Aryan gods like those of Aryan Persia and India. And why was this so important? It was because tin ore needed to make ductile bronze was there.

As R. D. Penhallurick points out in his exhaustive work on the subject, *Tin in Antiquity*, tin ore sites known in the Bronze Age were rare. The largest known lodes in the bronze-age world were in north-central Asia, one in southern present-day Uzbekistan, another in the western present-day Tajikistan, another on the south side of the Kirgizskiy Khrebet mountain chain that forms a border between Kyrgysstan and Kazakstan, and two more farther on in the northern Tien Shan mountain range foothills on both the northwest and northeast ends of the salt lake now called Ozero Issyk Kul in present Kyrgyzstan, and another site seventy-five miles northeast of the salt lake in present day Kazakstan, the last three in the foothills of the Tien Shan[12].

The bronze-age Egyptian Empire would have quickly collapsed without a source of tin ore. In tomb paintings one can see copper ingots in their ancient characteristic oxhide shape being carried along with tin ingots with shapes closer to the modern. These were vital commodities that were mixed to make bronze in the Late Bronze Age.

A debatable ancient Egyptian word for "tin," *dm*, as we shall see later, is strikingly close to our English-language word. One can only wonder at it. The "t" sound and the "d" sound can intermingle in common speech, and we can see it in the phonetic corruption of "the" to "da" in caricaturized uneducated speech, da cow instead of the cow. The "m" sound and "n" sound can similarly intermingle like we use the negating prefix "im" and "in" as with "improbable" and "incorrect" to mean the same thing. The Egyptian "m" and "n" glyphs appear even more interchangeable, and the probable *Gsm* in ancient Egyptian has come down to us as "Goshen." So the debatable ancient Egyptian *dm* may have common roots with our present English word "tin."

And in the mountain chain name "Tien Shan" is something equally tantalizing, a vaguely possible hint of an Egyptian-derived word, or alternatively a word from the local language that could conceivably have traveled south with the commodity trade and become the Egyptian word, in other words a connection from one direction or the other.

While in modern Chinese Tien Shan means "Celestial Mountains," the ancients loved plays on words and double meanings. Chinese *tien* and ancient Egyptian *dm* have close sound similarities. And one can even wonder, highly doubtful though it may be, whether after the demise of the bronze age and its strategic demand for the mineral tin, a new Chinese-language meaning was superimposed over sound similarities of an old local pre-Chinese one. This, of course, would have nothing to do with the Chinese word for "tin" itself, "*syi*" in modern Chinese, probably little changed. The ancient Chinese, who had their own tin ores near the ancient Shang capital of Anyang, would not have been forced to travel across difficult desert terrain to obtain the vital bronze-age mineral.

Without laboring this speculation about the name of the mountain chain extending out past the far western extreme of Chinese geographical nomenclature too heavily, it still must be noted that this area of the Tien Shan foothills was among the very few sources of the strategic mineral for the tin-consuming bronze-age West.

Moreover, coincidentally or not, the great Aryan invasion south into Iran and India originated if not precisely in this area then within its range of cultural and technical influence and, significantly, close enough to the time of the beginning of the Late (tin- alloy) Bronze Age to raise questions.

It does not appear to have been a military invasion as such but rather a mass migration southward of almost unparalleled scope, as if forced by a significant climate change. The enormous explosion of the Greek volcanic island of Thera came at about this time and would have had the same effect on climate as the explosion of the Indonesian volcano Tambora did early in the nineteenth century of our time. As a result of the ash cloud blocking sunlight, the year 1815 AD completely lacked a summer across the Northern Hemisphere. Crops failed to grow causing starvation and hardship, noted, by among others, Thomas Jefferson.

Something similar would have forced a mass migration south, but an enabling factor could well have included superior weaponry—swords, spears, daggers, chariots, and armor—derived from a new metal alloy tin-copper bronze that opposing forces lacked.

One can only wonder now, across the great dark age and after millennia, at plays on words and coincidence of sounds in the name of both the mountain chain with the tin-rich foothills, and the name of an offshoot people of the Aryan mass-migration who came to occupy a crucial area smack in the midst of the trade route to the tin-consuming nations and empires of the West, the Hurru or Hurrians, also called Mitanni—Horites of Haran in the biblical text.

While the Egyptian word for these people, *Mtn*, would seem to rule it out, the Hurrians might possibly have been called "Mitanni" as a play on words for something like *Meht-dm*, "Northern Tin People." Plays on words were fodder for ancient tongues, and even abbreviations are not impossible. *Mtn* is clearly not very much like *Meht dm*, but it is close enough to pause and reflect. It may, after all, be something like that. Tin began to play a vital role in Egyptian strategic considerations just as the Mitanni came into the picture, very likely out of the area around the Tien Shan, and there is that similar-sounding *tn* syllable in the name—"tan," "tin," "ten," or "tun" we do not now know because the Egyptians did not use written vowels, the convention being to use an "e" when otherwise unknown.

Tin was the single vital strategic mineral of the Late Bronze Age. Copper ore was not ubiquitous, but reasonably abundant. But tin, needed to make a strong ductile bronze with it, was rare.

Tin, which replaced arsenic as the metal alloyed with copper to make bronze in the late bronze age, beginning about the time of the Hyksos invasion—but possibly as late as the pharaoh Amose's conquest of them—would have been regarded, for national strategic planning purposes, exactly like petroleum is in our time. It was the single military-industrial mineral that ancient nations and empires required, would fight wars to get, would scheme politically to sequester—and would sink into colonial or economic subservience without.

There are, even now, very few known tin ore sources in the world. There are some small tin ore sites in present-day Egypt, but they seem not to have been known during the Bronze Age. Egypt, during the whole four-hundred years of the imperial period and the simultaneous tin-bronze age, had to obtain its tin from outside its borders.

In addition to controlling access to tin in north Central Asia, including the Tien Shan foothills, the Mitanni may have mined small amounts of tin ore within their own borders between the upper Tigris and Euphrates rivers. There are almost too many touches on tin and late bronze-age events affected by strategic tin trade to ignore tin in both the name and historical presence of the Mitanni. That curious syllable *tn* (tan) in the Mitanni name could conceivably be from *dm* (tin), the Egyptians nicknaming the Hurrians "Mitanni" for their source of strategic commodity in much the same way as we refer to "Oil Sheiks" of the Persian Gulf. Far-fetched as that may be, the fact remains that the land of the Mitanni was halfway between the largest known tin lodes and Egypt, and the Mitanni were thus one of Egypt's few options for access to the vital strategic mineral.

The marriage of Tuthmosis IV to Mutemwiya, a Mitanni princess and the daughter of the Mitanni king Tushratta, takes on, then, some strong political overtones. Realizing that he could not conquer the Mitanni, let alone all the way to the Tien Shan, Tuthmosis did what the Hapsburgs did, married his way into alliance and influence. In desperation to get Egyptian access to the single most vital strategic mineral of the late bronze age, he broke with long Egyptian matrilineal succession to the throne—broke even with having succession from any Egyptian woman—and allowed their first son, half-foreign Amenhotep III, to come to the throne as the next pharaoh.

In addition to Mitanni access to tin, the Canaanite land and sea routes for transport of this strategic mineral were vital to Egypt. Canaan had, by then, been Egyptian colonial territory for centuries. Generations of "loyalists" to the Egyptian crown had grown up secure under direct Egyptian colonial administration or suzerainty.

One of them may have been Prime Minister Yuya. Perhaps he was an elite chariot officer. Perhaps he came from a powerful international merchant family involved in the overland tin trade in donkey trains and in sea trade. If so, it is difficult to imagine his family as biblical donkey drivers as such, any more than Aristotle Onasis in our time was an oil tanker captain or a truck driver.

Whatever Yuya himself or his family might have been, he became, it must be emphasized, the second most powerful man in the richest and most powerful nation on earth, the prime minister who in those days had additional judicial powers. Only the pharaoh could overrule his decisions. Since he outlived Tuthmosis IV and continued to have influence through at least two other pharaohs, he may have been the *de facto* most powerful man in the bronze-age world.

Egypt and Egyptians prospered under his leadership. The pharaoh especially prospered from his land appropriation schemes. The careful mummification of his body and his rich burial indicates that his efforts were enormously appreciated, at least by the royal family and the Amon-Re religious establishment.

Whether he was the biblical Joseph or not, Yuya was a real historical person. Ahmed Osman makes a good archeological and biblical text case that Yuya is the Joseph of the final chapters of Genesis. Over and above Osman's conclusions, one can take the first syllable of Yuya's name and the first syllable of his Egyptian government title and get Yu-Seph, not far from the traditional pronunciation of the biblical character and a not unlikely condensation by foreign-speaking oral historians and early transcribers removed by distance and time from the real man and his times.

Fragments of history in the biblical text have been put in or left in to promote and emphasize theology. The text is at once both fortunate and unfortunate because on one hand we have some fragments of very ancient history preserved for corroboration by archaeology, but on the other hand unfortunate because belief may cloud and frustrate attempts to recover history through them. Genesis especially and the Old Testament in general would seem an abbreviated and generalized attempt to relate for promotion of religion the whole history of the world from its very beginning to the general area of time in which it was written.

The story of creation and beginning of the world was undoubtedly convincing to the people of the time because it was consistent with other contemporary creation stories like the epic of Gilgamesh, still in circulation in the timeframe. The subsequent genealogies seem careful enough to have reality bases even if lifetimes and spans of time seem exaggerated. "Lifetimes" may represent carefully preserved dynasty lengths of some yet unknown royal house or religious-astronomical institution. Confusion could further result from the misinterpretation of the Hebrew word *dor*, which means either "lifetime" or "cycle," and one of the several used, a Syric "cycle"—*dara*, obviously related—is 80 years. The biblical text four "lifetimes" between the Abraham and the term as prime minister of Joseph fits amazingly well with the arrival of the Hyksos, prior to their coup and appointment of northern pharaoh Maa-ib-re Sheshy in about 1650 BC, 4 times 80 = 320 years, and the term as prime minister and later retirement influence of Yuya that may have lasted into the possible "neo-Hyksos" Amarna period beyond 1350 BC. And one cannot but note a symmetry—symmetry religiously revered by the ancients—between that time and the time of Exodus, with the hypothetical smallpox epidemic in the Sinai, 4 times 80 = 320 years later, or its real counterpart, the historical appointment to prime minister and term of office of Yuya (c 1400-1375 BC) and the three-plus centuries to the great population decimation catastrophe and death of Rameses V of smallpox in 1141 BC.

But this is to some extent cheating. There were other "cycles" with different lengths of time, some also called *dara*, and this one just happens to fit nicely. What it means to show is that there could have been ancient attempts at precision and accuracy, not to mention symmetry, that are now lost like the measurement systems they utilized. The various "lifetimes" appear greatly exaggerated even considering remarkable genetic endowments toward longevity. They seem more to be eras or time-cycles than real human lifetimes, but the lifetime exaggerations could also have resulted from transposing between fundamentally different numerical systems.

Whether or not Yuya was Joseph, the much edited and revised Old Testament would still seem to contain a stylized attempt at accurate rendering of history as it was derived from the first the oral narrators and later by the first transcribers. It may, therefore, allow an edited view of the New Kingdom Egyptian Empire. Certainly the long line of people involved in orally preserving and then later writing down the Biblical stories saw something crucially necessary to the whole of the story in not only the Joseph story and the subsequent New Kingdom events leading up to the Exodus, but from much earlier in the Abram-Abraham story, the first excursion into Egypt, either Hyksos Egypt of New Kingdom Egypt.

What the biblical text omits about various people in contact with New Kingdom Egypt is almost as important as the information it gives. Moses, for instance, had to have been given, as a member of the royal family, a good upper class Egyptian education, almost undoubtedly including some military officer training. To have taken a significant part in the great war involving wide-ranging and powerful nations in Chapter 14 of Genesis, Abram-Abraham would have had to have been a man of some standing, a warrior-class feudal chieftain, or less likely but still possible, a merchant with considerable power and influence whose resources were drafted for or involved with military supply.

That ancient authors sought at very least to point to real places can be seen in the identical names found on an Ebla tablet contemporary with the fabled war, and in the same order as Genesis 14, Sodom, Gomorrah, Admah, Zeboiim, and Bela[13]. Abraham would have been no grunt private and unlikely even a minor tribal chieftain in that probably real ancient war. If archaeology has given us some corroborating historical facts, we must see the biblical text as having undergone normal alterations of oral transmission and editing of written material over time. But this story and others in the biblical text from Genesis until Judges (same word for title as Hannibal's) and Samuel also remarkably survived across a dark ages after the civilized world all but vanished.

The subsequent Joseph story appears to go some length to present authenticating material. While opening with material to establish his credentials as an unfortunate tough Canaanite kid from a very grubby and fractious family whose brothers got away with getting rid of him into slavery, it shifts slowly through his trouble with Potiphar's wife and his jail sentence to his awesome position of power, quite obviously a prime minister in the most powerful country then on earth. No real attempt to minimize this occurs. Through all the years of oral rendition and through all the editing of the written story, it was still terribly important that a local "proto-Jewish" boy made good, terribly good, became, quite possibly, the most powerful man in the world for a time.

From Genesis Chapter 11 on to the into the early parts of Exodus we catch a glimpse of imperial Egypt not through the eyes of insiders in pompous records on tomb walls and related papyrus scrolls, but through the eyes of outsiders kept at a distance from the powers that were in the royal institution and government bureaucracy. While Abraham, Jacob-Israel, Joseph, and Moses all would seem to have had direct contact with Egyptian royal institutions and power, the ensuing storytellers, oral and written, did not. Moreover, their audience did not, and this would have had some considerable influence on the stories. While we can accuse the great wasteland of Hollywood and TV-land of gratuitous sex and violence, the storytellers of the Old Testament were not immune to the same attention-getting techniques. These stories are notorious, with sex, incest, bloody violence, tribal wars, virtual genocide, and other devices that early Hollywood and television censors probably would not have permitted. But even with these instructional-entertainment story productions we get a glimpse of some ancient reality at the edge of imperial Egypt and on its adjacent borders.

For whatever reasons, the Genesis narrative seeks to connect the ancient civilizations of the Middle East, Mitanni (Haran), known locations in Canaan, and Egypt. Abram-Abraham, son of Terah, the ultimate patriarch on whom the whole story rests, came very pointedly from Ur in, by the time the story was written down, a country named Chaldea, probably known far and wide back then as the oldest city in the world. The story makes a point, in fact, of locating Ur there so as not to be confused with a number of similar sounding city names. Father Abraham, then, came from the city where civilization began and stands as a father-figure reference to it.

Because ancient storytellers wasted little time on unnecessary details, Abraham goes to Haran, the land of the Mitanni who played such a crucial role in New Kingdom Egyptian politics and history, the land of an offshoot of the great Aryan invasions across central Asia and eventually into India, possibly the land of people nicknamed something like "The Tin People."

Abraham's first stop in Canaan is Shechem, near modern Nablus. He then stops at Beth-on, later known as Beth-el. Then he stops at Mambre to erect an alter under the Oak Of Mambre. As Ahmed Osman speculates, this could well be a New Kingdom Egyptian temple of Amon-Re. Sound-corrupted over centuries of oral renditions, later transcriptions, and even more hidden in deliberate redactions, Amon-Re became "Mamre" or "Mambre" the very credible New Kingdom Egyptian temple of Amon-Re thus becoming the temple of Mambre. The time was, of course, during the period of time when Canaan was an Egyptian colonial territory, the very biblical text word Canaan apparently being an Egyptian administrative name for the province.

There follows a series of difficult to believe stories about his wife Sarai-Sarah and the pharaoh and then about a very old Sarai-Sarah giving birth to Isaac. The authors wanted it known that the patriarch and his chief wife (because like all the gentlemen of the day he clearly had several) traveled a long road into Egypt, stopping religiously at significant pre-Yahweh pagan shrines along the way.

As the story goes, Sarai was taken into the royal harem, becoming a "wife" of the monarch of the greatest nation on earth, no small accomplishment for even a beautiful young foreign woman not of royal or at least Egyptian upper class birth herself. And as Ahmed Osman points out, the change in her name reflects a change in her status. The name Sarah, an Egyptian language change, indicates that she was regarded as an Egyptian princess. Like Mutemwiya and Nefertiti, and many who were not chief wives, Sarai "married" into the pharaoh's harem and became a "princess," Sarah.

The story troubles itself with a morality tale about her release from the harem to her true husband Abraham. But royal harems probably underwent personnel changes for reasons not unlike those of a modern strip joint, and released harem residents would have gone back to their original families. In this case it seems to have been back to Abraham.

When they died, Abraham and Sarah were buried in a plot Abraham bought from the "Hittite" Ephron. The sons of Heth (Hittite) who sold the plot of land, repeated for emphasis, probably meant generic non-Egyptian and non-Canaanite rather than a Hittite as such, but whatever it meant, it shows, and seems meant to show, the ethnic diversity of the commercial Egyptian empire in Canaan and elsewhere. Abraham and Sarah are buried in a cave called Machpelah "before Mamre" (Genesis 25:9—not precisely "in" Hebron, but about five miles north of the ancient city center), in other words apparently properly buried according to Egyptian custom in burial grounds dedicated to Amon-Re. The corruption to "Mam-re," may at first have been accidental through lack of understanding, then later deliberate, to disassociate the patriarch and his wife from Ancient

Egyptian faith. Note, also, that it was first the Egyptian "princess" Sarah who was buried in the religious grounds of the god of the royal house of New Kingdom Egypt, Amon-Re.

A stab at a timeframe for this might be gleaned from the early church historian Eusebius, as noted in *Eusebius as Church Historian*, by Robert M. Grant. The year 2220 of Abraham, derived from jubilees, is the 251st year of Antioch, and the 12th year of Septimus Severus (193 AD to 211 AD, died in England) That would make Abraham 2220 equal to 205 AD, or in reverse, year Abraham 1 equal to 2015 BC.

That is centuries too early to fit well with this scheme of things, but it would be roughly consistent with the timeframe of great war of Genesis 14 happening at the beginning of the twelfth dynasty of Egypt, the dynasty of the pharaoh Sesostris, whom Martin Bernal (*Black Athena*) shows marched an army up through Anatolia, into Greece, across southern Russia, and down through the Caucuses before returning to Egypt with the loot apparently found in his tomb. Great wars between nations were taking place at this time, and large armies were being led over great distances.

But Amon-Re does not begin to figure prominently in Egyptian religious affairs until shortly before the Hyksos were expelled, circa 1550 BC. If there is only one Abram-Abraham, the burial names and images could be anachronisms. Isaac Asimov points out in *Asimov's Guide to the Bible* that there may be two Joshuas in the biblical text, the latter one being better known to us by his Greek-derived name, Jesus.

If we are to take the biblical text at its word, there is only one Abram-Abraham, who would seem to have entered Egypt in the Hyksos or New Kingdom periods. To resolve the contradiction we might venture a really wild guess that there are two different Abram-Abrahams, just like there are two ancient Mideast monarchs named Sargon, widely separated in time. Unlike the famous and amply recorded Sargons, the two Abram-Abrahams could have merged into one over centuries.

It is just a guess, but the change in the man's name itself hints at a second individual. The earlier one has a name appropriate of a chieftain who took part in the great war between nations in Genesis 14. The latter one has a name appropriate for a man who went down into Egypt with Sarai-Sarah in the early in the New Kingdom empire, or possibly at the end of the Hyksos Empire.

We can hope that he went, as the story goes, voluntarily. But this may be out of place for those times, and he went less than voluntarily or saw his chief wife taken, four generations, or about a century, before Joseph, just at the beginning of the reign of the "Napoleon" of New Kingdom Egypt, Tuthmosis III (1479-1424 BC).

To present a sense of the time and its ways, the campaign chronicler of militarily aggressive Tuthmosis III, the scribe Thaneni, writes: "He brought the chiefs of Zahi (in Syria) as living prisoners to Egypt and he conquered all their cities." Tuthmosis III conquered his way up through Canaan, through Syria, to the Euphrates, and brought back lovely young women from the conquered harems, three being listed in his tomb, Menhet, Menwi, and Merti.

It does not seem impossible that others not listed might include a beautiful young woman named Sarai, but there is no evidence for it and it is presented here only to render a feeling for the time. Later downsizing of this or another pharaoh's harem for economic reasons could well have released "Sarah" and returned her to the Canaan hill country. Or she may well have—as if the biblical text may have sought to make a point on ancient audacity and cruelty—grown fairly old, past normal childbearing age, and was unceremoniously returned to her pre-Jewish Canaanite family.

Looking at the name of Abraham's and Sarah's son from an Egyptian colonial perspective is also tantalizing. "Isaac" may not have been named for "laughter," as extracted from Hebrew, but could have had an even more pointed allegorical name. His life lacks the detail provided for both his parents and for his son, and his name, Isaac, is a strange one, not found among names in the ancient Middle East. It is almost as if a gap in time between generations was filled in by someone with a religious message.

But an Egyptian meaning dredged up for "Isaac" (the *sac*-sound comes through in all linguistic forms of the name) exquisitely fits the story. One of the few ancient Egyptian words coming down intact all the way into modern English is *sac*, exactly the same meaning as modern "sack." The Egyptian name "Isaac" might, then, mean "sack-carried," or "by sack," or something similar. The name has stumped biblical scholars because there is no ancient equivalent as there is with most other biblical names. The idea is certainly consistent with the story. Sarah is, with emphasis by use of exaggeration, said to be too old to conceive. But Isaac is born anyway.

Might we think the unthinkable and consider Isaac an adopted kid who could have been brought to Abraham and Sarah in a sack, the original message possibly that adopted or biological children are legitimate in passing down "family" inheritances, names and values.

Such things could conceivably have been later altered in the Jewish monarchy days when genetic heritage meant so terribly much. Original historian-storytellers (including Moses), later transcribers, and even later official editors seem to have been at cross-purposes at times.

Another less religious and less important point lost, but significant to this discussion, is the purchase of a piece of land on which to pitch his tent by Jacob, Isaac's son. Unlike Isaac, but like Abram-Abraham, Jacob's name undergoes a significant change to Israel. While his second name is vital to the very meaning of the Old Testament, his original one appears to have been a glossed-over or misinterpreted biblical name. Jacob was said to mean "heel," but the transcriber was no longer aware of "the original theophoric name," *Iahkub-ila* (may God protect)—as explored by Claus Westerman in *Genesis 12-36, Commentary*[14]. And, again, one of the Hyksos pharaohs was named "Yacov-el," (1645 to 1635 BC), virtually the same name but from Egyptian, and raising large questions about Hyksos influence in the family of Abraham, or, *vice versa*, the proto-Jewish heritage of the Hyksos rulers of northern Egypt. This, in turn, raises another question. Just as Mizraim is a direct translation of the Egyptian name Tarwy, both meaning Two Lands, we can wonder if "Israel" might be some long lost and still unknown direct translation from something in Egyptian, something so badly misinterpreted in the past that the original meaning has been lost?

To return to the piece of land purchased by Jacob-Israel, in Genesis 33:19, we see that he purchased it from Hamor, Shechem's father (eponymously the city?) for "a hundred pieces of money." The translators and editors may have lost something along the way, this time more recently. Not understanding a term, they used a common general word, money. But on still surviving ancient texts the word that no one understood is *kesita*. Since there was no known contemporary or ancient coin called a kesita, the authors of the King James version caved in and used the word "money," and got on with the rest of it.

In a footnote in the JPS translation of the Tanakh (most of the Old Testament), it is suggested that the word might be derived from the Hebrew *qesitah*, "to pay." But this would not seem consistent with the context, and contemporary with this JPS translation, the official Revised Standard Version of the Church of Scotland is so unsure of it that the word "sheep" replaces the King James Version use of "money."

Unknown to earlier biblical writers and translators, money as we know it—even coined money—had not yet come into existence in the late bronze age when Jacob was purchasing his land. The first metal coins were made well into the Iron Age, centuries later.

The ancient Egyptian economy had a monetary unit called *deben*, based on a weight of copper. Like our modern dollar-amount credit card transactions, no physical "*deben*" were actually exchanged. It was simply a fixed value written on papyrus or clay for accounting and bookkeeping purposes.

But this knowledge has been gleaned from recent archaeological discoveries. The early translators could not have known this either. Recent translators realized that bronze-age trade was done by contract and barter and began looking for a meaning of the word *kesita*.

A commodity in demand would have been the strategic metal tin, and it leads one to believe that by the late bronze age, with its extensive networks of trade, metal ingots, notably tin, had become, like *deben*, a standard for a medium of exchange, possibly even the one of preference.

Kesita looks temptingly similar to the Aryan word for tin, *kastira*, somewhere phonetically between that and the Greek word for tin, *kassiteros*, as if the word itself were in route across time and territory from the original Aryan homeland through Mitanni (Haran) to Greece. A large number of Greek words have Aryan derivations, and many familiar Greek gods appear to have been more ancient Aryan ones, Varuna becoming Uranus for instance.

If *kesita* did not come from the Aryan word, it may still be a corruption of another of the similar sounding ancient Middle Eastern words for tin. Oral renditions eventually taken down in writing and subject to creeping errors over centuries appear not to have changed it so much that we cannot recognize something that very likely signifies the vital bronze-age mineral. Rather than sheep, Hamor would seem to have sold Jacob a plot of land for an amount equal to a hundred-or-so ingots of tin.

This all suggests a vague possibility that during the dark-age transition from bronze age to iron age, oral renditions confidently portrayed Jacob as a businessman in the big lucrative multi-national bronze-age donkey-train tin-hauling business, as a son who had inherited it from his ancestors, as businesses typically were and still are. That further hints that Abraham, Isaac, and then even Jacob's favorite son Joseph (Yuya?) were all, at some point in their lives, involved in strategic metal hauling, internationally dealing with its politically sensitive suppliers and private and military buyers in ways not unlike British Petroleum executives have been doing with that strategic mineral in our century.

And if the Hyksos pharaohs, one of whose name is "Jacob," had been ancient multi-national corporate heads when they seized northern Egypt and ruled it for a century from 1650 to 1550 BC, just as the tin-bronze age was replacing the arsenic-bronze age, they surely would have been, among other things, tin tycoons.

It cannot help but leave one with a suspicion that Abraham, Isaac, Jacob, and later Joseph, were the bronze-age equivalent of corporate executives involved in strategic commodities production and trade, especially the crucial strategic mineral of the late bronze age, tin.

The fragment about Joseph loading up his brothers' pack-train may then take on a slightly different meaning pointing to something lost or omitted later when all the ancient innuendo about the excitement, contradictions, and ironies of the tin trade had lost its meaning and interest. Even the concept of a multi-national corporate executive—and such people would surely have existed in the massive complex production and trade that went on through the Late Bronze Age—would have lost its meaning in the barbaric tribal survival cultures economies that coalesced out of the catastrophe chaos. Credible characters for purposes of both religious teaching and storytelling would have to have been given tribal titles and traits.

Even if neither the biblical patriarchs nor the Hyksos were involved in the crucial tin trade, someone was. Some people and organizations would have to have gained outstanding wealth and power in it. We can only wildly guess at the biblical patriarchs and more soberly speculate about the Hyksos. But the late bronze age tin trade had to have made fortunes and given business leaders involved in it great power and influence in world affairs.

The location of the Mitanni land of Hurru (Haran of Abraham) on the way to the ancient world's largest tin-ore lodes, the Mitanni's evident Aryan ethnicity, their singular marriage into Egyptian royal succession and thus obvious strong political alliance with Egypt, the clearly half-Mitanni pharaoh Amenhotep III and his marriage to an apparently half-Canaanite, or possibly half-Mitanni, daughter of a possibly Mitanni or Canaanite, but certainly foreign, prime minister, the replacement of Egyptian polytheism with a solar-worshipping proto-monotheism of the Aten, whose name Shu is also the same as the Aryan sun god Shu, can certainly lead one to speculate on the power and influence of the strategic tin economy in late-bronze-age Egypt.

As DeLacy O'Leary boldly pointed out in his 1927 book *Arabia Before Muhammad*[15], apparently when the great Aryan migration began, they moved east "to the Hindu Kush (adjacent to the Tien Shan) and thereby into N.W. India" on a route "already known and of great antiquity."

The actual bronze-age route came to light with the discovery in the late 1970s of "Caucasian" mummies in Loulan, Tarim Basin, Xinjiang Province, China, on an ancient "silk road" route on the south side of the Tien Shan mountain range.[16]

Recent archaeology has uncovered at least this ancient trade route between China and Western civilizations four thousand years ago, and it lends authority to O'Leary's contention that the Aryans came out an area contiguous to, if not actually in, the known bronze-age tin-producing area.

The Aryans of Mitanni-Haran would probably have known the route and nearby routes into the tin ore lodes, and knowing this would surely have controlled the vital tin trade from there into the land of greatest consumer of the time, the late bronze age world's wealthiest and most militarily powerful empire, imperial New Kingdom Egypt. And it is a commentary on the collective human attention span, as well as sidelight on the near total devastation of knowledge and culture after the great population decimation catastrophe, that the crucial strategic value of tin and resultant political, military, and economic machinations of tin resource sequestering and tin commodity trading so totally dropped from historical consciousness after the demise of the bronze age.

Figure 8: Nefertiti, possibly widow of Amenhotep III, married his son Akhnaten. Jocasta? Photo used by permission of Cleveland Public Library Photography Collection.

Figure 7: Amenhotep III Wearing the Blue Crown. Egypt, Dynasty 18, reign of Amenhotep III. Granodiorite, 39.1x30.3x27.7cm. © The Cleveland Museum of Art, 2000, Gift of the Hanna Fund, 1952.513. (Laius?)

Figure 9: Akhnaten (Amenhotep IV), possibly "married" his father's final wife. Was he Oedipus Rex?

Chapter Six

Greek Seepages Across the Barrier of the Dark Ages

Only in the last century-and-a-half has factual historical material from the end of the bronze age become available through archaeology and literal cryptology to decipher written languages so thoroughly lost that they were completely forgotten. What little managed to seep across the barrier of the long dark ages and survive an additional three millennia to our time presented a fuzzy and distorted picture until then.

We presently live in an era of cheap genetic engineering technology, petty wars, political-religious fanaticism, enormous gaps between super-rich and abject poor, and related terrorism. So it seems fair to ask, what fragments of our own marvelous level of civilization might survive a similar catastrophe and seven hundred years of barbaric dark ages and functional illiteracy? A look at what may have survived the bronze-age catastrophe into what we see in biblical text literature and ancient Greek myth and drama seven to ten centuries later provides us with some unsettling clues.

Greek language would appear to have evolved from, among others, Aryan proto-Sanskrit. The language of Homer's heroes, proto-Greek Achaean (Mycenaean-Minoan, and linked with bronze-age Canaanite) had, for example, a word *potnia* (our lady). This would seem derived from Aryan proto-Sanskrit *patni* (lady).

One can wonder if the very name Mycenae (possibly pronounced something like Mikinni) might not be somehow vaguely related to a significant contemporary name in bronze-age political, military, and economic maneuvering. It is not so greatly different from Mitanni that generations of oral balladic historians between the fall of Troy just before the great catastrophe and Homer's poetic pen four hundred years later could not have let a syllable slip.

Real historical Greek mariners contemporary with Jason and his Argonauts certainly touched on territory that was probably under Mitanni control in the south Caucuses Mountains and along the southeast shore of the Black Sea. The tale itself has been brilliantly revisited by Tim Severin in *The Voyage of the Argo*. Severin built a full-scale replica Mycenaean warship that he also named the Argo and actually sailed what he considers the route, finding it to be a "story-map" to guide ancient sailors before the days of modern maps.

Sea trade must have been rather heavy along this route. One can even wonder at a real historical "Port of Colchis" at the eastern end of the Black Sea (to put the story-map fable into a realistic context) where overland metals, including vital tin, were transferred to ships, better suited for bulk hauling, especially of heavy metals.

But if legend-derived proto-Greek history hints at trade with the Mitanni, the same legend series plainly states that the proto-Greeks came from Canaan. Kadmos, the legendary founder of the Greek city of Thebes and "founding father" of Greece came from Canaan and brought the Canaanite alphabet with him—the alphabet foundation for all modern Western languages, including this one you read here, the Roman alphabet used for the English language.

The name of a king of the "Canaanite" city of Ugarit, Nikmed, who lived in this era, has a name very temptingly like Kadmos if you drop the first syllable, (Ni)-kmed and add a suffix the Greeks used for important personal names, *os* or *ous*, sometimes Latinized *us*. This is not to say he is the same person, but that only a little less clearly so than with the Hyksos pharaoh "Jacob" (Yakob-er), the name similarity shows a personal name fragment in use in the place and time of the story setting. It would appear that the ancient Greek dramatists, like the ancient Jewish biblical text authors, were working with nebulously known historical material and attempting to record and preserve real personal and place names, difficult as it may have been for them with tongue-troubling and unmeaningful foreign names and words.

By the time of the classic Greek dramatists seven centuries after the population decimation catastrophe, the bronze-age city of Ugarit was at best a ruins and more likely a mound of earth completely hiding the unknown city ruins under it. Farther south down the coast, the island city of Tyre, from where the Phoenician women of the play's Chorus have come, had survived the catastrophe and was apparently known as an ancient, and therefore bronze-age, city.

Euripides, something of a dramatic agitator, was not only aware of the legendary foreign origins of Greek Thebes, but would seem to have delighted in dramatically calling attention to it while risking audience rejection in ethnocentric classical Greece. Why, after all, title a play *The Phoenician Women* and have a chorus of Phoenician women from the island city of Tyre narrate historical material to remind everyone that Kadmos, the founder of the Greek city of Thebes, not only came from "Phoenicia" but brought from there that vital foundation for Greek and any other civilization, writing? Neither Aeschylus nor Sophocles appear to have needed this kind of foreign focus for their dramatic treatments of the same Theban folk-history material. For all his dramatic genius, because Euripides may have made audiences uncomfortable and annoyed the critics with reminders of common humanity like this, he walked away with only four known first prizes in his dramatic writing career.

The Phoenician Women, set in ancient times in what we call the bronze age, uses the contemporary Greek word "Phoenician" in place of its more proper bronze-age precursor "Canaanite," by then no longer in common use. Euripides and the audience knew the location, but used language of their day for the Canaanite people of the more ancient time.

Canaan, during all of the late bronze age, and thus in the time the drama is set, was thoroughly under Egyptian supervision, a virtual Egyptian colony. So who might these recurring Greek dramatic characters of the recurring dramatic saga of Thebes really be, old favorites Jocasta, Oedipus, Creon, Eteocles, Polynices, and Antigone? Might there be an Egyptian connection?

Euripides, as well as Sophocles and Aeschylus with their dramas, wrote this tragedy creatively drawn from obviously widely known folk-history of a royal house of Thebes, and this Greek folk-knowledge contains dim and sometimes partially obliterated awarenesses of Egyptian-Canaanite ancestral connections as seen in the legend of the founding of Greek Thebes.

According to the legend, Canaanite Kadmos had followed a cow to where it lay down to rest on the fertile Greek plain of Boiotia, inland northwest of Athens, the place name an approximation of "Cow-land," the legend and the place name recalling the Canaanite "sacred cow" worship and idols, the cast-metal calf that Moses railed against in Exodus 32. On this fertile plain Kadmos founded a city, originally called Kadmea after him, but later renamed Thebes (Thebai, same spelling as the ancient Egyptian city).

He fought and slew a dragon who was son of the war god Ares (Mars), and extracted its teeth and sowed them. From these sprouted warriors who fought and killed one another until only five were left, the Spartoi or "sown men," who became the founders of the noble families of Thebes.

If Kadmos were a Canaanite, he would appear to have been a Canaanite during the Hyksos occupation, thus more likely at least a cultural Hyksos-Egyptian if not an actual one, and possibly even an ethnic Egyptian. One may read into the story remnant surviving allusions to a dimly remembered Egyptian military venture gone sour or an Egyptian civil war skirmish on Greek or Canaan soil. Following the collapse of civilization, highly trained and rigorously regimented armies would have vanished from sight and then from memory. We now can see lifelike Egyptian "toy soldiers" recovered from royal tombs marching in step in military formation to show us Egyptian military discipline. But Dark

Ages warlords, who had to recruit what local gang-type toughs they could find, appear not to have had such disciplined fighting forces.

But it is easy to see how individual soldiers of a highly trained and disciplined military detachment could seem, and thus have been originally described as, "planted" in place like a carefully spaced row of sown seeds, and could "spring out of the ground" to fight, the metaphorical meaning subsequently lost when such highly disciplined soldiers no longer existed. Images that the metaphor or simile had conjured would have been increasingly reduced to literal denotations—mysterious and prima facie meaningless, around which myth would have gradually replaced the original interpreted observation. The dragon, whose teeth from which the "sown men" sprang, may have been corrupted from a typical Egyptian god-sponsor military unit name—after, say, the crocodile god.

The folk memory remembers Kadmos coming from Canaan, founding Greek Thebes, and bringing with him the knowledge of writing, so it is within the realm of possibility that a real Egyptianized Canaanite, or even ethnic Egyptian, arrived on the Greek plain of Boiotia with a small highly trained Egyptian military contingent during an Egyptian civil war, that there was a battle, and that the winners or the losers stayed on to begin the five noble families of Thebes. In other words, there may have been folk memory connecting the city of Thebes on the Greek plain of Boiotia and the imperial Egyptian capital that the Greeks much later called Thebes.

But which "Thebes" might the root of Greek folk-history have originally drawn from, Greek Thebes or the city that the Greeks centuries later, for some apparently fitting reason, called Thebes in Egypt—that the Egyptians themselves called No-Amon, the nominal royal capital of bronze-age New Kingdom Egypt?

Euripides would seem to have used Phoenician women as his chorus to stir recollections of Egyptian-Canaanite links to Greece. The Phoenicians repeatedly recall their ancestor Io, a princess of the Greek city of Argos who was loved by the Greek god Zeus and turned into a cow by Zeus's wife Hera for it. In the myth Io regains her human form in Egypt.

We see Io invoked by the Phoenician chorus several times as ancestor of both the Phoenician and Theban royal houses, for instance: "And Io, our horned ancestor, bore kings of the Kadmeans (Thebans)."

And earlier the chorus says of the imminent civil war: "...and Phoenicia suffers too if this town of seven towers (meaning Thebes) suffers in any way." If the kings of the Egyptian quasi-colonies and Mediterranean port cities of Ugarit or Byblos (ruins respectively north or south of the present Syria-Lebanon border) had said the same during an Egyptian civil war, we could understand it to mean weakened Egyptian military might was a threat to their own dependant power. The last line continues: "Shared blood, shared children were born of horn-bearing Io. I have a share in this suffering."

There appears to be emphasis, rather than mere mention, of a strong link between the drama's "Thebes" and its "Phoenician women" of ancient Canaan. On the face of it, this would seem to represent overt folk-knowledge of Canaanite origins of the Greek city of Thebes and accepted Egyptian links to Canaanite Tyre and Greek Argos through their connections with Greek Thebes.

But lurking under it may be Egyptian "Thebes"—given that name by the Greeks either before or after the classical plays were written, it does not matter. The Greeks gave the Egyptian city the name of their historical and legendary Greek city of Thebes—rather than use its easy-enough-to-pronounce Egyptian name, No Amon (*Niwt Imn*)—for some reason. It is as if they had some remnant morsel of ancient knowledge. So let us look at Egyptian Thebes, the nominal capital of the New Kingdom Egyptian Empire for all but a score of its over four hundred years, and poke around through some more intriguing connections between Egypt and Greece and especially historical Egyptian Thebes and the recurring Greek Thebes myth and drama sagas.

Some 900 years after the collapse of the experiment in monotheism by the pharaoh Akhnaten (Amenhotep IV, c 1360-1343 BC) in Egypt, and around 700 years after the fall of Troy and the end of bronze-age civilizations, Aeschylus, Sophocles, Euripides, and undoubtedly other dramatists now lost and forgotten, wrote repeatedly about an ancient royal house of Thebes. To put it in perspective, this is akin to us in our time looking back 800 years to the well loved legend of Robin Hood for an insight into the events surrounding King John (1199-1216 AD) and the signing of the Magna Carta in a desperate attempt for very tiny light on real history.

The last great war of the New Kingdom Egyptian Empire was the defeat of the Sea Peoples by Rameses III, roughly 1200 BC, and roughly at the same time as most would put the fall of Troy. A hundred years earlier, roughly 1300 BC, the Eighteenth Dynasty in general and an intriguingly possible "neo-Hyksos" encroachment into the Egyptian royal house in particular—begun with the "marriage" of powerful Egyptian prime minister Yuya's (Joseph?) daughter Tiya to Amenhotep III (circa 1384 BC)—came to an end with the death of the law-and-order pharaoh Horemheb in 1299 BC.

In other words, there were roughly a hundred years (1398—1298 BC) between the time Tuthmosis IV—"married" to the Mitanni foreigner Mutemwiya and served by an apparent foreign prime minister, the above Yuya—took the throne until the death of the last 18th dynasty pharaoh, Horemheb.

There were another hundred years of empire from Horemheb's death until Rameses III defeated the Sea Peoples, and about fifty more years (most of them under Rameses III himself) until Rameses V died apparently of smallpox and the civilizations of the late bronze age abruptly came to an end.

In the midst of these roughly two-and-a-half centuries, 1398 BC—1141 BC, came the two-decade-long experiment in proto-monotheism by the pharaoh Akhnaten 1360 BC—1343 BC, included in it the brief coregency of Smenkhakhare 1346-1343 BC, and the great virtual world war of the known world between the Egyptian and Hittite empires, circa 1300 BC. In the "world war" the Hittite emperor Muwatallish and the pharaoh Rameses II fought to a draw with armies of at least 20,000 men each and "signed" the famous first peace treaty as a result a few years later.

Both the war and the peace treaty show a powerful secure Egypt exerting enormous influence on world history, a continuing profound and unanticipated one when you consider probable influence of the three great Western religions on the present-day world. The Egyptian-Hittite War had its immediate national goals and its immediate political-military effect. To supply an army of this size marching up through Canaan to meet the Hittites virtually at the Canaanite border at Kadesh must have required Egyptian supply by sea, and must have required at least as many as the thousand ships of Agamemnon's fabled expedition to Troy apparently less than a century later.

The Egyptian capital city that the Greeks called "Thebes" was at the center of these powerful religious, political, and military events. Not only ancient Egyptian documents but a mention in the Biblical text, in Nahum 3:8, give the bronze-age name of Egyptian Thebes as No (from Egyptian Nut Amon, No Amon, or *Nwt Imn*, City of Amon).

It may simply be that the name Thebes grew from T-'pe, or T-Apit, the Coptic name for the shrine of the goddess Apit during the Hellenistic Greek period in Egypt, and this was mispronounced as "Thebes" by the Greeks. But even here there may have been a reason for the Greeks to designate the city "Thebes."

While the "City of Amon," No Amon, may have been called "Thebes before the Hellenistic Greek occupation that began with Alexander the Great (356-323 BC), the designation of the Egyptian city to resemble the name an early fabled Greek one apparently was acceptable to the Hellenistic Greeks. They kept it.

Nor was it the first time Greeks had renamed a city Thebes. Did they like renaming cities Thebes? Legendary Greek Thebes of myth and drama was originally named Cadmeia, after its mythological founder Cadmus. The legend has it that one of the kings, Zethos, married a nymph named Thebe, and thus the name. But the name Thebes is gnawingly similar to the Egyptian word for a sacred walled enclosure, and this is consistent with the legend in that at the time of renaming a wall was supposedly built around the city. Either way you look at it, there seem to be a number of connections between Greek and Egyptian Thebes, and thus it would seem no accident that No Amon became known to later Greeks and to us as Thebes.

During the Egyptian Empire period, the Egyptian capital Thebes must have been either singularly the greatest and grandest city in the known world, like Rome during the Roman Empire, or at least among the greatest and grandest, like London during the recently departed British Empire.

As prime minister to Tuthmosis IV, non-ethnic Egyptian Yuya ran Egypt from "Thebes," the City of Amon, the capital of southern Egypt from which a century and a half earlier the pharaoh Amosis had set out to successfully conquer the Hyksos.

Even if Joseph were not Yuya, we see in Genesis 42:6 that Joseph was governor over at least a jurisdiction or nome of Egypt. It would seem from the story that he was a governor of Egypt itself, like Yuya and a few other foreigners in the New Kingdom period, the prime minister, and therefore had to do his governing from Thebes.

The early storyteller teachers and preachers seem to have sought to convey through their tales an innate human ability to change for the better coupled with a sense that things are going to happen if they are fated to happen, no matter how unlikely it would seem—in a way the very story of life on earth and its resulting human life and intelligence. In the story base on which Western religious belief depends we find that, among others, both Moses and Joseph—both destined for awesome power and greatness—ran into trouble with the law in what we must assume to be their wild youth. Moses killed an Egyptian and had to flee the country. Joseph was accused of adultery with his boss' wife and sent to jail. Both later rose to leadership positions, and both had enormous effects on history, Moses, of course, profoundly, while Joseph merely ruled the wealthiest and most powerful nation on earth, an empire and a time destined, ironically and as everyone knew by the time the story was written down, for the trashheap of history. In our day of increasingly computerized criminal records, credit data banks, widespread records of the most minute details of people's lives, and official scrutiny that locks out, even from mere jobs to make decent livings, all who might not conform to very narrow standards, these stories should be carefully considered—even by the secular storytellers of our time.

It is difficult in our time, and was back then, to accept a foreigner, after being thrown into jail justly or unjustly for adultery, interpreting some nightmares and being pardoned, and then being appointed to the most powerful nation on earth's second most powerful position. But that is, of course, what makes it a good story in either the religious or the Hollywood sense.

People and places in the biblical Joseph story betray New Kingdom Egyptian nomenclature and lend the story authenticity. Potiphar (the guy whose wife got Joseph in trouble) and Potiperah (his father-in-law) are probably both *pir-di-per-re,* he whom Re gives, a common Egyptian personal name. If Joseph married Asenath, daughter of a priest of On (Anu in Egyptian), Potiperah, by coincidence (?) the same personal name as Potiphar, it would have put him directly into some circles of influence and power. The biblical storymakers did have historical concerns to paint their own picture of the world from its beginning until the now of that ancient time. There would seem to be elements of historical fact woven into the story.

We are left with the tantalizing possibility that the real historical Egyptian prime minister Yuya was the biblical Joseph. Yuya, as Ahmed Osman points out, was also married to a daughter of the high priest of On. The temple of On—at Memphis (Hikaptah, which the Hellenistic Greeks turned into the very name of Egypt, Aegyptos)—was the temple to the sun, a very important, if not the most important, religious temple in Egypt. And it should be noted that apparently Yuya's son, perhaps his grandson, or even brother, who later became the pharaoh Ay, was the high priest of the temple of On.

Yuya's daughter, Tiya, did become the powerful chief wife of Amenhotep III, and their son, Amenhotep IV, who changed his name to Akhnaten to promote his new proto-monotheism, was probably, therefore, Yuya's grandson.

Sigmund Freud and others have long speculated that Akhnaten was actually Moses. Immanuel Velikovsky, however, wrote an even more highly speculative—and haunting and even chilling—book about Yuya's grandson, Akhnaten. Velikovsky championed wild speculative theories throughout his life. Sometimes he came close to a truth, and he certainly provoked thought. Sometimes he was out on the periphery, but with thought-provoking kernels of similarities to modern accepted scientific theory.

His *Worlds in Collision*, while flagrantly in opposition to the geological record, has been partially exonerated by the "neo-catastrophism" of Walter Alvarez which shows a meteorite impact probably wiped out the dinosaurs and three-quarters of all the life forms then on earth. But the sheer wildness of Velikovsky's *Worlds in Collision* theories branded him an intellectual kook in his lifetime.

An exception is Velikovsky's 1960 book *Oedipus and Akhnaton*.[17] While speculative, it is far more level headed. Here he is more at home in his educational background of history, linguistics, and Egyptology. Whatever reasons that the Greeks had for linking Greek Thebes and Egyptian Thebes, we are now left to ponder with our imaginations.

In *Oedipus and Akhnaton* Velikovsky demonstrates a possibility that the famous tragic king of Greek drama may in fact have been drawn from the real Egyptian pharaoh Akhnaten.

If this should some day turn out to be historical fact, this could make the legendary tragic monarch of Greek Theban dramas, Oedipus, the grandson of the biblical Joseph, not only tying Western religious and secular story-bases together but raising larger questions. When civilization literally fell apart, was there an effort to preserve the greatness that had once been by telling stories to next generations, stories that underwent drastic changes as time went on and generations died off? Three to five centuries later the still loved and circulating stories were finally written down and have come down to us in this form. But by then they had been adapted to religious, political, and social needs, as well as artistic demands and modifications for ancient box-office acceptance.

A look at the imaginative link between Greek drama and biblical text raises tantalizing questions. Homer, writing around 800 BC and closest of the ancient writers on this side of the great catastrophe, took down in written words a docu-drama oral ballad created and modified for popular entertainment. For both dramatic effect and box office appeal, between about 500 BC and 400 BC, Aeschylus, Sophocles, Euripides, and we should include Aristophanes, took increasingly wider artistic liberties with the popular storybase.

If these Greek dramatists were using stories derived from real people and real events, those people lived and those events happened eight or nine centuries earlier, in a timeframe centering around 1300 BC, with the balladic and folklore-derived dramas reaching back a millennium to people living and events taking place from about 1500 BC up to the crashing down of civilization not long after 1200 BC. The last Classical Greek dramatist was therefore writing up to thirty or forty generations after the events. To place this span of time in perspective, it is as if a Native American in our day were to attempt to dramatize Scandinavian court gossip stories told by Leif Ericson's crew members to American Native Peoples, long after a huge Amerindian population decimation, due largely to smallpox, and after little remained of pre-European-contact civilization and social structure, and even language, except Mexican and South American pyramids and archeological edifices.

As noted earlier, in the real historical ancient Egypt, a princess whom the Egyptians named Nefertiti may have come south to Egypt from Mitanni to marry the great builder pharaoh Amenhotep III. She apparently made it to

Thebes before he died, possibly of liver cancer. How the dead pharaoh's son, Amenhotep IV (later changed to Akhnaten) came to marry one of his father's wives, Nefertiti, and appoint her his chief wife is not known. But if the sculptor of her famous bust rendered her features accurately, she was an exotically beautiful and would seem a sharply intelligent young woman, and the new young pharaoh no doubt had his pick.

Like Oedipus marrying Jocasta—called Epicasta by Homer—Akhnaten married his father's wife, Nefertiti—although probably not, as the tale goes, his own mother, who was apparently Amenhotep III's chief wife, Tiya. Queen Mother Tiya, however, apparently did continue to play a dominant role in his reign, possibly not only because she was the chief wife of the late pharaoh but also because she was the daughter of a former powerful and highly regarded prime minister, thus giving rise to later stories.

The model for the dramatic character Jocasta may have been, then, a synthetic contraction of Tiya-Nefertiti, or it may simply have been Nefertiti, wife of Amenhotep III and not long after, wife of his son, Akhnaten, the original story material mellowed and sensationalized over the centuries.

Oedipus, like many of the Greek dramatic characters, is not a real Greek personal name but simply a descriptive name. In Greek it means swollen or fat feet. Egyptian language did not carefully distinguish between legs and feet, so coming from that language "Oedipus" also could have meant swollen or fat legs. A quick look at any of a number of surviving painted or sculpted renditions of Akhnaten seizes first on his very unusual features, then on his strange laid back (in a Californian sense) pot belly, and then on his wide fat hips and legs. Especially after the overthrow of his proto-monotheistic religion by the bitter conservative religious establishment, it is possible that he could have been known scurrilously in popular gossip as Fat Legs. Whatever the case, Akhnaten literally fits the descriptive name Oedipus, meaning Wide Legs in Greek.

Akhnaten's father, Amenhotep III, is also a strange looking man, oriental or Russian looking. To native Egyptians this half-Egyptian pharaoh may have seemed very female looking, in much the same way as Spanish explorer Francisco de Orellana failed to differentiate the smooth-skinned Tapuyan tribe adult males and females of the Amazon valley and therefore named the river after the fighting women of ancient Greek mythology, the Amazons.

Perhaps Amenhotep III was bisexual, but he never officially emerged from the ancient closet—if such was even felt necessary by Egyptian god-monarchs. Gay or not, his unusual physical appearance must have caused popular comment even in his own lifetime. This might explain a name Laius, which Velikovsky shows means Impudent Effemination. The dramatic character Laius was deliberately cast as a homosexual in a related Mycenaean saga, so Velikovsky's interpretation of the meaning of the name would seem correct. In all the dramas, Laius is the father of Oedipus, just as Amenhotep III is the father of Akhnaten. That part fits—real Egyptian history linked tantalizingly with Greek folk history.

If we continue this link between Greek drama and Egyptian history, Creon would clearly be the caretaker pharaoh Ay. In Greek Creon simply means Ruler. Ay, very much like Creon, not only became pharaoh following the deaths of the brothers Smenkhakhare and Tutankhamon—both of them briefly reigning and notably young pharaohs—but may have assisted in a regency with young Smenkhakhare when Akhnaten was either dead or totally incapacitated by blindness from gazing at his sun god. There are strong hints that Tutankhamon and Smenkhakhare may well have died fighting each other, as Polynices and Eteocles did in the Greek drama.

Polynices simply means in Greek, "Belligerent," which dramatically, of course, he was. It is difficult to say which real brother the character Polynices was meant to be, Smenkhakhare or Tutankhamon. Eteocles, whose name means True Fame (or, Just Glory), was the reigning monarch of Thebes in the dramas, against whom Polynices led an army, and therefore Eteocles would seem to be the real Egyptian pharaoh Smenkhakhare, who reigned for a year or two. On the other hand, the denial of proper burial to Polynices would seem to favor Smenkhakhare for two reasons, one, he did not have a proper tomb, and two, he appears to have been an Amen-Re reconversion who was denied that burial and was instead given an Atenist burial, evident on his coffin. This would fit the Greek dramatic character Polynices.

Sometimes myths and legends are deliberately composed and disseminated for devious purposes, and since Tutankhamon's tomb remained successfully hidden until archeologist Howard Carter discovered it on November 4, 1922, the story may have been part of the greatest literary and literal coverup in all history. Whichever brother it was, Polynices, whose name means belligerent, remained unburied in the Greek drama, meaningful lesson being more important than potential irony to the original storyteller.

The other brother's name in Greek drama, Eteocles, is more curious. Eteocles (from *eteos*, just, true, and *kleos*, fame, glory) may not have been just one more Classical Greek descriptive name like the others, but a real Mycenaean-era Greek name. Contemporary with the reign of Akhnaten, a personal name very much like it, Etewoklewes, was found in clay tablet records in the ruins of what was apparently ancient Pylos (a real bronze-age name, in those tablets, *pi-ro*). A known real Mycenaean name may, of course, have been the origin of the character Eteoclus, son of Iphis, one of the Seven Against Thebes opponents of Eteocles, but the ancient name similar to one of the two brothers, from apparently ancient Pylos, has an *ese* final sound that the later Classical dramatists seem to have sought to preserve. Etewoklewes seems closer to Eteocles. But what might the dramatists have been trying to say, or what might have been understood without further comment by ancient audiences?

Important to Western religious history as well as Greek drama, a real tragedy may have taken place with Antigone. Velikovsky describes a live pit burial near one of the tombs and demonstrates how this may have been the pharaoh Akhnaten's daughter Meritaten, wife of the young pharaoh Smenkhakhare. The first half of her name hauntingly resembles a later Merit (Mary), the wife of a later Joseph (Mary is Meriam in Coptic Christian!), both of whom fled as political refugees to Egypt rather than elsewhere in the Roman Empire for some good reason, hinting a novel reinterpretation of New Testament biblical meanings if Meritaten were Antigone, in some ways suggesting the female counterpart of a suffering Christ.

It is all thoughtful but wild speculation, of course. Meritaten, daughter of Akhnaten and Nefertiti, granddaughter of Amenhotep III and Tiya, and great granddaughter of Yuya, our hypothetical Old Testament Joseph, may not have been the tragic young woman who died literally buried alive in a pit. But there is a reasonable possibility that she very well might have been.

If the character Antigone was drawn from the historical Meritaten whose name means "Beloved of the Aten," the holy sun disk, the character Polynices would seem to have been drawn from Smenkhakhare rather than Tutankhamon. Both of these young pharaohs who succeeded Akhnaten would have been required by Egyptian matrilineal succession custom to marry daughters of the previous pharaoh's chief wife to legitimize their succession to the throne. Whether they were brothers-and-sisters or merely cousins, both Tutankhaten and Smenkhakhare indeed married Akhnaten's daughters Ankhsenpaaten and Meritaten, respectively.

Like his sister, half-sister, or cousin Meritaten, the former's reign name Tutankhaten included the name of the Aten sun disk until he allied himself with the Amon-Re political and religious conservatives, possibly to gain their support for the overthrow of his brother, and changed it to Tutankhamon. The treasures of his fabulous tomb have traveled on tour through many of the famous museums of the world and indeed have shed a great deal of light on his time.

The mummy of Smenkhakhare seems to have been found in his brother's tomb, but there is some question. But there is that other possibility that would make the apparent Egyptian historical confrontation compatible with that of the Theban dramas. Smenkhakhare, forbidden a funeral as an Amon-Re believer, was buried as an Atenist. It would seem consistent with the story in Theban dramas. If Meritaten, disobeying an order given by a neo-Hyksos pharaoh Ay now surrounded by Theban conservatives—a man riddled with fear and political anxiety as the victorious Theban Amon-Re forces were gnashing their teeth and drooling over regained power—publicly defied her uncle and had her Aten monotheism-supporting stepbrother husband properly mummified, the insecure and tenuously legitimate pharaoh may have felt it politically necessary—for the greater good and to maintain peace—to punish her publicly in this horrible way.

These conjectures would in the balance have the pharaoh Kheperu Neb-Re Tutankhamon as paralleling the dramatic character Eteocles. Akhnaten, Nefertiti-Tiya, Meritaten, Smenkhakhare, Tutankhamon, and Ay act out their lives in Egyptian Thebes, perhaps tellingly in the same timeframe setting in which the dramatic characters Oedipus, Jocasta, Antigone, Polynices, Eteocles, and Creon act out their parts in Greek Thebes.

But fascinatingly lurking behind the Greek dramatic characters and their parallel Egyptian historical figures is the biblical text figure Joseph, who could be the same person as Egyptian prime minister Yuya, grandfather of Akhnaten, great-grandfather of Meritaten, Ankhsenpaaten, and possibly great-grandfather of Smenkhakhare and Tutankhamen. Was the impact of the Egyptian era so powerful that anecdotal and narrative material about it seeped across the barrier of the dark ages into two different cultures and locations in two strikingly different ways?

Martin Bernal found numerous Egyptian and Canaanite words in Greek place names, river names, implement names, and personal names, including those of Greek gods and titans. He uses these words in conjunction with Greek legend to show that early Greek civilization arrived from Egypt. Kadmos, the founder of Greece according to the Greeks themselves, came from Canaan. But in the ancient Greek drama *The Phoenician Women* by Euripides we can see a suggestion—if the above consideration of Egyptian equivalents of Greek dramatic characters can be believed—that Canaan (Phoenicia) may only be a euphemism for Egypt, Hyksos Egypt. And we are led from there to our hypothetical "neo-Hyksos," or "crypto-Canaanite," period antecedent to the Amarna period and running through it—perhaps to the end of the New Kingdom Empire.

This period apparently began with Tuthmosis IV's marriage to Mutemwiya from Mitanni (Haran) with, at the same time, control of Egypt coming under his powerful foreign prime minister, Yuya. If not then, it started with the next pharaoh, Amenhotep III, who loudly and widely proclaimed marriage to Yuya's daughter, Tiya (Te-i-i in foreign cuneiform diplomatic documents). In all, Amenhotep III reigned from about 1390 to 1350 BC, about forty years, and combined with the decade of his father Tuthmosis IV, a total of a half century, long enough to firmly establish change.

Change continued even more radically with the experiment in protomonotheism by his and Tiya's son, Akhnaten, until it collapsed either after that pharaoh's death or during a coregency with Smenkhakhare, who appears to have been ousted by conservatives supporting his brother, Tutankhamon. In the third year of Tutankhamon's reign the city of Akhet-Aten, the temporary "New Thebes" of Egypt, the new capital city that Akhnaten had built for himself in honor of his sun-disk god, really was, like Greek Thebes in Epigoni, abandoned. Nefertiti may have died there, even possibly, like Jocasta, took her own life after everything had fallen apart. The Hittite emperor Supililiuliumas had captured the Mitanni capital of Washukani and put an end to the Mitanni kingdom of which her father had been king. In her adopted country, Egypt, all that she had worked for had come to a grievous end. At last, the city she and her husband had built was abandoned as an enemy army in a religious civil war advanced on it—if the story of Thebes is drawn from this. It takes little imagination to see the fate of Jocasta ominously building up for Nefertiti.

When, a few years later, the period of neo-Hyksos Canaanite-Mitanni influence at least temporarily came to an end with the death of the pharaoh Ay, the model for the Greek dramatic character Creon, Egypt was in turmoil. A military general named Horemheb took over, claimed legitimacy to the throne through marriage, and restored law and order, and apparently sought to eradicate the foreign religious and political influences. He had the former capital city of Akhet-Aten sledgehammered down. At the end of Horemheb's reign, however, came an apparent brief period of chaos, ending with a new name in the long line of Egyptian monarchy, Rameses. The old man, Rameses I, reigned only one year and was followed by a pharaoh named Seti, an Egyptian name equivalent of Canaanite Baal or El, a strongly suggesting return of the neo-Hyksos.

The political chaos, the return to power of the "neo-Hyksos" or whatever nomenclature one might chose for these foreign-connected traditionoclasts, and the generation length of time bring to mind the next drama in the Theban saga, Epigoni (Younger Generation or Later Generation), where the sons of the fallen return to military action at the gates of Thebes.

The dramatic setting time period from the play *Oedipus the King*—that is, from the reign of Oedipus' father, King Laius (Amenhotep III?) to Seven Against Thebes, would seem to fit the last years of the Egyptian Eighteenth Dynasty. The next drama in the series, Epigoni, would seem to virtually bring in the Nineteenth Dynasty, following the law and order conservative interim period of the reign of Horemheb.

The Theban dramatic series began with Canaanite Kadmos, the mythological founder of Greek Thebes and the Theban dynasty, who may have come from Canaanite Hyksos Egypt, and the classical dramatists, aware of their Phoenician-Canaanite roots and apparently also their Egyptian, would seem to have refocussed on the revival of Canaanite Hyksos influence in Egyptian Thebes from the middle to the end of the Eighteenth Dynasty.

Following the time setting of the Epigoni, the end of which would probably mark the real beginning of the Nineteenth Dynasty of Seti I in about 1300 BC, a rash young man from Troy with a good old Hittite name of Alexander (Alakshandush), otherwise known as Paris, started the Trojan war by running of with a young woman named Helen, someone else's wife. Exactly how many years is unknown.

This brings in another famous Greek saga, contemporary with the dramatic events of Thebes, the Mycenaean saga, a link between them providing a comparison of characters and timeframe. While the Theban stories begin with Kadmos, founder of Thebes, the Mycenaean stories largely begin with Pelops, for whom the present Peloponnese island-peninsula is named. It begins slightly later in time but is very much within the same timeframe.

Pelops is the son of Tantalus, a king in Lydia (now western Turkey), and father of Atreus, founder of that house which has, like the Cadmean Theban house, its own central dramatic theme of a curse. Important here, though, is that the family of Pelops and Atreus arrived in Greece not from Egyptian colonial Canaan but from Anatolia, at the center of which was the Hittite empire and at the far western end of which was Mitanni, Haran of the Bible. Conquered by the Hittites as the reign of the pharaoh Akhnaten and his Mitanni wife Nefertiti was coming to an end, the similar sound and geographical location suggest that it may have survived or revived and become the country of the Medes (Medoi), Media of the iron age. Then who might Medea be, Jason's wife brought back to Greece from this area? Is this another Mitanni princess married not to a Greek but an Egyptian?

In contrast with the Theban saga, which derives perhaps even its very name from Egypt and began with Kadmos arriving from Egyptian colonial Canaan, the Mycenaean saga looks west for its beginnings. Moreover, it continues links west through the Black Sea to Tauri (Crimea). Both in this saga and in the story of the voyage of the Argo lurks a hint of Mitanni—lurks a hint of an Achaean-Danaan-Argive empire or alliance that looks on a map not unlike the middle Byzantine empire of thousands of years later, basically Greece and then an area far to the west in the southern Caucuses and the far eastern part of Anatolia to the land between the northern Tigris and Euphrates. Either Turks in modern times or Hittites in ancient times occupy the center of Anatolia. In other words, Mycenaean Greece and Mitanni (which, again, sounds very much like the pronunciation of Mycenae, Mikinni) were in this model a unified nation or at least political-economic hegemony deeply involved in metals trade, especially vital bronze-age tin. Not only does Mycenae bring to mind Mitanni, Dan, Danaan, and Danaus sound like roots of Mi-danni (Mitanni). A real alliance by political marriage of Mitanni and Egypt may thus be preserved in fictional form.

Atreus, son of Pelops, had two sons, both deeply involved in the Trojan War, Menelaus and Agamemnon. To connect the two stories, Laius (Amenhotep III?—whose mother was a Mitanni) fled for a while to the protection of Pelops. Laius, like most of these old heros, lacked restraint, fell in love with Pelops' son, Chrysippus, abducted him, and was cursed for it. But the story allows a time comparison. Laius and Pelops have sons Oedipus and Atreus respectively. Oedipus (Akhnaten?) has, himself, two sons, Eteocles and Polynices (Tutankhamen and Smenkhakhare?). Interestingly, Atreus also has two sons, Agamemnon and Menalaus.

One can only guess that it must have been a young Pelops and an old Laius, because other than a certain symmetry in sons and grandsons, these two families' generations do not quite, historically or dramatically, match up. The mythologized Trojan War took place a generation length of time after the dramatic Epigoni, but the real events may have been farther apart in time.

The Trojan War was over somewhere around 1200 BC, perhaps as late as 1150 BC. The much later ancient Greek historian Eratosthenes (circa 276 to c 194 BC) devised a chronology that fixed the date of the fall of Troy at our equivalent of 1194 BC. The balladized war thus took place either as bronze-age civilization was imminently poised to come crashing down, or was indeed, during the legendary decade of the siege, already in the throws of the unparalleled population decimation catastrophe.

The Greek dramatists appear to have set their Theban and related dramas from a time beginning around the "neo-Hyksos" encroachment into the Egyptian Theban dynasty, which would seem to be between 1400 BC (Tuthmosis IV), to a time shortly before the Trojan War around 1200 BC, putting it during the reign of Merneptah or Seti II, following Rameses II of the great battle of Kadesh, and before the reign of Rameses III. At the center of these known historical events, Oedipus-Polynices-Eteocles, paralleling Akhnaten-Smenkhakhare-Tutankhamen, can account for almost thirty years. Creon, paralleling the pharaoh Ay, can account for another few, and coincidentally the pharaoh Ay reigned for about five years, not unlike King Creon. That leaves a little over a hundred years for the rest of the dramatic action—through the fall of Troy. Time, therefore, must have been dramatically and poetically condensed—not at all unacceptable after between five hundred and a thousand years had elapsed to mellow real historical events.

In the Greek Theban sagas there are only nine kings from Kadmos to Creon, and one more after that. Each would have reigned a hypothetical average twenty-five years to make a total of 250 years. In the real world of the same time period, there were as many as (give or take a few unknowns) twenty pharaohs from the fall of the Hyksos dynasty, which Kadmos would logically represent, until 250 years later at the beginning of the reign of Rameses III (c 1200 BC), the victor over the Odyssey-resembling Sea Peoples, the last logical pharaoh who might possibly have been minorly involved in Homer's epic poetic docu-dramas.

Thus while a one-to-one relationship between Egyptian Theban pharaohs and Greek Theban mythological kings is not quite possible, the timeframe and time lengths are reasonably similar considering distortions of time, poetry, and drama. If so, tempting sketchy one-to-one survivals may still be included. Pentheus, the second king of Greek Thebes, might possibly be, in the tradition of Kadmos coming from Canaan a Canaanite-Greek conglomerate, Ben-theus, roughly Son of a God, not too unlike Tuth-mosis, Son of (the god) Thoth, and therefore could conceivably be a historical pharaoh like Tuthmosis II, Tuthmosis III, or some other real pharaoh.

In Aeschylus's prize-winning drama *Suppliants* (not to be confused here with *The Suppliant Women* by his contemporary Euripides), the story, set in Argos, probably the most ancient Greek city-state, draws on an event that would seem widely known mythic folk-history, the literal military pursuit across the eastern Mediterranean Sea to Argos of evidently Egyptian women by their Egyptian cousins, whom they prefer not to marry.

Preposterous as it may sound to us, and may have sounded with some levity to the Greek audience in the early fifth century BC, Aegyptos (clearly either a pharaoh or personification of Egypt) is attempting to forcibly marry his fifty sons to the fifty daughters of his brother Danaos, a name, like that of Aegyptos, with that *os*, *ous*, or *us* suffix, indicating personification of a nation or an abstraction.

Not all names in the myth or drama have this "personification" ending. Aegyptos and Danaos are sons of Agenor, monarch of the ancient Canaanite mercantile city of Tyre, a bronze-age city that survived across the population-decimation catastrophe's dark ages, and thus "Agenor" could have undergone normal pronunciation modifications over centuries from the name of a known historical person.

The personification or person of Aegyptos is clear, Egypt, most likely a pharaoh of Egypt, but conceivably a folk-history known Egyptian prime minister or military general. Danaos is less clear, but in the drama represents a royal person, a brother of Aegyptos, and by inference a personification of a national people named "Dan" who show up in late New Kingdom Egyptian military recordings as a "nation." If myth and the resultant drama tie Aegyptos and Danaos together as "brothers," nephews of the Canaanite-Hyksos god Baal (Egyptianized as Seth or Seti, and the name of at least two New Kingdom pharaohs), one might infer a link to Egyptian colonial Canaan. "Brother," it should be noted here, was an address used in bronze-age official written correspondence between two equal monarchs.

Of the two personified national names, Danaos may be the more contemporarily precise. It shows up in Egyptian records even if now the people and their location have slipped through the cracks of history. On the other hand, the character we can identify with Egypt, Aegyptos, is derived from a Greek mispronunciation of the Egyptian name for the city of Memphis, Hakeptah, Residence of the spirit (ka) of Ptah, one of the main Egyptian gods. The best the Greek tongue could do with "Hakeptah" was "Aegyptos," and the name was applied to the country as a whole. The ancient Egyptians called their country Taawy, "The Two Lands," which is directly translated to biblical Hebrew "Mizraim," meaning "The Two Lands." The pharaohs called their country Taawy and are always pictured wearing two crowns, representing authority over both Upper Egypt and Lower Egypt.

So "Dan," while we now have lost track of exactly what it may have meant, is approximately a real contemporary bronze-age name, while "Egypt" is an iron-age anachronism and not even a correct name, having been derived from a later mispronunciation of an Egyptian city name and then that mispronounced word applied to the country as a whole. But Aeschylus either did not know this or chose to utilize the accepted Greek nomenclature of the fifth century BC for clarity to his Greek audience.

We see two national names implying the names of monarchs of Egypt and "Dan." Martin Bernal points out in *Black Athena, Volume One*, that the title *Suppliants* could be a pun, a play on words. *Hikes(ios)*, meaning "suppliant," and Hyksos (*Hka Has{o}th*) mean one in the same and refer to the proto-Greek Minoan-Canaanite trading peoples who established an Egyptian dynasty and built a Nile Delta capital, Avaris (Hwt Waret), later conquered by the first New Kingdom pharaoh, Ahmose, and long after that rebuilt (at least nearby), reoccupied, and nominally honored by the pharaoh Rameses II. Aeschylus may have known some historical and etymological roots, not merely unknowingly borrowed a word and a key meaning from earlier sources.

According its translator Janet Lembke, citing a papyrus found in 1952, *Suppliants* was probably first performed in either 463 BC or 466 BC, which may place it after the war-related destruction of the ancient temple of Hera near Argos, the most ancient temple in Greece, in about 468

BC—the two to five years allowing about the right time for written composition and rehearsals leading up to performance in the two weeks around the most sacred day in the ancient world, the Spring Equinox. Thus there may have been dramatic, religious, and sentimental reasons for its apparently intentional archaic-style. The primitive style of *Suppliants* may be due to it being a very early work of Aeschylus, circa 490 BC.

Argos was almost certainly known at the time of the initial performance of this first, and sole surviving, play of a tragic trilogy as the most ancient civilized site in Greece and thus appropriate for the ancient time-setting of the drama. Its ancient mythological monarch, King Pelasgus—another name having a personified *os*, *ous*, or *us* ending, thought to refer to earlier peoples who populated Greece, the Pelasgi—would seem, if we consider the title's innuendo, to save fifty Hyksos girls and their daddy, Danaos, when they flee to Argos in Greece and are given political asylum by King Pelasgus after a popular referendum permits the citizens to vote in favor of it, all the workings of a nice patriotic melodrama with distant historical overtones.

Greek myth relates connections between Canaan and Greece, and one may be free to wonder about the Pelasgi, from whom Pelasgus is named, and a people whom the Egyptians called—in the same trumpeting of military triumph containing "Denyen" (Danyan) and Carcamesh—"Peleset," now thought to mean ancestors of modern Palestinians, who show up as defeated Sea Peoples foes Rameses III.

The inclusion in this list of Carcamesh on the Euphrates River, clearly in what had a century earlier been Mitanni territory, before Mitanni had been conquered by the Hittites and Assyrians, may give an idea of the geographical range in which one may have to look to find the mysterious "Dan."

As *Suppliants* plays out on the stage, the drama calls back to a yet earlier myth and another connection between bronze-age Egypt and Greek civilization. Io, the princess of Argos and mistress of the chief Greek god, Zeus, turned into a cow (resembling the horned Egyptian goddesses Hathor and Isis) by the wife of Zeus, Hera, and restored to human form in

Egypt, where she became—interestingly because in Egypt royal succession was matrilineal—the four-times great grandmother of both Aegyptos and Danaos, is repeatedly recalled.

Interestingly, Io is the mythological mother or grandmother of Epaphos. And the mythic Epaphos is thought to be fictionalized from the real and fifth (second last, and last undefeated) Hyksos pharaoh to rule northern Egypt from Avaris, the famous Hyksos pharaoh Apophis (c 1485-1545 BC) who reigned a thousand years before the ancient Greek play was written, the name undergoing a slight adaptation and becoming the easier to pronounce and remember Greek meaning for "touch" or "caress" and possibly the myth-story of his birth later built around the meaning.

It would not be unreasonable to speculate that the mythological Io, whose mythical name would seem to have been derived from a lament *ioioioio*, used by women in Greece today to express great grief and sorrow, could have been a real person, possibly a Greek wife of one of the previous Minoan-Canaanite multinational corporate heads who styled themselves as Hyksos "pharaohs" and who may indeed have traveled widely to far-flung Hyksos-Minoan-Canaanite corporate holdings with reluctant wives, as Io was forced to travel widely. Perhaps, one might speculate, there had originally been a widely known and somewhat bitter folk-ballad account authored by the real "Io" when there had been literate civilization, essentially lost in the long dark ages, and even if not functionally lost, mythologized and embellished over the millennium between Hyksos Egyptian rule and classic Greek drama.

Hyksos pharaohs as far back as number two, "Jacob," or in Egyptian Mr-wsr-re Ya'kob-har (later called Bnon or Pachan), number three, Swsr.n-r' Khyan (later called Iannas), or number four, with an erased first name followed by Yansas-X (later called Assis) could conceivably qualify as a "husband" of Io and thus grandfather or father of Apophis-Epaphos.

As noted earlier, our present word "pharaoh" for the ancient Egyptian god-monarchs is corrupted from the Egyptian words *per-o*, "great house," probably the combined royal residence and administrative center for the Egyptian Empire during the New Kingdom. "Great House" was used in much the same way as we presently use "White House," as for instance: "The White House announced a new peace initiative today."

In ancient Egypt it was customary—and probably required—to address the person we call the pharaoh (and thus a self-styled Hyksos pharaoh), who was regarded as a living god on earth, as "The God," and a later Greek misinterpretation of the word and custom could have resulted in the mythological Epaphos becoming a child of "the god" Zeus and Io.

Even at best, wives' names rarely come down to us, and even one of the chief goddesses of ancient Egypt is simply known as Hathor—Hat Hor, House of Horus, the word "house" meaning, even as it does today in Egypt, "wife," hence "Wife of Horus," a strange non-name, we would think today, for a powerful goddess. (Biblical Hebrew transposed the Egyptian custom and nomenclature, as one can see, for instance, in Genesis 50:22.)

The play's title, *Suppliants* (*Hikes(ios*, punning Hyksos), its characters "Egypt" and "Dan," and its internal myth-historical throwbacks to Io and Epaphos, would seem to place a real historical event from which it was fictionalized back in Hyksos and possibly running into New Kingdom times, and Danaos, as personalizing a nation or ethnic-corporate group of Dan, would seem to unite the post-catastrophe proto-Greek and proto-Jewish nations, both of which sprang from the powerful cultural influence of pre-catastrophe ancient Egypt and would later themselves have such powerful influences on Western civilization.

Interestingly, in Genesis 49:16, without a doubt contemporary with some time in the Hyksos and New Kingdom Egyptian centuries and thus the two time-settings of the play, we see a tribe named Dan, earlier authenticated and eponymously personified as a son of Rachel's maid Bilhah (Genesis 35:25), apparently honored by inclusion into the tribes of Israel.

Suppliants is the first play, and the only extant one, of a tragic trilogy. No one knows how the combined three dramas played out, but the theme and climax would seem, as with other surviving tragedies, to have been constructed around those fateful moral paradoxes that permitted nothing but tragedy. If, then, there may be a historical basis to the mythology and drama, it may include one or both of two awesome catastrophes that struck Argos and Greece in particular, and the eastern Mediterranean in general, one about ten centuries earlier, the other about six centuries earlier, the explosion of the Greek island volcano Thera (that myth calls Calisto) and its destructive tsunami, and the great population decimation catastrophe, apparently caused by smallpox—mythologized in nebulous folk-memory and then this knowledge classically dramatized as the wrath of the gods for moral infractions.

A tantalizing hint of perhaps something anciently known like this may be seen in the chorus of Danaos's daughters repeatedly crying, as Janet Lembke translates it, "Lighten me healing hillpastures." Lembke's note explaining her coined word "hillpastures" for the Greek *Apian bounin* points out that the adjective *Apian* summons the healer Apis who came to Argos and cured the polluted earth, and *bounin* is a rare word that calls to mind the word for cow, *bous*.

Perhaps, then, one or both of the lost last two plays in the trilogy would have given us additional material to shed light on a smallpox epidemic, as material in Exodus, Joshua, and related biblical books seems to have done. *Suppliants* by itself is useful, though, to link Greek, Egyptian, and Jewish historical material that survived across the centuries-long dark ages.

And some speculation about Aegyptos, Danaos, Io, Epaphos, and the Hyksos and post-Hyksos—perhaps neo-Hyksos—may bring in another multinational trading corporate head.

The play's utilization of Egyptian and Canaanite characters also raises questions of where the real historical, and probably tragic, events on which the drama was eventually based might have taken place. Was it in Greece? The location of ancient Argos looks transported and contrived to please Greek audiences. Was it coastal northern Canaan, possibly a city-state like Ugarit, the name of which has corruptible word-sounds similar to those in "Argos" and which was one of many cities that burned down to permanent ruins at the time of the population decimation catastrophe?

If it were, the Mitanni land of Haran—of the patriarchs in Genesis—this would hint of a Canaanite-Mitanni alliance—proto-Greek Palestinians, Mi*tanni*, and Amarna-era Neo-Hyksos. But no matter which of these three possibilities may have been the real historical location, the play betrays ancient knowledge that Egypt and Canaan played folk-history and mythological known parts in pre-catastrophe Greek history.

The use of sons of Aegyptos and daughters of Danaus also show remnant knowledge of the adamant Egyptian position on marriage of royal daughters. Egypt had a matrilineal line of succession. Royal daughters absolutely did not marry foreign monarchs and princes because that would have automatically allowed a foreign husband and possibly following that a half-foreign son to become pharaohs.

While the numbers of daughters and sons of the two "brothers" are undoubtedly exaggerated, harems did provide a great many sons and daughters to monarchs of the Late Bronze Age.

Aeschylus may, with some folk-knowledge of the past, be poking fun at ancient days of great harems, great numbers of sons and daughters to be married off. Fifty seems a great many offspring to have to find spouses for in our monogamous society, but it may actually understate the problem since many pharaohs are on record as having more. Rameses II, who reigned for sixty-six years and lived to be 97, had one hundred eleven sons and sixty-seven daughters. In 1987, American archaeologist Kent Weeks digging in the Valley of the Kings discovered a tomb of the sons of Rameses II, and ten years later had uncovered 108 rooms in it with possibly more to be found. No parallel tomb of daughters, however, has yet been discovered. If this tomb had been known in the time of Aeschylus, it could conceivably have influenced the drama *Suppliants*.

Even if fifty offspring of each gender, all at the same approximate age and all getting married on the same day, does dramatize and exaggerate—perhaps originally with some levity—an ancient-past reality, it does deal with the late bronze-age problem of properly marrying off a large number of royal offspring. As in *The Phoenician Women*, this dramatist sought to include a popularly recognized Greek national past that included Egypt, Canaan, and other ancient nations and empires.

In notes on a translation of *Suppliants*, a spurious note titled "Sons of Egypt" refers to how the Suppliants describe the Egyptians as animals. Io's grandsons are: dogs, carrion crows, spiders, pit vipers, a winged horde, a black dream out of Egypt. But what may have the real intended metaphor? The Egyptian gods Apis, Anubis, Set(h), and Thoth?

The sons of Egypt's torsos are human, but their heads are animal—bull, jackal, snake, lion, vulture, baboon, crocodile.

The Egyptian army literally named its military units after gods like these, possibly the various units' patron gods. We see this military unit nomenclature spelled out in the recorded Egyptian account of the great battle at Kadesh. Maybe these are not stage monster metaphors. The drama could therefore preserve a remnant of Egyptian expeditionary force names handed down in oral tradition over six or seven centuries of dark ages.

But if Greek epics and dramas, especially the Theban dramas, really represent Egyptian history in fictional form, they would seem to curiously omit a very important part of history, even Greek history. Either that, or maybe a whole tragedy saga has been tragically lost.

Rameses II became embroiled in a war with the Hittite Empire which culminated in the great battle at Kadesh, certainly within the timeframe of the dramatic series about the tragic Theban house and its anachronistic sequel the Homeric ballads. Why would this be so thoroughly erased from ancient Greek literature, whether it is derived from Egypt and Egyptian Canaan or not? Two ideas come to mind. If maritime Greeks took part they would probably have done so as naval units and naval supply rather than contributing large numbers soldiers in a land army.

While the great battle at Kadesh was fought far from Greece, far from Egypt, and far, for that matter, from the heartland of the Hittite nation, it was part of a larger war. It is difficult to see how some dramas that may have mentioned it were so completely lost as not to have even mentions made of them survive. What may make sense is that the Trojan War represents another, more minor, battle in that last great war between empires before empires disappeared from earth for centuries and ancient civilization vanished. If the Greeks were allied with the Egyptians, this would be a militarily reasonable opening of a two-front war, or at least a skirmish to draw Hittite forces and supplies away from Kadesh. Alternatively, if the Danaan-Achaean-Argive Greeks were on the other side, it would make sense to capture an Egyptian-allied fortress protecting a bottleneck in the trade route north where considerable amounts the vital bronze-age mineral tin appear to have originated.

The former would appear to be the case. In Rameses II's pompous Egyptian records of the battle of Kadesh, the *drdny* were one of many nations that fought on the side of the Hittites at Kadesh. Homer's epic calls the people of Troy *Dardanoi*, and this coupled with the Hittite name of Helen's Trojan lover, Paris/Alexander, would make Troy a Hittite ally. Moreover, as Bernal has shown, Greece was dependent on Egyptian grain to feed its population and the various Mycenaean Greek kings could not have turned against Egypt if they wanted to. Thus if the great battle of Kadesh is in some way represented in Homer's ballad and Greek dramas concerning the Trojan War, the Achaean-Argive-Danaan Greeks were protecting the vital tin route for the Egyptians and opening up a second front in the war with the Hittites.

It is nevertheless curious that if Velikovsky has hit upon a real historical Egyptian source for the Theban dramas, and that if many of these and other contemporary Greek dramas do hark back to historical Egypt, something so memorable as the great battle at Kadesh, theoretically occurring at a time between the Epigoni and the beginning of the war with Troy, involving a hundred thousand bronze-age soldiers, enormous casualties, a great drain on imperial treasuries, and ending in a stalemate and peace treaty, would be so thoroughly overlooked by bardic poets and later Classical dramatists. It is all the more curious if there were extensive Greek borrowing from ancient Egyptian history and literature.

Hellenistic Greeks in Egypt seem to have identified Rameses II with Memnon, and even in the early nineteenth century proto-archaeologists like Giovanni Battista Belzoni, who first arrived in Thebes in 1816, six years before Jean-Francois Champollion translated the first hieroglyphics, mistakenly called Rameses II Memnon. In the *Iliad* there is minor character named a Memnon, an Ethiopian king, on the Trojan side, but more curious is the name Agamemnon, as if not an unlikely real historical name with wrath (aga) in it, but slightly corrupted from Aka Memnon, "Named Memnon." Is it possible that the *Iliad* poetized and personified the Hittite-Egyptian War or great terrible battle of Kadesh itself, and that Agamemnon is really Rameses II? Or, might Agamemnon have been an Egyptian military commander of the great tin-trade-protecting fortress Mycenae, who had one of those terribly unpronounceable Egyptian names and became known in lore as the "Wrath of Rameses II" (or III)?

While the fortress of Troy that Agamemnon launched his thousand ships against overlooked the Dardanelles stranglehold on a vital tin route—from what is now central Germany and from Cornwall to Egypt—the battle there and all ancient wars and battles had to be dwarfed by Kadesh, an enormous military confrontation even in modern terms and with its own ironies.

It reasonably should be there somewhere in ancient literature. But the walls of Troy stood in poet-tempting outstanding ruins for centuries as a monument to ancient folly as well as a great poetic and dramatic irony in a later iron age when tin was no longer a mineral vital to the survival of nations and empires. Is the Trojan War, then, a poetic-dramatic euphemism for a remembered fragment of the long Egyptian-Hittite conflict that culminated in the great two-day battle at Kadesh, resulted in a peace treaty, but flared up again in terrible additional irony on the eve of the great population decimation catastrophe at this strategic tin-trade stranglehold fortress?

The earlier conquest of the Mitanni by the Hittite emperor Suppiluliumas toward the end of Akhnaten's reign cut off Egypt from tin coming from the east. Rameses II and the Hittite emperor Muwatallis fought the great indecisive battle at Kadesh to gain control, among other things, over the eastern tin route, and the battle at Troy was fought either at the same time or shortly after for the same reasons but over another vital tin route.

Nevertheless, there was a focus on Egypt. Both the Greek secular storybase of modern Western culture and the Hebrew storybase of modern Western religion include more than passing references to Imperial New Kingdom Egypt, the greatest, wealthiest, most sophisticated culturally and artistically, and the most powerful nation on earth just prior to the great catastrophe that wiped out perhaps three-fourths of the population. There is a hint of a powerful social and religious lesson, increasingly lost as time went on, about not only the greatest and most powerful being humbled by gods and nature, but the hopes, dreams, and expectations of humans in general being so thoroughly put to the test. If it might one day be shown that Joseph was indeed the grandfather of King Oedipus, there would be a whole new tale to tell.

And this story may not only be of Joseph-Yuya, Oedipus-Akhnaten, and a foreign Mitanni-Canaanite influence in Egypt beginning with the Canaanite prime minister of Egypt during a time his pharaoh was married to a Mitanni princess. It may be of Danaus of Greek drama, and Danaan of Homer, one of the three Greek peoples who along with the Achaeans and Argives fought at Troy. The people referred to as Dan not only show up not in Greek literature and Egyptian documents but, as Bernal points out, in the Bible, and even way up in Ireland as a pre-Celtic people.

Who were these people who not only show up in widely separated documents but over a wide geographical range? Might they have had something to do with tin, the tin trade, protection of the tin trade. The word Dan would appear to be not too different from the ancient Egyptian and modern English word for tin. One might look, for instance, at the Mitanni, who if they don't have tin in their name, then at least would seem to have Dan.

The Mitanni empire which originated with the Aryan onslaught of 1550 BC or earlier came to an end at the same time the religious experiment Akhnaten and his Mitanni queen Nefertiti came to an end. It suggests tin-trade-oriented military alliance and political marriage—not only of Nefertiti but going back to Mutemwiya and Tuthmosis IV, and possibly having something to do with his prime minister Yuya-Joseph. The rest of the known world came to an end two to three centuries later in the apparent great smallpox epidemic.

From the time of the defeat of the Hyksos—either an Aryan nation like the Mitanni, or Canaanites pushed into Egypt under pressure from the Aryan onslaught to the north, or a mixture of both—to the time of the disastrous apparent smallpox epidemic, Egypt dominated the political and economic fortunes of both Greece and Canaan. Greece had at very least become dependent on Egypt for the net difference in food not produced at home. Canaan was an Egyptian colony. Mitanni women married into Egyptian royal-religious power and must have had something to do with the ill-fated religious experiment in proto-monotheism since the Aten's name was Shu, the same as the Aryan Mitanni sun god's.

Centuries after the great population-destroying catastrophe, when only orally transmitted stories and monumental ruined structures remained, survival-level existence grew again into tenuous levels of civilization and literacy revived. For centuries the stories had been sung and told for entertainment value and altered accordingly. When some of the stories began to be preserved in writing—the poet called Homer apparently taking great pains to preserve them as accurately as possible—much of the factual base had not only been lost but could no longer be understood. It would be centuries more before great empires formed, and even then levels of sophistication in the arts and sciences, in government and living standards fell short of that which had been lost.

If the Classical Greek dramatists knowingly or unknowingly utilized ancient Egyptian historical characters and events, their concern was with dramatic effect. Even today these are some of the most powerful dramatic psychological insights ever written. Simultaneously in what had once been Canaan, Hebrew writers began transcribing stories that had been transmitted orally for centuries. Their concern—and even more so with later editors—was for the religious meaning and a political-religious state doctrine more than preserving history. We are left with piecing together links. Caphtor, Egyptian Keftiu, is Minoan Crete. The characters in The Phoenician Women are not about Egyptian colonial Canaanites (anachronistically Phoenicians) as about a foreign Mitanni-Canaanite insertion into Egyptian government itself.

Great poetic, dramatic, and religious-lesson ironies may have been lost on us. For some reason there is a sphinx at the beginning of both the Joseph-Yuya story and the Classical drama of Oedipus Rex, the very word Rex (king) perhaps a language remnant reflecting the fact that all the ancient pharaohs had Re (the sun god as part of their names).

If Joseph is not Oedipus' grandfather, Oedipus really being the radical pharaoh Akhnaten, grandson of Yuya/Joseph, and if Akhnaten/Oedipus is not Moses, as both Ahmed Osman and Sigmund Freud believed and demonstrated, at least they all came close. King Oedipus may not therefore be Moses, but these real people and dramatic characters all lived or were all set in the same time in either imperial Egypt or its Greek zone of influence.

The rediscovery of an ancient smallpox epidemic could shed some light on these. An understanding of the absolutely vital need by bronze-age nations and empires for the mineral tin may shed some more.

Figure 10: Illustration from early Harper's. Obelisk of the Temple of the Sun, Heliopolis (On).

Figure 11: Early American illustration. Sphinx at Thebes, from "Short History of Art."

Figure 12: Known tin ore in the Bronze Age. Note tin ore where the Aryan Invasion seems to have originated.

Figure 13: Closer view of central Asian tin ore. "Ar" in "Aryan" appears to have the same Indo–European root as "ore" in English, hence Aryan = "Ore People," or "Metal People."

Chapter Seven

Tin, the Petroleum of the Late Bronze Age

The vital strategic mineral which late bronze age nations and empires sought to access and control was comparatively rare tin, absolutely necessary to alloy in about a one to ten ratio with more prevalent copper to make military and industrial quality bronze. Without it military forces and industrial economies were doomed to the bronze-age equivalent of third-world status. Tin was the petroleum of this Tin Bronze Age, and nations fought and schemed to secure supplies of it for themselves and to deny it to rivals.

It is probably not coincidence that the dates of the tin-bronze age and the dates of imperial New Kingdom Egypt appear about the same. And the initial appearance of the bronze alloy made with tin instead of arsenic may into the time of the Hyksos occupation of northern Egypt. So a combined era that includes both the Hyksos and the New Kingdom Egyptian Empire virtually defines the Late Bronze Age. For five centuries, from the Hyksos coup to the population decimation catastrophe, Egyptian and other contemporary political, economic, and military strategists must have spent considerable energies in matters surrounding the discovery of new tin ore lodes, the smelting of these ores, the shipping of tin ingots, the alloying of tin with copper to manufacture industrial-and-military-quality bronze, and the ever constant needs to secure strategic tin supplies and their delivery routes.

Imperial Egypt, the singularly most powerful and influential late-bronze-age nation, had to defend not only its imperial might but occasionally its very national borders. Egypt may have gotten some of its strategically vital tin from as far away as Cornwall in England, from Erzgebirge along the present Bohemian-German border, and earlier from the area around the Tien Shan mountains in Central Asia. And possibly of some interest here, when Mitanni was overrun by the Assyrian and Hittite empires toward the end of the Aten religious experiment in Egypt, the Egyptians would have been forced to scramble for new political-economic-military arrangements to acquire strategic tin and for alternative sources of tin ore.

Some possibly relevant fragments of political, economic, military, and psychological international trade maneuvering that have been unearthed are intriguing. In the peace treaty following the final Hittite-Egyptian war fifty years after the death of the last Aten pharaoh Ay, the Hittites appear to have insisted on a significant clause. That clause forbade trade by the Ahhiyawa —almost certainly the Achaeans of Homer—with the Assyrians through the ports of Amurru. Homer's heroes were poetically idealized sword fighters who in reality were national leaders of an extensive strategic trading hegemony. Very likely the clause in the treaty was meant to blockade copper and tin for making bronze because the Ahhiyawa and their Mycenaean-era Greek contemporaries appear from marine shipwreck archaeology and land-based evidence to have been both seagoing warriors and metals shippers and traders.

Mycenaean-era Greek trade with Egypt appears to have been extensive. In *Black Athena* Bernal shows that Mycenaean Greece had become dependent on Egypt for food, largely wheat at the end of the era. In exchange, Greece supplied Egypt with pottery, manufactured goods, and metals. Not all these metals would have been mined in Greece, and there is no tin ore there.

As an illustration of how extensive this trade was, when archaeologists began digging in the ruins of Akhnaten's capital city of Akhet-Aten, the "New Thebes" of the quarter-century Aten-worship period, they found a street lined with so many Mycenaean-era Greek pottery vessels they dubbed it "Greek Street." Two-way trade was extensive, but Egyptians would probably have shipped not only perishable food, but also flax fiber and linen cloth in exchange for archaeologically lasting pottery.

Ancient late bronze-age shipwrecks show the involvement with metals. A huge ancient population on the small, now lifeless, desert island of Pseira, off Crete, shows how heavy and extensive this seagoing trade was. And Egyptian words surviving in Greek language show how extensive, influential, and persuasive imperial Egyptian culture had become.

Since rare tin was vital to military power and industrial strength in imperial Egypt—which apparently never discovered the small amounts of tin now known to be within Egyptian borders—acquisition of foreign tin was necessary for the very survival of the nation and empire. Egyptians, therefore, had to go out in the world to secure tin resources for their nation and empire, had to construct delicate trade arrangements over vast areas, and had to back those with trade incentives and even military power in much the same way as modern industrialized nations now do the same with petroleum.

In doing so, they may even have left a few words that survive to this day even in the far hinterlands of mainstream Egyptian awareness. A few Egyptian words seem may even be found in present Germanic languages, possibly as a result of extensive tin and the amber trade through central Europe. If speculation about Egyptian words in German stretches credibility and the imagination too much, the trade routes themselves, especially concerning amber (Greek *electron*), are widely accepted.

One of the routes would have followed an old and well known amber trade route up the Danube, up tributaries to near present Nuremberg, portage to the Main River tributaries, and then down the Rhine to the cold misty North Sea where we see modern Holland. Trading ancestors of the Dutch may go back a long way. To the east along the Danish and German coasts was amber. To the west in Cornwall and Brittany was tin. Distantly to the south were the manufactured goods of the great empires.

Not very far above the present German city of Regensburg the Danube begins to flow too swiftly for commercial shipping, but several tributaries that flow into the Danube within fifty miles of that city that virtually connect to—by means of portages—tributaries flowing into the Main River system, and in fact an extremely costly shipping canal now connects the two river systems.

Near the portages between the Rhine-Main system and the Danube system there must have been another great bronze-age trading center of considerable wealth and size there, perhaps beneath the present city of Nuremberg itself. There was additional tin in the Erzgebirge mountains on the present German-Czech border and therefore one would expect a protected tin-oriented trading center near the mining and smelting operations there.

Since the forests of northern Europe provided plenty of wood from which to make charcoal—prior to the discovery of coal the only fuel to smelt ores—tin ores were probably smelted as near the sites of extraction and milling of tin ore as possible, and tin from the north and from the east would surely have arrived at the hypothetical proto-Nuremberg trading center in the form of ingots.

Moreover, a garrison would have been required at this midway point along the long hazardous river route where men and goods were forced to leave their ships for several miles of overland journey with their goods, or if their ships themselves were portaged, to protect them at this vulnerable juncture. And if there had been a garrison there, whose interests would they primarily have been serving? Ultimately imperial Egyptian—even if possibly under more direct allied Mycenaean-era Greek military control. Thus one is brought to wildly speculate even about the name of the present city of Nuremberg itself, which has a root "nu" similar to the Egyptian word-root for rope—rope which would have been a singularly crucial necessity for portaging goods and ships.

Who were the people living in hypothetical proto-Nuremberg? We can only guess. But while the historical iron-age Celts, as we know them, had not yet evolved in the tin-bronze age, the area around Nuremberg is known to have been the early iron-age Celtic central homeland. And this homeland would not seem to have been far from their earlier bronze-age central homeland somewhere in the upper Danube valley. So by extension, the Celts or proto-Celts, who like the present Germans, many of whom would appear to have descended from them, spoke an Aryan language. And these Celts may have played a role in trade, and especially tin-trade, at this trading center in its midst.

The Aryan and basically Indo-European word for tin is *kastira*, not surprisingly not much different from the Greek *kassiteros* or the late Babylonian *kassitira*. Latin *stannum*, Spanish *estanyo*, and modern Irish *stan* retain the st of the word as if to hint at some past fusion or confusion. Cornish is similar to Welsh, *staen*. And tin ore is *costaen*, literally "wood tin" because grainy fibrous tin ore in Cornwall often resembles wood. But a Welsh word may not only be *staen* but *tyn*. And French is *etain*, and German is *zinn*. Two different word bases for the metal, one close to the Indo-European, the other from something else would appear to be the case.

While there is some heated argument about it, let us assume for the sake of discussion that the ancient Egyptian word *dm* meant tin. James D. Muhly in the second chapter of *The Coming of the Age of Iron*[18] tersely states that *dm* means the naturally occurring gold and silver alloy called electrum, not tin.

Muhly's argument is with Ethel R. Eaton and Hugh McKerrell, whose watershed 1976 report in *World Archeology*, "Near Eastern alloying and some textual evidence for the early use of arsenical copper," changed thinking about the bronze age[19]. Spurious to the main thrust of their thesis, they show that Egyptian *dm* means tin. Assuming they are correct in cleverly resurrecting an important word from a long dead language, the ancient Egyptian word *dm* (written *d(m* in their paper, the second character apparently signifying the unknown unwritten vowel) is very close to our word tin after three thousand years. The "d" can easily be lisped as "t", and the "m" becomes "n" just as the ancient Egyptian *gsm* becomes our familiar land of Goshen, so *dm* is "tin." It then certainly seems reasonable to theorize—and while astounding, not surprisingly—that we English-speaking people still use the same word that the ancient Egyptians used for the vital strategic metal of the late bronze age. And whatever their origin, "*dm*" and "tin" are clearly not the Indo-European words evolved out of proto-Aryan *kastira*—a noteworthy anomaly in our Indo-European derived language.

The thrust of the paper by Eaton and McKerrell is to show that only the late bronze age was a genuine bronze age. The earlier alloy, used extensively in the early and middle bronze ages, was arsenical bronze, an alloy of arsenic and copper. This metal is similar to tin bronze but is more brittle. Perhaps horse-warfare military considerations entered into the spread of tin bronze. Tin bronze allowed, among other things, tough bronze wheels, axles, and bearings for military chariots and bronze fittings to control horses, especially bits. Simultaneously with widespread use of tin bronze came horse-and-chariot warfare. A connection must be suspected.

While tin bronze was discovered earlier, the late bronze age, from the Tumulus Culture of central and eastern Europe to the mighty and magnificent civilization of Egypt, began after 1600 BC and ran strong for about five centuries until the great population decimation catastrophe brought bronze-age civilization suddenly crashing down between about 1150 BC and 1050 BC. The late bronze-age actually struggled on for a few more of the subsequent dark-age centuries until iron-making technology became adequate to supply a usable replacement metal, but its heyday of rare strategic tin resource sequestering and behind-the-scenes related political, economic, and military maneuvering was gone.

More properly the Late Bronze Age should be called the "Tin Bronze Age," or the "True Bronze Age," or possibly the beginning of a genuine metals age in which we are still living, where to support our present enormous population level life itself depends on malleable strong structural metal.

But while a genuine metals-age began with the tin bronze age, true technological metallurgy from which it eventually evolved initially appeared fifteen centuries earlier, around 3000 BC in the Tigris-Euphrates Delta region of all those ancient Sumerian cities like Ur. Muhly and most others link it to the discovery of writing, after the controlled use of fire, probably the single most important discovery by human beings, from which all others spring. First came writing and then metallurgy, as if this aid to memory and thought processes was necessary to allow enough understanding of processes.

You see an Arsenical Bronze Age growing into a tin-bronze age in a core area of Mesopotamia and the eastern Mediterranean, the literate part of the Western world, while on the periphery a copper age dragged on and yet like economic colonies supplied the tin to make the new bronze.

The mummified ancient man found in the Alps on the border between Austria and Italy and radiocarbon dated at around 3000 BC was probably a typical copper age man. He used stone and copper tools and weapons similar to those found all over Europe but which were found with their wooden handles, fiber and leather carrying cases, and even arrow feathers freeze-dried and intact. Not long after this ancient man's death, areas far to the south and west in the eastern Mediterranean and in Mesopotamia began experimenting with metal alloys. When the experiments created a more useful metal in the form of an arsenic-copper alloy, the copper age graduated into the Arsenical Bronze Age, and almost a millennium-and-a-half later, with the discovery of a far superior tin-copper alloy, graduated into the Tin Bronze Age.

While the continuing experimentation eventually led to the age of iron, both the requirements of very high temperatures and the elusive several-step peculiarities of iron smelting and carbonization, and the different properties of iron ore itself delayed it for centuries. The most important factor, however, appears to have been necessity, primarily economic necessity. It was all that many centuries after the great population decimation catastrophe that iron replaced bronze, and the necessity that created the new Iron Age would appear again to have revolved around tin.

Clearly a major disruption in negotiated trade and protection arrangements concerning the supply of comparatively rare metal ores, especially extremely rare tin, took place and had a great deal to do with decreasing availability and increasing costs of bronze implements to the point where new experimental, but brittle and inferior, iron products were eventually reluctantly chosen as substitutes. All the political structures and economies had collapsed more profoundly than anything we can imagine today short of a nuclear war, but those built around tin and tin-bronze had collapsed and never recovered in the West because tin ore mining was so distant from large scale users and thus difficult for them to obtain.

Tin and copper miners, traders, buyers, trade-policers, bronze military-industrial utilizers, government and corporate leaders, skilled technicians and labor, and common everyday users suddenly died off in droves. From twenty-five to thirty-five percent of the total Old World bronze-age population survived and were still there, but governments, manufacturing and distribution networks, and economies were in shambles.

Survivors cared about surviving. The crucial factor now missing was incentive to mine tin in distant lands and haul it in long dangerous overland journeys or in hazardous small ships and trade it for something desirable where a goodly barter return could be got for it.

In the good old times of the late bronze age, by the time tin reached places like the Egyptian Empire after wear and tear on the equipment, including donkeys and rowing slaves, and paying the help for months of travel, and after payoffs across the long route to feudal lords and other gang-leader types, the hypothetical profit margin must have been slim indeed. After the population decimation catastrophe it appears to have been just not worth the effort and danger anymore.

Reward had fallen too low. Mines fell into disuse. Help could not be obtained. Protection that had formerly been bought could no longer live up to the old agreements. The formerly marginal but recession-proof tin-hauling business went down the drain, and that set the stage for the iron age.

Iron ore is ubiquitous. Unlike copper ore, and even more so for all tin ores, it can be found close at hand. The difference is that to smelt and refine it into something useful much higher temperatures than for copper, tin, and their alloy bronze are required. Moreover, it must be dealt with thoughtfully. An understanding of metallurgy is absolutely necessary. While a blob of copper melted out of ore is immediately useful, a blob of iron obtained the same way will be brittle and, for all practical purposes in the ancient world, useless. Knowledge about working it further into something even minimally useful had to be carefully gained and recorded over generations. Then even after knowing how to do it, much hard physical labor had to go into making a useful iron implement, tool, or weapon.

Since even this hard-won iron product was at first inferior in every way to good tin bronze, necessity had to nudge it further. That nudge would seem to have been reviving population levels and demand.

After carefully negotiated trade agreements and routes for tin came to a sudden end, surviving experienced metal workers and their generations of offspring widely but slowly began to experiment with iron to make both weapons and practical tools and implements. Even after generations of experimental improvements and slowly acquired technical knowledge, iron technology was still on an insecure base of fumbling with bad and almost unusable product and competing with hordes of at first considerably superior bronze implements, tools, and weapons in excess of a surviving and only slowly growing population needing to utilize them. Probably due to an excess of bronze amid a decimated population, the surviving or arriving Greeks returned to the bronze age for a while after flirting with the iron age briefly.

A look at the trade routes should give an idea of some of the reason the bronze age came to an end following the great population decimation catastrophe. In his mythoclastic and exhaustive *Tin in Antiquity*, R. D. Penhallurick shows that western Asian bronze-age tin came from an area ranging from the north foothills of the Tien Shan mountains in Kyrgyzstan to the modern city of Bukhara in Uzbekistan. Early in the tin-bronze age there would not have been any other major ancient tin sources in western Asia, debunking many earlier proposed sources said to be in Iran, upper Mesopotamia, and the Caucuses. Aryan—and offshoot Mitanni—power may have been derived from this, or the Mitanni may have controlled the profitable and power-brokering tin trade into imperial Egypt, but this was certainly an area dominated by the Aryans.

Penhallurick also notes other tin sources in Europe, the Erzgebirge on the Czech-German border and as far away as Cornwall in Britain and Brittany in France. Tin could conceivably have come from as far away as Thailand, especially to bronze-age Persian Gulf ports and thus into the Mideast market, but this does not seem likely. Spanish tin may have been discovered after the end of the bronze age and utilized, but it does not appear to have been.

Even the known Asian Kyrgyz-Uzbek and European Erzgeberge and Cornwall-Brittany tin would have traveled a long and therefore difficult route to reach imperial bronze-age Egypt. One can only imagine the negotiations and strategies and how this may have affected the growth of Western thought and knowledge.

The bronze-age Shang Chinese, however, had both copper and tin ores within fifty miles of their capital city of Anyang, and it is telling that the bronze age lasted much longer in China as a result of this.

To maintain the same imperial military strength and economic power as the Shang Chinese, the New Kingdom Egyptians and other early Western civilizations had to obtain vital tin from distant places, negotiate trade agreements, depend on shipped supplies from very distant foreign lands and climates. In Egypt and in the West when the great population decimation catastrophe struck, vital tin routes and agreements were disrupted.

New Kingdom Egypt and its Hyksos-century predecessor thus defines the total timeframe of the tin-bronze age. In China the Shang dynasty came to an end apparently as a result of the catastrophe, but probably due to easy access to both tin and copper, the Chinese bronze age simply continued on through the next dynasty.

In the West there was a permanent disruption. One can now only wonder what effect the required reaching out to distant lands for copper and especially tin had on bronze-age Western civilization. Resulting experience in negotiations, experience in land and water shipping, experience in international politics, widespread interchange of people and ideas, and rudimentary risk capital investment all may have given the West an economic, social, and technical development edge on the East, but it is difficult to say what of it may have lasted through the long dark age. But one element of it apparently did, and if so that element, the "story map," formed the basis for modern Western literature.

As Tim Severin has so nicely examined in *The Ulysses Voyage,* much of the *Odyssey*—unlike the war-chronicling *Iliad* and a very different story—may be the best surviving "story map" of sea trade routes in existence. While there are a few scattered ancient architectural maps, the concept of a genuine map would not develop for centuries. To fill the need for a guide across great distances, especially sea distances, the "story map" was developed. In a "story map" notable landmarks are integrated into a story in the order in which they appear along a known route. The context of the story both kept the pattern of landmark appearances in order and provided a "secret code" to locations for those who knew it. Those who knew the code knew the way.

It would appear that to avoid Hittite control of what is now the Syrian and Turkish coast, the New Kingdom Egyptian-Mycenaean Greek trade route, especially in strategic minerals like tin, cut across from Africa to Crete, and from there to Greece. After the Hittite conquest of the Mitanni midway through the tin-bronze age, there must have been a desperate scramble by the Egyptians to find new sources of tin and to protect the routes to and from these sources. Moreover, coastal Canaanite trade must have suffered and shifted for survival to that route or a more hazardous Ugarit to Cyprus then dash along the south Anatolian shore to Rhodes route.

To the north of Greece, through the Dardanelles—again that ancient Egyptian *dn*-or-*dm*-word, *drdny*—and Bosphorous, up the west side of the Black Sea, and up the Danube River system lay the mineral wealth of central and northern Europe, especially the tin ores of the Erzgebirge—which literally "Ore Mountains" in modern German. Penhallurick, in *Tin in Antiquity*, points out with the assistance of one of his many fine maps that high tin-content late bronze-age bronze arrowheads are plentiful in the vicinity of the Erzgebirge—and it can be said by extension around portages near Nuremberg—and that a squandering of otherwise valuable rare tin on expendable arrowheads shows it was so cheap and available that it must have been heavily mined nearby.

In view of the apparent foreign control over tin sources, tin trade, and tin prospecting, one would not expect to find many Egyptian words or names in the Central European or Cornish tin areas. But one is led again to wildly speculate on very marginal possibilities. Curiously surrounding portages near Nuremberg there are many rivers with names beginning with "re." This "re"—as opposed to the sun god—means "mouth" in Egyptian and was used as we use it for the mouths of rivers and canals. For instance, the mouth of the Nile was Re-ha-t or the entrance to a canal at Abydos was Re-peqr. Re-set could have originally meant a baudy bar-lined barge-port area of a canal mouth in Memphis where sailors hung out and fought drunken brawls because it later became Egyptian slang for the grave.

In the area where potential portages not only to the north but toward the Erzgebirge tin mines exist you have German rivers named Rezat, Regnitz, and Regen. Might these by some wild stretch of the imagination have been named by ancient Egyptians? It is not very likely, but the thought is intriguing.

Tin would not only seem to have been mined there in the late bronze age, but practical considerations would dictate that it would also have to have been smelted there, and there would have been economic reasons surrounding the availability of wood for charcoal fuel that it would have been alloyed with copper and cast as unfinished bronze tools, implements, and weapons there.

It is thus unlikely that the tin-bronze arrowheads were the only items cast in the bronze-age proto-Nuremberg-Erzgeberge corridor. The availability of northern European forest-cover wood for charcoal and the unnecessary bulkiness and difficulties of shipping both it and loose tin ore would have made it economically necessary for fairly extensive tin and alloyed bronze smelting and casting to have been done on location there.

If so, an image of persistent foul sulfur smelling smog hovering over valleys and making the area a bronze-age air-polluted environmental disaster springs to mind. But that area was the bronze-age equivalent of the Third World, and off in distant imperial Egypt it would not have bothered anyone. Tin ingots and unfinished cast bronze goods would have been shipped south down the Danube to the great hungry markets there and elsewhere along the eastern Mediterranean.

Connecting the Danube system with the Rhine River system, there were portages near modern Nuremberg. These portages have been used up until comparatively recent times. Up from where the Rhine-Main system takes water from the Regnitz River there branches off a small stream called the Schwarzbach, just south of modern Fuerth-Nuremberg, and it ends at a portage, or land-ferrying place, where there are two telling names to English speakers, corruptions of original Germanic that we can easily understand, Oberferrieden and Unterferrieden. Not very many meters beyond that is another Schwarzbach that flows down into the Altmuehl River, which flows into the Danube. In this area, though, there are several good "overland ferrying" points, portages. Another possible one would have been above the junction of the Vils and Rosen Rivers at Amberg. Near Neukirchen a potential portage goes across to the Hersbruck, which flows into the Pegnitz.

Shippers from the Eastern Mediterranean coming through the Dardanelles to the Black Sea and up the Danube could portage across to the Rhine-Main system and access distant additional tin from southwestern

Britain as well as amber from Lower Saxony and Denmark. A number of late-bronze-age implements seem to connect bronze-age Erzgebirge and proto-Nuremberg sites with Cornwall. Penhallurick describes a bronze pin with an amber head in a style from the Czech-German border area that was miraculously, after all the modern heavy machinery mining, found in the tin fields of Cornwall.

Trade clearly existed. A wild speculative imagination might then picture occasional Mycenaean-era Greek warships plying the Danube, maybe also the Main-Rhine, maybe sometimes carrying imperial Egyptian military and civilian officials, protecting the vital strategic tin trade and its routes. Far-fetched as it may sound, it is not completely unreasonable and not impossible.

This was not the dying dark-ages petty-warlord era of Homer and Hesiod, but a time a full three centuries earlier when a Greek confederation could launch a fleet of a thousand ships, or at least a sizable naval expedition as seen in the "Catalogue of Ships" in the *Iliad*, generally regarded to be a reliable historical document. Moreover, the great fortress of Mycenae and others like it still to be seen in Greece betray the prolonged existence of sizable disciplined military forces in the late bronze age, of which hints like the "Sown Men" may still survive. That these sizable disciplined military and naval forces would not be used to protect the vital strategic tin routes should boggle the mind even more than images of Mycenaean-era warships plying the Danube and possibly even the Rhine. But the world awaits the discovery of a sunken Mycenaean-era Mediterranean ship at the bottom of a European river.

Throughout the north there was ample wood for charcoal, in days millennia before Marco Polo brought coal back to Europe the only fuel to smelt and refine metals. Wisdom would have it, therefore, that metal was smelted into ingots at or near the mining locations where wood was plentiful. One might wonder at the large numbers of rivers in the area beginning with Re, not so much the Egyptian sun god as the word commonly used for a river or canal mouth.

Could ancient New Kingdom Egyptian river names and route designations possibly have survived so long? Or, what kinds of mills were on the Alte Muehle (Old Mill) River? Or, we see Dan (*dm*-tin?) in the name of the Danube (Danau, Danuvius), and although this is not the ancient Greek name, it would appear to be a very ancient name. The ancient Greek historian Herodotus writing in the middle of the fifth century BC, four centuries after the end of the bronze age, states that the original homeland of the Celts was in the upper Danube valley. That Ireland and therefore probably Britain also were inhabited by people already speaking an offshoot continental Celtic dialect at the time of the Celtic invasions of the fourth century BC has been demonstrated in linguistic studies.

And that brings us back to the Israelite-Canaanite tribe of Dan. Bernal points out that the "Danites" were said to have lived on ships, and that the Israelite tribal league admitted them only late, and that they were the last tribe to establish their own territory, originally on the coast between two known Sea Peoples, the Philistines and the Tjeker.

All this in addition to a noticeable lack of detailed genealogy for the Tribe of Dan in the biblical text, reinforces a notion that the tribe was not an original member of the Israelite confederation.

So what is Dan? Are they people called the "Dan" in documents of Rameses III referring to the raiding Sea Peoples as the Denyen? Bernal rattles off a whole list from the ancient Mideast and Mediterranean: Tin^3y, Tanaya, D^3-in, Dene, Denyen, Danuna, Danaan, Danaos, and Dan from Egyptian, Akkadian (the international diplomatic language), Canaanite, and Greek during the Late Bronze Age.[20]

Bernal also names rivers, suspecting an Indo-European origin: "Dan" found in the Danube and the Dnieper; "Don" found in a Yorkshire Don and the Ukraine Don. And Irish legendary people—from about this time!—the Da Danaan, who arrived in Ireland from the south.

He admits being puzzled and concludes that they may have been Mycenaeans. But given the strategic value of tin and postulating a lively trade in tin, it is not unthinkable that the names came from peoples and places having something to do with that, especially with voracious Imperial Egyptian tin demand.

But if we glance at a map showing Eurasia between the Tien Shan Mountains and the Atlantic Ocean and allow our imagination some freedom, there may be some answers in the vital strategic mineral of the late bronze age. Heavy metallic tin, or heavy tin ore, from the Asian source could well have been brought by boat down the Syr Darya River and across the Aral Sea. From there would be an overland journey to the Caspian Sea. Then up the Volga River to around present Volgograd. Then a short journey across to the Don, a friendly river flowing west with the heavy material, where the Mycenaean Greeks may have picked it up and taken it by way of the Sea of Azov into the Black Sea, and from there into the Mycenaean Greek trade zone to Egypt.

Bernal overlooked another river with "Dan" in its name, the Dnestr, which flows from near the tin ore of the Erzgeberge on the Czech-German border east and south into the Black Sea. And the Danube flows not only near the Erzgeberge, but would serve as an artery, by way of a portage near present Nuremberg, to the Main, then Rhine, and on from there to the rich tin fields of Cornwall.

That could conceivably explain the river names. There may be no way of ever knowing. As for the peoples, in the Bronze Age tribes could easily have become specialized in trading and shipping a commercial and strategic commodity like tin.

Again, there is no way of knowing. But when demand for their highly specialized lifeblood commodity began to evaporate and the world economy began to crumble, they surely would have turned to raiding and seizing territory to survive. And that might explain raiders called "Dan" from Egypt and the Levant to Ireland.

Where, for that matter, might the name Britain have originated? The much later Greeks in Roman times seem to have derived their Pretanikai from the local Celtic name, even if the Celts as we know them were fairly late iron-age arrivals long after the great population decimation catastrophe. It is tempting to imaginatively read into this an earlier Egyptian *p-re-dm*, the source or "mouth" of tin and at any rate there is the suspicious tan in the word that eventually became Britain. If this name goes back to the bronze age, it may be like Mitanni, where one can speculate on a meaning derived and corrupted from something like "north tin" (*meht dm*) people. Were the original Britains and others associated with tin sources called Tin People much as we now refer to Oil Sheikdoms? Two bronze-age tin ore producing places, the southwest corner of the island of Britain and the northwest corner of France called Britanny, even today are associated with name-sounds that may be derived from "tin."

A look at Erzgebirge leads one unto the same temptations. The tin ore in these "Ore Mountains" on the present German-Czech border is in rock. Even alluvial tin from these rock sources may have been largely broken-off rock.

The Egyptian word for copper is *hemt*, but copper ore (rock copper) is *hemt her setf*. Might we stretch our imaginations to the limit and find a hint of something in the German "*erz*" left over from the Egyptian "*her setf*," especially since the tin ore of the Erzgebirge is in rock?

Even more interesting is that the German word for "brass," usually *Messing*, may also rarely be called *Erz Metall*, either the same first half as the German word for ore, *Erz,* or possibly suggesting an "archmetal," as with the German word for "archbishop," *Erzherzog*. The more important point about brass, however, is that modern word "brass" is used for an alloy of copper and zinc. But the mineral zinc was isolated and discovered in modern times. In 1597 AD one Andraes Libavius obtained a sample of zinc from India and called it "a peculiar kind of tin." Zinc smelting was done in England as early as 1730, but was not done in continental Europe until 1807.

In short, the alloy of zinc and copper we know as brass was unknown in ancient times. What was historically often called "brass"—until virtually the last century—was actually "bronze," the tin-copper alloy. Only in our time and after the discovery of zinc have we used the word "brass" for the alloy of zinc and copper to differentiate it from the alloy of tin and copper that we now call "bronze." But bronze as we know it was often in earlier times called "brass." Might the Erzgeberge be translated, therefore, "Bronze Mountains," rather than "Ore Mountains" in some convoluted etymology of ancient reference to what was made from the tin ore extracted there?

There are a number of English-Germanic words that look strangely Egyptian other than tin-*dm*. Some are clearly accidental, such as the ancient Egyptian word so and our English word so being identical in meaning. But some may have come from extensive late bronze-age trade between Egypt and northern Europe, mainly vital tin trade.

The Egyptians used *she*, meaning "waters," as a word for lake, as in an artificial lake named She Hor, Waters of Horus. In modern German the word for lake is *see*, as in Bodensee (Lake Boden, or more commonly Lake Constance), virtually the same word, or seen modified in the Dutch *zee*, and in English "sea." Is this another accident?

The Egyptian word for a small temple is *hwt*, and their word for house is *hat*. The former could possibly have been pronounced "hauth," and this is virtually the same as the modern German *haus* and our own English house. The ancient Egyptians (and modern Egyptians still do) also used this word to designate a wife, and you can see this in the goddess Hathor, wife of Horus, which is more properly Hat Hor, House of Horus. But we are after the word for the structure itself here, and it is tantalizingly the same word.

This wild speculation is pretty far-fetched. But then the imperial bronze-age Egyptians had an undeniable strategic interest in keeping large scale amounts of vital tin ore flowing into the empire. It leaves one wondering if in the wake of the great population decimation catastrophe and sudden collapse of Egyptian influence there may have been many small abandoned temples up through the Egyptian dominated trade routes to fetch tin, and these became houses to the less religious. The German and English words for hut are also suspiciously Egyptian sounding in this regard.

You also might look at the biblical city of Pithom in Exodus. In Egyptian it is Pi-Tum, City of the God Tum, a deity of the solar temple of Heliopolis also called Atum (the temple of On in the Bible). Just north of Chemnitz in an area of the Erzgebirge where in ancient times alluvial tin mining could have taken place is a hamlet named Thum. Probably it is sheer accident, but one has to wonder.

I have gone from words to hamlets here because it is necessary to focus on the Germanic-British connection. for instance, the Egyptian word for a canal is *pi-khen*, but it is derived from voyage and our English *can*al comes from Latin-French, and *can*oe comes from African-French much later. And quite possibly neither of these came from Egyptian anyway.

The Greek goddess of sorcery, Hecate, surely comes from the Egyptian *heka*, magic, the medium through which ancient Egyptian gods operated. Whether this is one or not, Bernal has loaded *Black Athena* with ample examples like this. Greek language is filled with Egyptian-derived words. These naturally have come into English one way or another.

How the ancient Egyptian words *sak* might have become our sack, or *dsrt* might have become our desert, or *nuh* (cord or rope) might have become our noose or noodle one can only guess. It would seem through Greek and Latin.

But *she* and *see*, *hwt* and *haus*, *dm* and *zinn* or tin would all seem to hint at the ancient strategic tin trade up through central Europe and into Cornwall in Britain. Or what about Egyptian *sepy*, "to bind," first used for reed ships that had to be bound together, but later used by the Egyptians for wooden boats? It sounds enough like ship to make one wonder. Even more interesting is the Semitic-Canaanite word for ship, *zi*, which comes directly from the Egyptian word for ship, *za*. It sounds very close to the same word we still use.

Along this line, the name George seems terribly German-British to us—the name of monarchs and an insignia of the Order of the Garter, the latter showing Saint George and the famous dragon. But this is an ancient Egyptian story, Horus and the crocodile god. And if you pronounce

George in modern Spanish, you can see where the name comes from: Jorge (pronounced Hor-hey in Spanish). George, especially the saint of the dragon story, is none other than Horus, the hawk-god, patron of all the ancient pharaohs. While the name itself may come into English from Greek, the story may possibly have been more direct.

Similarly, the closest surviving derivation anywhere in the world of the ancient Egyptian chance-and-skill board game of *senet* may be the British children's game of hop-scotch, and an Anglo-Saxon game called Snakes and Ladders may have been derived from *senet*. There would appear to be a tenuous connection between these games.

At first glance it boggles the mind that far-off cold and dreary primitive ancient Britain would have anything to do with hot, dry, desert-hugging magnificent imperial Egypt. But connections have been found. Mycenaean Greek daggers, swords, and implements have been found in bronze-age Wessex culture sites in Britain. Egyptian-style faience (proto-glazed ceramic) jewelry and neckwear have been found in southern Britain, and while it probably was not actually made in Egypt, it is unmistakably ancient Egyptian style. The climate of Britain is not like dry desert Egypt and has allowed very little to be preserved. What has been found, however, does show a frail British trade connection with New Kingdom ancient Egypt.

It would appear that the Mycenaean Greeks were the main middlemen in the vital tin trade with late bronze-age Egypt. In fact, tellingly, Muhly points out that small amounts alluvial cassiterite tin ore exist in dry streambeds even today in Egypt not far from where they had ancient gold mines. Since Egyptians could simply have picked up lumps of it, they seem not to know what it was. It would therefore seem that the ancient Egyptians simply relied on foreign sources and foreign technical knowledge for this vital bronze-age commodity and used their military and economic power to assure access to these.

The Mycenaean Greeks were linguistic siblings to the colonial Egyptian Canaanites and these would have been the ore, ingot, and knowledge sources. Egypt kept Canaan under colonial control and Greece a heavily dependent on Egyptian grain trading partner. This arrangement for tin then seems secure throughout the tin-bronze age. Classical Greek poetry and drama preserves more ancient links between all three. One can therefore venture that even if Egypt were not directly involved in obtaining tin from Cornwall in Britain, some Egyptians had to be involved in procuring tin for their national defense and their civilian industrial needs and knew of far away Cornwall.

If so, a number of minor military and civilian officials and enterprising individuals undoubtedly traveled there. A remote possibility exists that Egyptian officials actually lived in Cornwall for standards assurance and other administrative purposes. There would seem to be a strong handed-down folk-memory of Canaanite-speaking Mycenaean Greeks in the wealth of popular references to Phoenicians having lived in Cornwall in ancient times.

Why did a few farmsteads begin to make their appearance toward the end of the late bronze age? The answer would seem to be deforestation. Enough land had been cleared of trees by then. Looking at scenes of the moors of the Cornwall and Devon tin fields today one sees a dreary mournful desolation in great contrast with the lush farm country of southern England. It has to remind a Californian of the recent similar desolation virtually in our own time around the gold fields there and provoke speculation of ecological disaster beginning in ancient times.

At the onset of the tin-bronze age, Cornwall was probably non-tropical rain-forest not unlike that still found at the same latitude on the Olympic peninsula in the State of Washington. It may have been warmer then, even tolerable for ancient Egyptians. But it would be tolerable even now as Cornwall juts out into the Gulf Stream current and certain hardy palm trees and Mediterranean plants grow there.

The ancient discovery of tin doomed the idyllic rain forest. For at least three centuries bronze axes felled trees for charcoal to smelt the ore and more to build mining towns. Air pollution resulting from this, land and water pollution resulting from mining, and apparently heavy population related to extracting and smelting tin ore in the late bronze age would appear have brought on the haunting desolate dreariness of ancient ecological disaster we seem to see today, a setting for ghost stories amid the ghosts of ancients forests, ancient civilizations, and tough boisterous ancient tin miners.

When ancient Egypt succumbed to the great population decimation catastrophe it would appear to have left the same ecological disasters that modern civilizations leave.

Bronze-age ruins show reasonably heavy tin working, and one has to ask about the market for this, especially in competition with the Erzgebirge. While northern Europe surely consumed some of it, most must have gone to fill the demands of the empires and densely populated kingdoms of the eastern Mediterranean, especially Egypt, preeminent among them all. It would appear that not too long after vicious and ambitious exploitation and excavation tore into British fields, forests, and hills the variola virus brought a sudden end to it. Generations of gentle lives ruined by backbreaking mining labor ultimately contributed little more than undecipherable statements carved on monuments sinking into desert sands in far away lands.

In Cornwall itself little remains because almost two centuries of fossil-fuel powered machinery tore into the earth. Curious farmers also tore into it before history and archaeology entered rural vocabularies. In *Naenia Cornubai*, published in 1872, William Copeland Borlase tells of the discovery of a bronze-age tomb by a thoughtful and careful man named Matthew Williams in 1716. While a brief description survives, one can only wonder what was lost. The early eighteenth century discovery by Matthew Williams is at least recorded. Much must have been lost to treasure-seekers and souvenir salespeople in addition to plowing, construction, and mining and its related efforts. What has been salvaged shows not only some eastern Mediterranean contact with southern Britain, especially Cornwall, but some central European contact as well.

If Cornwall had tin, Ireland had gold, silver, and copper, also very much in demand in the late bronze age. It is hard to imagine that if ancient Mycenaean-Canaanite-Egyptians had set up shop in Cornwall that prospectors would not have soon ventured just a little further to Ireland. Some Mycenaean artifacts have been found there and similar social and ecological disasters must have taken place prior to the great apparent smallpox epidemic.

In *The Origin and History of Irish Place Names*, Third Edition, published in 1871, P.W. Joyce relates some bardic histories that claim the first person in Ireland was a woman named Ceasair or Cesar who came with three men, Bith, Ladhra, and Fintan forty days before that unexplainable deluge that goes through histories. The men died, but one of their names remains on Bith Mountain (Sliabh Beatha) in the north of Ireland. Joyce continues:

> The first leader of a colony after the flood was Parthalon, who, with followers, ultimately took up residence on a plain anciently called Sean-mhagh-Ealta-Edair (pronounced Shan-va-alta-edar), the Old Plain of the Flocks of Edar, which stretched along the coast by Dublin, from Tallaght to Edar, or Howth. The legend—which is given by several ancient authorities—relates that after the people of the colony lived there for 300 years, they were destroyed by a plague, which in one week carried off 5000 men and 4000 women; and they were buried in a place called, from this circumstance, Taimleacht-Mhuin-tire-Parthalon, the Tarlaght, or plague-grave of Parthalon's people. This place lies about five miles from Dublin; and on a hill, lying beyond the village, there is to be seen to this day, a remarkable collection of ancient sepulchral tumuli, in which cinerary urns are found in great numbers.[21]

This is remarkably similar to descriptions of late bronze age burial sites across the mainland of Europe where one finds Tumulus burial sites being utilized for Urnfield burials after 1200 BC. One can find in *The Bronze Age in Barbarian Europe*, for instance:

> Moreover urnfields are not always found in isolated necropolises that are characteristic and belong to a well defined period: often urns appear in cemeteries that were used over a long period, and are interspersed with inhumations of the middle Bronze Age Tumulus culture and Iron Age burials.[22]

The cinerary urns seem to be Urnfield Culture urns, contemporary with the final days of New Kingdom Egypt and the catastrophe that brought an end to the tin-bronze age in general. Heretofore the Urnfield Culture was not thought to have reached Ireland, but not only the ancient ballad but Irish names and descriptions suggest otherwise. Joyce points out a number of Irish place names with the word *taimhleacht* (plague-monument) in them, Tamlaght, Tamlat, Towlaght, Derryhowlaght, Doohallat, Magherehowlet (in a patent of King James I, Machaire-thaimhleachta (Field-of-the-plague-grave).

While the bardic ballad fits beautifully into the time and events of the proposed great smallpox catastrophe, it may, of course, have been derived from an ancient bard wandering through an Urnfield burial site and inventing a story . But it raises questions. If these are Urnfield sites contemporary with the fall New Kingdom Egypt and the termination of widespread mining at the height of the bronze age, why are the words plague is such widespread use in the nomenclature? While an Urnfield burial site may have provoked a bard to conjure up a poetic plague, so many sites with names like this suggest something else. May there have been some long oral-tradition handed-down knowledge of the great smallpox epidemic that brought an end to the tin-bronze age and New Kingdom Egypt?

As with Borlase's book, Joyce's, written at about the same time, touches on nineteenth century historical interests before twentieth century archaeology came of age. Only later did we all learn that there were Irish and Cornish connections with the lands of Homer's heroes and more tenuous ones with the great civilization of New Kingdom Egypt.

The connection was Irish and British metal, especially Cornish tin to make bronze for the armories and industries of bronze-age empires. The appetite for metals, especially tin, kept growing right up to the great population decimation catastrophe.

While access to Cornish tin could possibly have been by way of the Atlantic Ocean, rough seas and frail ships make it is less likely than river routes through Europe. While The Rhone-Seine system might possibly be less difficult and surely was used, the earlier amber trade to the Baltic, the presence of tin ore in the Erzgebirge, and the Danube outlet into virtual Mycenaean Greek territory would cumulatively favor a Danube-Rhine route to the British Isles.

At the advent of the great catastrophe, either a new people or a new burial tradition called the Urnfield Culture suddenly replaced the Tumulus Culture that had stretched from the mouth of the Danube to the British Isles. A few centuries later and coincidentally as new iron-age civilizations began to tenuously appear to the south and east, the Urnfield Culture was replaced by the Hallstatt Culture, sometimes called the "Celtic Empire," a linguistic and cultural entity spread across Europe in the early iron age. One has to suspect that a smallpox-decimated Tumulus-Urnfield Culture slowly revived and evolved into this Celtic Empire.

This is not new or wild speculation. In *Celtic Civilization and Its Heritage*, Jan Filip cites Lantier as an additional author supporting his view that the Tumulus Culture evolved through the Urnfielders to become the Celts.[23]

It is difficult to imagine how a like language and similar culture could spread itself out across the continent of Europe so quickly and so thoroughly, especially in view of the failure of the mighty Romans to do the same in four hundred years and the failure, following them, of any hint of a United Europe right down to the present. How could these ancient Celts do it—unless they were already there?

If they were already there—there with the tin of the Erzgebirge on the Czech-German border and Cornwall in southwestern Britain—there is no question that they were involved in some way in the tin trade with Mycenaean Greece and Egypt. At Rameses III's temple at Medenet Habu the naval battle scenes with the Danann (Denyen), Peleset, and Shardana, show their ships with birds' heads on the prows. These bird boats show up in tin-bronze-age Urnfield Culture designs in the Danube Valley.

If they were involved in the tin trade, they must have participated in defense arrangements concerning it. That would surely have brought contingents to fight at Kadesh and at its possible offshoot, Troy. This would lead one to suspect that the references to Dan, with its suspiciously tin sound, especially in Egyptian (*dm*), were basically Celts, many of whom would have been involved in river and sea shipping of the vital metal. This would explain Homer's Danaan, Dan among the tribes of Israel (a late arrival with no biblical genealogy) Dan in Egyptian documents, Da Danaan in Ireland, and other references in ancient Mideast documents.

Moreover, King Danaos of Greek drama seems not only to have a Mitanni derivation, the Mitanni—*Hurru*, Hurrians, Horites, etc., of Haran—certainly at a vital crossroads of the early tin trade and related to Vedic Aryans controlling the route to the Tien Shan region, might well be the North Tin People. And if not, the dan or tan in the name would seem to link them to the Celts. Celtic language is certainly Indo-European. A careful study of Celtic legends in this light might, then, reveal some surprising links to Aryan Vedic gods and stories. Of course all proto-Celts were not dan or tan. Nor do all modern Arabs have petrodollars from being Oil Sheiks. But ancient popular impressions may have survived into present nomenclature.

It is, at any rate, not difficult to see how people deeply involved with tin ores from Central Asia would prospect for, locate, migrate to, and extract and trade tin ore from farther west in central and western Europe.

Is it simply a historical accident that the tin-bronze age, or late bronze age, arrived contemporaneously with the great Aryan invasion from the north down into Iran and India, with an offshoot into upper Mesopotamia called the Mitanni? It would seem that the Aryans sat on some valuable tin for centuries without knowing what it was. Just about the time they found out what it would do for copper, found out what this alloy could do for chariot wheels, found out what horse-and-chariot warfare could do against unprepared infantry, a historical accident *then* may have happened. The volcanic island of Thera exploded, turning a Siberian summer into a Siberian winter. With food as a motivation and chariot warfare as a means, they headed south where there was food and the weather was better.

In the process they created something of a reputation for themselves in addition to maintaining control of tin prospecting knowledge, tin sources, and tin trade routes. Especially as we can see with the offshoot Mitanni, great empires had to deal in a businesslike way with them. As part of this process, they married off royal sons daughters into foreign palaces to gain both security, political leverage, and undoubtedly military intelligence. But they undoubtedly grew fat and uncautious like all great nations eventually do. Their decline and fall appears to have been swift. During the reign of part-Mitanni Akhnaten, with his chief wife the Mitanni woman Nefertiti, the Hittite emperor Supiliuliulimas saw his chance, invaded the land of the Mitanni, and conquered them. One can only imagine what this did to internal Egyptian politics not only struggling with an imposed proto-monotheistic religion probably derived from the Aryan Mitanni sun god but royally married into a secure tin route.

Very likely the new tin resources of the Erzgebirge and Cornwall had become available by then, and the conquest of the Mitanni by the imperial rival Hittites only served as a good excuse. Whatever the case, the pre-Amarna and Amarna period in Egyptian history soon came to an end.

To keep tin flowing down the Danube from new sources in the north, the new dynasty of pharaohs named Seti and Rameses and their middlemen in Mycenaean Greece had to constantly deal with the Hittite Empire in the center of Anatolia. The fortress city of Troy, overlooking the most vital part of the tin route, probably culturally and linguistically allied with the Hittites but also tied to Mycenaean Greek city-states, may have been swing-vote pivotal power.

It can only be speculation, but the original artist from whom eventually, fifteen to twenty generations later, Homer took down the *Iliad* might have seen the grand irony. The leaders of Troy threw in with the Hittites in the war that resulted in the battle at Kadesh. During or following that, they threw their military and naval strength into blocking metal, especially tin, coming out of Europe. The Mycenaean Greek city-states, dependent on Egypt for food and fine goods, with some commercial, linguistic, and ethnic ties to the earlier overthrown Mitanni, went through an undoubtedly painful and difficult political process of agreeing on military action, amassed an enormous military and naval force of which a catalogue of ships survives to show the scale, and launched a war to topple this obstacle to free access to the Black Sea and points north, the fortress of Troy.

They succeeded at some great cost, both militarily and with regard to their homefront frail domestic economies, and Troy fell. But just as Troy fell, after all that, civilization was wiped out by something the gods sent. People died like flies. Empires crumbled and vanished forever. Trade agreements and national strategic posturing came to nothing. It was all for nothing. When patches of tenuous civilization began to reappear, the tin god was gone. Tin sources were no longer vital. Tin was no longer needed for national defense and industrial might. Iron had replaced it—by the time of Homer completely. Only the deeds and misdeeds of people—heroes and anti-heroes—might in themselves matter for anything.

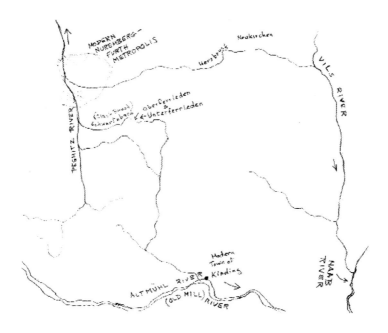

Figure 14: Portages at Nuremberg connection Black Sea and North Sea. How extensively was this used by tin traders in the Bronze Age?

Figure 15: "*My name is Ozymandias, king of kings;/Look on my works, ye Mighty, and despair!" Pharaoh Usermaatre Rameses II, name corrupted through Greek, Latin, Arabic to English as "Ozymandias." 3000 years later, Egyptians still knew who their great king was.*

Chapter Eight

After the Smallpox Epidemic and Disruption of the Tin Trade

We know now that the stars are violent storms of hot gases fueled by great hydrogen bomb reactions. We also know that the plant kingdom is in a constant state of chemical warfare with other plants and with animals. And even the ancients knew that the animal kingdom was a violent place of biting teeth, tearing claws, kill or be killed.

Still, even with that knowledge, we can relax under the violent stars twinkling over us in the serene stillness of the silent night sky, wondering and reflecting. We can also stop in a sunlit meadow to sniff the chemical warfare of roses and sigh at the beauty of a landscape, for a moment marveling at it all.

Only because we are distanced from the violence and brutal warfare of nature can we relax and reflect on the universe and our place in it. And only when we distance ourselves from our own animal beings struggling for life support and striving in pecking orders—ultimately, animal-like for our progeny—can we think those thoughts that cumulatively contribute to an understanding of ourselves and communicate it through art, literature, music, and science to others. In an otherwise violent universe, the very human soul would seem to be derived from this distancing, contemplation, and communication, especially and importantly where we give something to provide it for others.

In this, there was something gained that bridged the great smallpox epidemic and continues to this day. As a result of the catastrophe and the destruction of all social order, a natural political, economic, social, and religious revolution took place. The masses never rose up, but after masses and masses of people died there was little left of the old ways to follow or respect. By default, new ways had to take the place of the old. Most obvious to us was the fall of the Bronze Age and the gradual rise in its place of the new Iron Age, but there were other widespread and lasting subtle changes for the good.

To Homer it must not have seemed so. Comparatively low population levels and continuing petty gang wars between feudal warlords in Greece and western Anatolia precluded any hope that the greatness of the past would ever return. To his contemporary Hesiod, it clearly did not seem so. He metaphorically put the past in terms of increasingly nobler metals, iron men, bronze men, silver men, and golden men—the iron age in which he lived being preceded by a bronze age, then a silver age, and finally a golden age. Amid rampant petty wars and warlordism, the greatness that bits of evidence everywhere hinted had once been Mycenaean Greece could not possibly return with these new iron men and their gang values as ugly as their black rapidly rusting metal.

But even there and then the seeds of democracy were taking hold. A few centuries later the Classical Greek dramatists may have been making a conscious attempt at continuity with the bronze-age past by dramatically interpreting what they thought might be lessons of history, especially concerning New Kingdom Egypt. And by then modern civilization's tenuous experiment with pseudo-democracy was well under way in Greece.

Contemporary to Homer in what had been Canaan, early Jewish scribes began to record old stories dating to this significant time. Not only monotheism but the great experiment in human-oriented religion for the common people began. It had been spawned by Akhnaten and the Atenists, but was clearly enunciated by Moses (whether or not he was Akhnaten) only after the Exodus. Perhaps as early as Moses himself it began to be written down in forms we could recognize. Certainly the Atenist Hymn to the Aten, from which Psalm 104 is clearly derived, was already in writing at the end of the bronze age. If Moses wrote anything himself, it was probably, like this, written in Egyptian hieroglyphic or hieratic.

Seven hundred years later, at the time the Classical dramatists were working in Greece, Hebrew religious scholars were amending and reinterpreting stories that had previously been recorded and were probably writing them—as with the Classical Greeks and their script—in a Hebrew script that could be easily read even today. The social, moral, and religious values of Western society were spelled out in writing for all to read and follow even up to our own time. Over a span of five to seven centuries, a great catastrophe obviously caused by a sub-microscopic virus had caused a great unintended revolution to take place.

Not only did the metal basis for the physical infrastructure of our present civilization grow out of the tenuous transition across the great population decimation catastrophe, our democratic governmental institutions, our individual-worth-respecting religions, and our individual-worth and psyche-exploring literature and arts also sprang from it.

Through both the sacred and secular runs a thread to warn the dreamers and sentimentalists that the old and great was also tawdry and evil and that it deserved to go, and we are still influenced by that view to this day. Certainly there were some unpalatable aspects to bronze-age civilization.

In both the Bible and in ancient Greek poetry and drama we see references to religious human sacrifice. It is unnerving to observe that this horrible anti-human practice only came to an end in the Old World after population levels had dropped so far that every human being was desperately needed and could no longer afford to be sacrificed. And it only came to an end in the New World when Europeans got here to spread smallpox and religion dating from their own great smallpox epidemic. And might we not still be practicing it with artful capital punishment excuses?

If so, some of our present civilizations are not greatly different from the great bronze-age civilizations and we can hardly condemn them solely for their cruel fear-generated practice of ceremonially killing fellow human beings to satisfy demands of social order artfully disguised as abstractions of religion.

Religion, however, genuinely evolved. While it grew into virtually present forms in the secure institutions of the late bronze age, it was the catastrophe-initiated revolution that altered the altar.

First cautious steps took place before civilization crashed and amid the ease of life-support abundance, libraries, religious temples, laid-back palaces and other bronze-age institutions of imperial Egypt. The protomonotheism of Akhnaten may have been fanatic or highly politicized, but it is very obviously linked to Judaism, from which both Christianity and Islam grew.

Paradoxically, in the very wealth, ease, and social stability that allowed the experiment a temporary free hand there were also the usual suppressed powerful conservative cravings for a return to normalcy. The change was too abrupt and too sweeping and the movement resulted in civil strife that destroyed it and was brutally put down. But while the revolution failed in imperial Egypt, the seeds of its success were soon to be sown in the desert as empire came crashing down.

By fortunate accident the experiment occurred only shortly before a mutated microorganism brought monumental chaos and enormous irreversible social change, and the seeds of real religious revolution had already been planted. Whether Atenism became Judaism because Moses was really the pharaoh Akhnaten, or whether it more likely evolved from deposed, persecuted, and sentenced-to-hard-labor Atenists and Aten priests after the heavy-handed restoration of the Amon-Re polytheistic religion, Judaism has strong roots in the Amarna period of New Kingdom Egyptian history. But only after mighty Egypt collapsed did a small cult of outcast upper-class intellectuals and lower-class workers begin the first steps toward the religious values that dominate the world today.

Literally just as the epidemic consumed ancient bronze-age civilization—but growing out of that civilization and not its demise—Moses, a remarkable man by any measure, embarked the world on a new and far more human-oriented religious course. Just looking at it in cold disinterested terms, monotheism is more mentally compact than polytheism and a more efficient use of mental energies. This may or may not be better, but monotheism and assumptions of equality under The Deity appear to have led directly to the slight edge that allowed Western civilization to dominate the world.

As remnants show in Exodus, the Hebrews worked for a while as laborers. The six-day work week, with an obligatory day of rest for religious reflection found in all Western religions, has all the earmarks of a labor union demand. Prior to it one can only suspect that no such thing existed. Workers worked seven days out of a seven day week, probably until they dropped. While not strictly followed until modern times, the six-day work week was a social as well as a religious advance. Not only the social elite but all people were given an opportunity at that distance from worldly cares that allows for cumulative understanding in the arts and sciences as well as personal religious introspection.

One can only speculate at the origins of this. It would appear that deposed religious and white collar people of the Amarna period had been put to work in minimum-wage labor in the transition from the Eighteenth Dynasty to the Nineteenth Dynasty and therefore felt first hand its devastating effects, discussed it as educated intellectuals, and arrived at a good solution. Calamities that throw large numbers of educated people into grumbling situations where their educations and skills are not fully utilized create hotbeds of intellectual unrest that result in revolutionary changes.

Out of the sunset of bronze-age civilizations came the seeds of the present world, not the following time of people's subsistence and survival lives being run by feudal war lords (i.e. gang-leaders). After the last people of the well educated generation died off, after the well-oiled social institutions that supplied ease and knowledge to the privileged few were gone, and after societies that had promoted get a good education to get a good job had vanished into thin air, rudimentary and homespun philosophical speculation replaced the former educated and academic discourse.

One can read into the books claimed to have been written by Moses but transmitted, if they were, orally for five to eight centuries, the ideas of New Kingdom Egyptian religious intellectuals, including Moses, bent on both religious and social reform. One can also see early uneducated misinterpretations and subsequent accumulating inaccurate feedback from both oral transmission and written redaction over about ten centuries.

Technology is more resistant to such corruption. What works is accepted and what does not is rejected, and the iron age progressed slowly but relentlessly through those centuries. Some experimentation with iron had been done in the Bronze Age, but iron products were simply uneconomical. As long as rare tin and copper flowed in from remote locations, bronze could be alloyed, cast, cooled, and immediately used.

Only after trade was thoroughly disrupted and tin sources cut off was there an economic incentive to utilize ubiquitous iron ore resources. Early iron was poor in quality and generally inferior to bronze in every way. Knowledge of how to make a consistently usable iron metal slowly accumulated over several centuries after the great ancient empires fell, and even then, unlike easily cast and immediately usable bronze, iron had to be wrought, worked over with great difficulty, and could not be cast.

It is not surprising then that what we call the Iron Age did not arrive in full force until centuries after the great depopulation catastrophe. Delicate political and economic arrangements concerning mining, transport, and trade of metals had fallen apart, and tin to make bronze was no longer easily available. But there was plenty of bronze around and only one-fourth to one-third of the population survived to consume it. Empires had vanished, and gluttonous tin-consuming defense industries no longer existed to demand it. So both civilian and military demand shrank amid plentiful supplies, and there was little immediate impetus for research to utilize widely available iron ore resources.

Then populations grew again. When you look at North and South America in the last two hundred years, you can see how fast populations grow to the limit of available resources to support them. A similar time period stretched out from the great population decimation catastrophe to a real beginning of the Iron Age. During this time, even durable as it is, bronze wore out, was lost, went down in shipwrecks, and was dispersed in reestablished trade to wider areas. Demands for tools, implements, and weapons increased but not enough to drive prices to up to levels to encourage investors to recapitalize and restart the old tin supply pipelines. Proto-investment, public and private, such as it was, would seem to have gone to experiments with the by then not so new but increasingly promising iron technology.

It appears that the first pre-catastrophe and early post-catastrophe intentional iron was made from iron-rich sands on the north shore of Anatolia. But if entrepreneurs of that area hoped to get a handle on an iron monopoly just as others had gotten on the tin trade, they must have been in for a great disappointment. Once the knowledge of certain smelting, refining, and working techniques leaked out as they always do and there is really nothing such as a long-term trade or military secret—there was, unlike tin and copper, iron just about everywhere. Knowledge spread. Iron ore was virtually everywhere. As bronze implements wore out there was a growing demand. The Iron Age was on.

The bronze alloy was easy to make and immediately use. Very loosely and imprecisely, the ancients mixed about one part tin with nine parts copper, cast it, cooled it, and used it. There was no hard pounding with heavy hammers and working in forges and on anvils. Nor was second or third step refining or quench hardening involved. And importantly, there were no mysterious and misunderstood technical tricks involving carbonization.

The only drawback to bronze throughout the Late Bronze Age was the comparative rarity of copper and tin ores, especially very rare tin ore. Only when emerging nations again demanded metal for industry and war following the great depopulation catastrophe did a crisis occur that forced widespread research and development of the difficult to manufacture and use metal from its ubiquitous ore. And during these research and development centuries, unless this new iron was thoughtfully and skillfully handled, bronze was still a superior metal to the often brittle and mysteriously unworkable iron well into the iron age.

Iron required more work in obtaining fuel for higher temperatures. Once it had been reduced from ore and charcoal in a furnace, it might turn out to be too brittle to use. If it turned out useful, it had to be tiresomely and painstakingly worked to remove slag and to shape it into tools, implements, or weapons. The only real advantage of early iron at the end of the bronze age was that the ore was virtually everywhere and easily accessible.

Experiments in making iron had been going on for centuries prior to the unparalleled catastrophe, but it was all accidental iron and no one really knew how to make it. In the undisturbed tomb of Akhnaten's son, Tutankhamon, two daggers were found beside the famous pharaoh's mummy. One was gold. The other was iron. Iron was, at the time of his death in about 1300 BC and throughout the ancient world, regarded as a rare metal as valuable as gold.

Iron implements and weapons existed throughout the Bronze Age, but they were valuable and ceremonial objects, things given as gifts from one monarch to another. The disruption of the tin trade forced enough experimentation to discover how to make cheap and useful iron tools, implements, and weapons in reliable duplicable processes. For years becoming decades becoming centuries, inferior though early iron was to bronze, our ancestors were forced by sheer necessity to put large effort into continuing to manufacture these ugly and inferior iron weapons and tools.

Over time, of course, they learned how to make, refine, work, and use iron. But it took many more centuries after that before they learned how to cast it like bronze. And it took twenty-five centuries—into virtually our own time—to learn how to intentionally make and mass produce genuine steel from the ubiquitous ore. Most of us plod like ants through our short lives and contribute little of nothing new. Civilization results from the accumulated efforts of a very few brilliant, deducing, questioning, experimenting human minds who just as often as not get things wrong as right.

When you consider the thirty centuries between the early experimental beginnings of the iron age and the first mass-produced steel, it is appalling how slow our species learns and discovers, even basic useful things. The who and how and where and why of the discovery of useful iron making thirty centuries ago should therefore interest not only historians but all of us, including philosophers and even politicians.

Early historians speculated that this or that tribe or nation of barbarians had accidentally hit upon useful iron technology and with weapons and military hardware made from this they swept down and conquered ancient civilizations. But the technical knowledge to make consistently useful iron grew slowly over centuries following the collapse of civilization.

There is no evidence that the Hittites acquired an early adequate knowledge of iron technology to allow for their imperial expansion, and indeed they were gone from the scene long before the genuine iron age began. Nor would it appear that the Chou were iron-smart, allowing them to overrun the Shang civilization. In fact, the bronze age in China lasted longer than in the west because the Chou acquired the easily accessible tin and copper sources around the Shang capital of Anyang, and it is therefore unlikely that they regressed and reentered the bronze age following a conquest facilitated by some unknown accidentally acquired iron technology. Through most of the Chou dynasty the bronze age simply continued on—for centuries longer than in the West. The significant difference was that the West had an enormous appetite for bronze goods, and prospectors and miners ranged widely over Europe and western Asia to satisfy it, but in the East bronze goods were limited to the upper classes and their military needs, and unlike the West, Chinese commoners remained in the stone age until the invention of cast iron.

Far from barbarians hitting miraculously upon complex iron technology and overrunning civilization, it was the collapse of civilization and the disruption of tin demand supporting the long frail thin tin trade routes that forced iron experimentation and a gradually increasing use of iron. Because the tin supplies were so distant and inaccessible in the West, this induced an early iron industry there. But while necessity forced a several-century jump in the use of iron in the West, the lack of it permitted a continuity of civilization and its leisure institutions as population regrew and institutions regrouped in China. And this tenuous continuity, allowing a select few the resources to reflect, think, experiment, and discover, apparently gave China the real edge in iron technology.

While the bronze age continued on longer in China due to the availability of both copper and tin, when that ancient country did enter the iron age, researchers there happened on a way to make cast iron and therefore mass-produce iron tools, implements, and weapons that put them centuries ahead of the West.

In the West there are a very few early iron artifacts at the boundary dates of the great catastrophe in the late twelfth and early eleventh centuries BC. If very late in late bronze-age Mycenaean Greek-Cypriot civilization some iron technology had allowed for a few new weapons, they could hardly have been so superior to bronze and so plentiful as to make significant military differences. If they and the Hittites had indeed crossed several thresholds of iron technological knowledge, they were doomed by the great population decimation catastrophe just as they reached these. And Greece for a while reverted to and remained in the bronze age even while others were developing economical and useful iron products. It would seem unlikely that some hypothetical iron-smart Dorian invaders would abandon iron making after having militarily succeeded due to it.

In reality, the iron age did not immediately succeed the bronze-age civilizations. There is a gap of centuries between the fall of bronze-age nations and empires and the emergence of real widespread use of iron. First something brought an end to bronze-age civilization, and that broke the overstretched tin trade routes and economies, and that brought on something less than a flurry of activity to find a replacement metal amid a glut of useful bronze. Finally, as population levels were restored and demand increased even as iron technology had fortuitously grown to meet it, iron became the reluctant replacement for bronze.

As time and experimentation went on it, slowly replaced dwindling supplies of bronze. Over centuries iron technology improved and iron knowledge spread where smallpox had apparently spread throughout the Old World. In the New World, marvelous pre-bronze-age nations and empires continued to grow, unwary of the catastrophic implications both of these spreads held for them over a millennium into the future.

Muhly and Wertime illuminatingly observe that the element iron is born in the dying of stars, and is the most common solid element in the universe. They also note that if you exclude the gases hydrogen, nitrogen, and oxygen, we humans are mostly that same carbon-iron alloy that makes good iron and steel, hemoglobin and hydrocarbons. But though the ancients of the late bronze age were familiar with the concept of alloying from centuries of working with copper alloys, especially the tin alloy bronze, the ancients pursued the idea that truly good steel was somehow very pure iron. We know now that it is another alloy, one of iron and carbon.

In the West throughout the Iron Age the metal was made from a mixture of ore and charcoal in small furnaces. The hot reduced sponge of iron with slag impurities was taken out and immediately beaten to remove as much slag as possible. The result was wrought iron, and until new furnaces were developed not terribly long before Columbus sailed for America, the Iron Age was, in the West, a Wrought Iron Age. The clever Chinese invented the mini-blast furnace and thereby mass-produced cheap utilitarian cast iron tools and implements, and even inserted low-carbon wrought iron into molten baths of higher carbon casting iron to make steel on a proto-mass-production basis.

In the West every useful thing of iron was made, as it was in early iron-age China, from labor-intensive wrought iron. Proto-steel was made by baking iron arranged in charcoal. Useful iron tools and implements were made on forges by beating carbon from hot charcoal into them, sometimes picturesquely under spreading chestnut trees, but with the sweat of many brows.

Theoretical misconceptions about purity in the West forced frantic attempts to cast iron that resulted in useless material more brittle than most rocks. It simply could not be cast like the old bronze, and researchers abandoned attempting to accomplish it. It just had to be worked and worked even to produce an inferior product. Not until after Marco Polo came back from China over twenty centuries after the iron age began (whether he brought it or not) did cast iron enter European economies. After the tin trade dried up and bronze began to disappear one can imagine that it must have been terribly frustrating.

The frustration, though, eventually reaped its rewards, and we still live in a world dominated by iron and steel. But iron making was not the only material advance of transition through the bronze age to the iron age. The world is also still dominated by two other materials that developed simultaneously with iron, glass and cement. Both were known prior to the great catastrophe, and probably from the same late bronze age research into higher temperatures along with iron, fired brick, glass, and cement mass production altered the human environment.

Glass windows permitted civilized expansion northward into cold climates of northern Europe. Cemented stone and brick structures cut construction costs and spread leisure for contemplation and thought to larger numbers of human beings.

Adversity may have added some impetus to discovery in the West, but we must keep in mind that in China the bronze age continued for several centuries after the fall of the Shang Dynasty simultaneously with the collapse in the West. It would appear that while the Shang Chinese succumbed to the same smallpox epidemic at the same time as the great bronze-age civilizations in the West, a lack of urgency in better conditions for research and development there eventually brought about a superior iron age.

During the lengthened bronze age in China careful and unharried research continued into iron processes. Unlike in the West where bronze tools and implements spread down to the masses, bronze there was an elite metal even prior to the great catastrophe. Except for the power elite, China remained in the Stone Age. Peasants and common people continued to use stone and pottery tools and implements until they were suddenly directly from Stone Age into Iron Age by the discovery of cheap mass-producible cast iron.

Because some Chinese researcher discovered the trick of high-carbon iron casting, their world went suddenly from stone age to widespread use of iron tools and implements, bypassing the powerful influence that the bronze age had on Western civilization and the quantum jump an earlier metals age for the masses gave to the arts, sciences, philosophies, and institutions of the West.

Long before a scarcity of tin for making bronze brought on an early iron age in desperation in the West, it had forced trade over wide geographical areas, forced peaceful contact and intercourse between widely divergent peoples and cultures, forced proto-risk-capitalism to finance far-flung overseas and overland trade ventures, brought varieties of religious philosophy and worship into contact with one another, and expanded the literal and figurative horizons of the Western mind.

The availability of both copper and tin in north-central China compelled no such desperation there and allowed the Bronze Age to continue for the elite and the Stone Age to continue for the masses. For centuries after the great drop in population and the crumbling of civilized social structures, the elite survivors continued to use bronze and the everyday people continued to use stone and pottery. And yet it was the Chinese who first really learned to cast iron and therefore mass-produce it to permit widespread peaceful uses of the metal.

Adversity and economic incentives growing from desperation forced an early iron age in the West. But it would seem that a civilized climate that allowed for necessary thoughtful speculation and reflection—if even for a very small group of people—brought a far superior iron age when it finally did come to China.

In the West iron required hard labor but was adequate. It rapidly became inexpensive and widespread in use, and over two or three centuries became the metal of choice over increasingly scarce bronze. While no one knew why it worked, knowledge of how to beat iron into steel spread widely. Not only did new iron and steel weapons arm new military machines, iron and steel tools felled forests and plowed the tough clay soils of northern Europe, permitting population growths beyond pre-catastrophe levels there.

Horse-drawn carts with two or four wheels could go farther carrying heavier loads with iron wheel rims and iron hubs and axles. The Celts built networks of log roads across northern Europe to accommodate what must have been a large and growing number of inexpensive vehicles. Later the Romans would use them to move and supply their armies to conquer the Celts and then claim them as their own.

In Greece, civilization revived over centuries. Using iron tools and constructing with lead-insulated iron reinforcement, Greeks built temples of modified basic Egyptian design, the Parthenon clearly showing descent from the likes of Luxor or Hatshepsut's tomb. While some Greek gods derived from ancient Egyptian ones, this occurred prior to the great catastrophe. Minoan and Mycenaean era tablets show the same names for a number of deities, enough to assume that the rest were also about the same as in Classical times. Essential elements of the old time religion would appear to have been retained and passed on by survivors. The essential contributions of post-catastrophe Greece were not in religion but in poetry, drama, and government accentuating individual worth of each human being against the backdrop of mighty natural and social forces.

A real revolution occurred out in the Sinai desert apparently in the midst of the epidemic. While it clearly had its roots in relaxed philosophical discussions in the security of institutions of imperial Egypt, its success began in an obscure ethnically heterogeneous cult out in the desert. Fearful sacrifice to a multitude of animalistic and nature deities was replaced by worship of a unitary abstraction whose very name was the concept of destiny and under whom the essences of all human lives were equal. Post-epidemic seizure by determined cult members—apparently amid massive population decimation and attendant chaos—of a small eastern block of the former Egyptian colonial province of Canaan gave the revolution a territorial foothold. Thirty centuries and at least a hundred generations later it covers the world and continues to evolve.

Slowly the Egyptian-based Greek and Egyptian-based Hebrew contributions merged. Phoenician-Greek trade was followed by Hellenistic Egypt, was followed by imperial Rome. Then came Christianity, Byzantine and Coptic Christianity, Roman Christianity and Islam. Then there were the great universities of Caliphite Islam, and then the great early universities of Christianity, both with Hebrew scholars directly or indirectly attached, both studying and preserving ancient Greek literature. Finally these headed toward secularization and disinterested academic creativity and research, that distancing from historical, social, and natural forces and violence that permits reflection and the free mind.

Coming out of the knowledge base at the end of the Bronze Age and impelled somewhat by necessities brought about by epidemic-caused social collapse were glass, high-fired ceramic and brick, cement, and iron technologies and a very obvious resultant freeing of larger and larger numbers of people from consuming all of their time to satisfy survival needs. Less obvious is the accumulation of knowledge resulting from efforts to improve these, especially iron and steel. From that technical knowledge base came the physical sciences and a myriad of technologies giving human beings increasing ease and comfort.

Northern latitudes were opened to large civilized population with iron saws to remove the forest cover. Iron-tipped plows opened difficult northern European clay soils to increased food production to support the growing populations. Large cities could grow at trade junctures due to better transportation and because iron tools and implements could build inexpensive but structurally sound housing and infrastructure.

Increasing numbers of largely city dwellers were freed to create and entertain, study, learn, and accumulate knowledge, and improve technologies and their knowledge bases.

If we were anciently wrong about a unitary Deity, the various ancient gods may still look down at us. What might they say? Beings made of the spent fuel of stars came this way to eventually tap the thermonuclear reactions of the stars, leave the planet with its iron core and go out in space and look back at the bright blue of the extremely thin and delicate life-support biosphere surrounding it, and see themselves alone on this tiny spec in the vastness of lifeless space better than any of us might have been imagined to see them.

But we short-lived mortals who require this delicate biosphere life support have also not socially and ethically progressed to keep up with the technologies we have concocted.

Due entirely to human efforts and human technologies, smallpox itself is now dead. But a danger still lurks that could cause history to tragically repeat itself. The only live viruses are in vials—about 500 vials stored in freezers in the USA and the remnants of the USSR. The last naturally occurring smallpox case was in 1977. Two more cases came from an accident with one of the vials in 1979, but there have been none in the world since then. The disease that once destroyed civilization and came near destroying the human race is now dead. Or is it? So convinced of this were world health officials that they had millions of doses of cowpox vaccine to prevent smallpox destroyed.

And there sit the vials, in lightly guarded places while social turmoil seethes around them—as well as genetically engineered biological warfare research and its products stored in vials. And added to them are nuclear weapons, the mounting greenhouse effect, the erosion of the ozone layer, the destruction of the rain forests, and the growing dependence on high-yield, low-resistance food crops on increasingly soil-eroded farmland.

To trigger such a disaster we have the population explosion itself— adding to these stresses and making people increasingly desperate for food, water, clothing, shelter, and decent living standards. If the ancients were baffled at the wrath of the gods, we know that there are human-made catastrophes looming, and yet we add to these threats rather than seeking to prevent them. Consider Rameses V stopping his chariot for a reflective moment before the great temple at Karnak and contemplating it as the Nile flowed lazily by. All that he knew and loved would come crashing down in a very few years—to vanish forever. But it was, at that moment, still a viable and almost modern civilization. His bureaucrats shuffled papyrus. His farmers grew food not only for his nation but to feed the nations of his allies. His roads and waterways were filled with commerce. His schools were full of teachers and learners. His musicians, artists, and architects produced works of beauty. His policemen kept order. His military forces guarded the nation. His industries produced goods for defense and for a better standard of living. It was not all that different from what goes on today.

And you have to think back to the various pharaohs' boastful deeds of wiping out whole nations so that their seed is no more, especially Merneptah's apparently mistaken boast that the seed of the Habiru (Hebrews?) was no more. Not long after that, in a cataclysm that only such pharaohs might really appreciate, seeds and seeds and seeds were no more, whole genetic pools ceased to exist, and it was all apparently due to a microorganism that only a pharaoh with an electron microscope could have seen, the Variola virus. And those of us reading this are the descendants of those who survived this apparent great smallpox catastrophe and slowly rebuilt civilization over three millennia.

Appendix—
Other Added Bits

COMPARISON OF THE PRESENT CALENDAR WITH EGYPTIAN AND HELLENISTIC (MACEDONIAN) CALENDARS.
(note similar sounds, Egyptian "R" & "L" being the same sound)

BEGINS (in our calendar) (roughly)	MACEDONIAN Month Names	EGYPTIAN
December 18 30 days	Apellaeus	Rekhur
January 17 30 days	Audynaeus	Rekh-Netches
February 16 30 days	Peritius	Reunutet
March 18 31 days	Dystrus	Khensu
April 18 31 days	Xanthicus	Heru-Khenti-Khatat
May 19 31 days	Artimisius	Apt
June 19 31 days	Daesius	Heru-aakhuti
July 20 31 days	Panemus	*Tekhi* (New Year)

August 20	Lous	Ptah
30 days		
September 19	Gorpiaus	Het-Hor (Hathor)
30 days		
October 19	Hyperberetaeus	Sekmet (lion goddess of war)
30 days		
November 18	Dius	Menu
30 days		

It is said that Julius Caesar brought the Egyptian calendar of twelve months with thirty days back to Rome. It may have been a Ptolemaic modified Egyptian calendar. The Ptolemies were, as we know, Macedonians and probably used this calendar, probably in itself Egyptian-derived. The Egyptian calendar of twelved thirty-day months and a five-day year-end celebration began around July 18, the average start of the annual Nile flooding. The date is suspiciously close enough to the Summer Solstice, and one must conclude that the Egyptian Solar Temple at On (Memphis) would have made that the start of the year. But July 18 is adequate for our non-solar and non-astronomical comparisons.

Words from Various Dictionaries and Sources:

This section is added here not entirely with tongue in cheek. There are, for instance, several ancient Egyptian words regularly used in modern English that are pointed out in *Egyptian Galleries*, a 1999 brochure of The Cleveland Museum of Art. These include the name "Susan," which is *sheshen*, meaning "lotus flower" in ancient Egyptian. Our modern English word "ebony" comes from *hebeny*. "Sack" comes from *sac*, a "container," and its verb-form "to collect," or "gather." Our "adobe" comes from *djobet*, a "mud brick." Our "desert" comes from *deshret*, the "red land" of the

Egyptian desert. Our "gum" comes from *kemyit*, "tree gum" or "resin." Our "oasis" is from *wahet*, a "basin" or "well." These are known.

The following words are largely wild speculation. Someone may come along and be provoked to do research. The power, influence, and reach of the bronze-age Egyptian Empire has been under-researched, underestimated, and overlooked, and therefore influences of ancient Egyptian language on the etymologies of modern languages have been considered minimal. Plausible Egyptian-derived etymologies, therefore, may well have been ignored or overlooked. There may be nothing at all to the following curiosities, but who knows what dogged research may turn up in some this direction.

The Egyptian root for time is *ses*, and their word for season is, *sesu*. Like ours?

Besides the Egyptian Lake of Horus, *She Hur*, there is another use of the word similar to the German word for lake, *see*, in the original name of Fayyum, *Ta She*, Land of the Lakes.

One of the seventy-five names for Re is *Qa-Ba*, Exalted Ba, or spirit. It is probably only accident that it sounds like the Islamic holy shrine in Mecca, but it is curious.

The Egyptian for boat or barge is *qur*, and one has to wonder not only at our quay, but Gaelic *carrack*. Moreover, men who work on boats, boatmen (maybe porters) are *quru*. Is it accident that we use the almost identical-sounding word "crew" for the same?

If we *stem* the flow of a river we build a dam to do it. The Egyptian for to dam is *stena*.

The Egyptian word for sparkle, flash, or scintillate, as tin might do, is *tehen*. There is a river flowing out of the tin fields of Cornwall-Devon with the name Teighn. If it might not come from *dm*, it might not come from *tehen* also, but it is curious.

The Egyptian word for cut, hew, or dig out, as in mining, is *m'antt*, and sounds a bit like our verb mine.

The Egyptian word for green, *wrd*, looks like the Latin-derived words, as in *verde* in Spanish.

Might cot come from the Egyptian *khty*, bed? Might *sntr*, incense, have become our sensor? Could *bit* (pronounced bee?) have become our honey-making insect, bee? Might *gary* have become our jar? How about *tr* (door) becoming our door? How about *dwa* (morning) becoming our dew?

A couple words with Latin similarities are interesting. While standard etymologies say nothing about it, the Egyptian word for to build, is *khns*. It looks like the Latin root of *cons*truction. Similarly, the Egyptian word for monument is a self-explanatory *monu*.

In Nuzi Hurrian-derived (Mitanni-derived) personal names we see a female name Akap-elle. *Akap* means is brought, and *elle* means sister. The baby was named A sister is brought. But can we see the Mitanni word for sister is pretty near the same as the name of the young woman Paris-Alexander ran off with and thereby started the Trojan War, Helen?

Why is one Egyptian *heqat* about the same as one English bushel? And why is one Egyptian *hin* about the same as one English pint—and in fact possibly even the same word in feminine form with an definite article, *p-hin-t*, the *hin*-pint? Are these simply convenient sizes? Or might there be something left over from the ancient tin trade through northern Europe? The ancient Egyptians may well have drunk their beer out of a *hin*-bottle, a pint. Have another pint? asked the ancient Egyptian bartender. If the ancient Egyptians did not invent beer, they certainly seem to have brought the art of brewing to a high level. And the hieroglyphic character for beer is a pottery flask, a characteristic shape. Given human nature, one might expect to find shards of these beer containers littering ancient highways, possibly a good way to identify ancient trade routes.

The proto-monotheistic god of the pharaoh Akhn*aten*'s new religion, the Aten (the sun disk), was not only part of his name but part of the name of his new capital city, Akhet-Aten (Horizon of the Aten). A variety of pronunciation was apparently Athen, and one has to suspect the name of another city in the ancient Egyptian trading sphere, in Greece, a country which over time became dependent on Egyptian grain for survival. Taking a very speculative long shot, might Athens (not much different in Greek) have once been another new city named after the Aten (Athen)?

Moreover, the Aten's name was Shu, the Aryan god of the sun. Do we see something of this in the main Greek god Zeus (contractual Shu-ous), and derived from it the Roman god Jupiter (Shu-pater)? That is to ask, in addition to the very good possibility that deposed and persecuted Atenist religious professionals of the former state religion were in the cult led by Moses (even if Moses were not Akhnaten himself), might Atenists escaping persecution and then the smallpox epidemic have influenced Greek and Roman religion? These are wild questions, but if you don't ask questions, you don't get answers.

A number of people have remarked about the parallelism between The Hymn to the Aton[24] and Psalm 104. While it would appear to be loose, the style of ancient hymns in general is retained in the Bible. We therefore have a glimpse into ancient minds and ancient worship there even if much, if not most, ancient Egyptian common everyday religion slipped away from us after the catastrophe.

By the time Psalm 104 was actually written down, five hundred years had elapsed since the composition of The Hymn to the Aton. If Psalm 104 contains any direct elements of The Hymn to the Aton, these would have been filtered and altered by word-of-mouth transmission over at least five centuries and poetic translation from at least one language to another. A comparison provokes its own thoughts and the comparison I have used is from the King James Version because it is in the style of the *The Ancient Near East* text translations. At very least, the evolution of religion across the barrier of the dark age that resulted from the great catastrophe comes through beautifully in this quick comparison.

THE HYMN TO THE ATON*

*(In) Pritchard, James B. (edited by), *The Ancient Near East; An Anthology of Texts and Pictures*, copyright 1958 by Princeton University Press. Reprinted by permission of Princeton University Press. (Hymn, on Pgs 226-230, translated by Professor John A. Wilson, University of Chicago. Several lines slightly readjusted and commentaries slightly adapted.)

(A prefix precedes the actual hymn:)
Praise of Re Har-akhti, Rejoicing on the Horizon, in his name as Shu Who Is in the Aton Disk, living forever and ever; the living great Aton who is in jubilee, lord of all that the Aton encircles, lord of heaven, Lord of earth, Lord of the House of Aton (remote possible meaning: wife of Akhnaten, Nefertiti, or Akhnaten's mother, Tiya, my comment) in Akhet-Aton (the capital city); (and praise of) the King of Upper and Lower Egypt, who lives on truth, the Lord of the Two Lands: Nefer-kheperu-Re Wa-en-Re; the Son of Re, who lives on truth, the Lord of Diadems: Akh-en-Aton (Akhnaten), long in his lifetime; (and praise of) the Chief Wife of the King, his beloved lady of the Two Lands: Nefer-neferu-Aton Nefert-iti, living, healthy, and youthful forever and ever; (by) the Fan-Bearer on the Right hand of the King...Eye. He says:

HYMN TO THE ATEN

Thou appearest beautifully on the horizon of heaven,
Thou living Aton, the beginning of life!
When thou art risen on the eastern horizon,
Thou hast filled every land with thy beauty.
Thou art gracious, great, glistening, and high over every land;
Thy rays encompass the lands to the limit of all that thou hast made:

As thou art Re, thou reachest to the end of them (*poetic play-on-words with* er-ra, *to the end*);
   (Thou) subduest them (for) thy beloved son (Akhnaten).
   Though thou art far away, thy rays are on earth;
   Though thou art in *their* faces, *no one* knows thy going.
   When thou settest in the western horizon,
   The land is in darkness, in the manner of death.
   They sleep in a room with their heads wrapped up,
   Nor sees one eye the other.
   All their goods which are under their heads might be stolen,
   (But) they would not perceive (it).
   Every lion is come forth from his den;
   All creeping things, they sting.
   Darkness *is a shroud*, and the earth is in stillness,
   For he who made them rests in his horizon. (Psalm 104:20-21)

At daybreak, when thou arisest on the horizon
When thou shinest as the Aton by day,
Thou drivest away the darkness and givest thy rays.
The Two Lands are in festivity *every day*,
Awake and standing upon (their) feet,
For thou hast raised them up.
Washing their bodies, taking (their) clothing,
Their arms are (raised) in praise at thy appearance.
All the world, they do their work.   (*Psalm 104:22-23*)

All the beasts are content with their pasturage;
Trees and plants ate flourishing.
The birds which fly from their nests,
Their wings are (stretched out) in praise to thy *ka* (spirit).
All beasts spring upon (their) feet.
Whatever flies and alights,

They live when thou hast risen (for) them. (*Psalm 104:11-14*)
The ships are sailing north and south as well,
For every way is open at their appearance.
The fish in the river dart before thy face;
Thy rays are in the midst of the great green sea. (*Psalm 104:25-26*)

Creator of seed in women,
Thou who makest fluid into man,
Who maintainest the son in the womb of his mother,
Who soothest him with that which stills his weeping,
Thou nurse (even) in the womb,
Who gives breath to sustain all that he has made!
When he descends from the womb to *breathe*
on the day when he is born,
Thou openest his mouth completely,
Thou suppliest his necessities.
When the chick in the egg speaks within the shell,
Thou givest him breath to maintain him.
When thou hast made him his fulfillment within the egg to break it,
He comes forth from the egg to speak at his completed (time);
He walks upon his legs when he comes forth from it.

How manifold it is that thou hast made!
They are hidden from the face (of humans).
O sole god, like whom there is no other!
Thou didst create the world according to thy desire,
Whilst thou wert alone: (*Psalm 104:24*)
All men, cattle, and wild beasts,
Whatever on earth, going upon (its) feet,
And what is on high, flying with its wings.

The countries of Syria and Nubia, the *land* of Egypt,

Thou settest every man in his place,
Thou suppliest their necessities:
Everyone has his food, and his time of life is reckoned. (*Psalm 104:27*)
Their tongues are separate in speech,
And their natures as well;
Their skins are distinguished,
As thou distinguishest the foreign peoples.
Thou makest the Nile in the underworld,
Thou bringest it forth as thou desirest
To maintain the people (of Egypt)
According as thou madest them for thyself,
The lord of all of them, wearying (himself) with them,
The lord of every land, rising for them,
The Aton of the day, great of majesty.

All distant foreign countries, thou makest their life (also),
For thou hast set the Nile in heaven,
That it may descend for them and make waves upon the mountains, (*Psalm 104: 6, 10*)
Like the great green sea,
To water their fields in their towns (a note points out that this means rain in foreign countries, unknown in dry desert Egypt),
How effective they are, thy plans, O lord of eternity!
The Nile in heaven, it is for the foreign peoples
And for beasts of every desert that go upon (their) feet;
(While the true) Nile comes from the underworld for Egypt.

Thy rays suckle every meadow.
When thou risest, they live, they grow for thee.

Thou makest the seasons in order to rear all that thou hast made, (Psalm 104:19)

The winter to cool them
And that *they* may taste thee.
Thou made the distant sky in order to rise therein,
In order to see all that thou dost make.
When thou wert alone,
Rising in thy form as the living Aton,
Appearing, shining, *withdrawing or approaching*,
Thou madest millions of forms of thyself alone.
Cities, towns, fields, road, and river—
Every eye beholds thee over against them,
For thou art the Aton of the day over *the earth*...

Thou art in my heart,
And there is no other that knows thee
Save thy son Nefer-kheperu-Re Wa-en-Re,
For thou hast made him well-versed in thy plans and in thy strength
(*note says the pharaoh was the intermediary between the people and their gods, the concept here applied to the new proto-monotheism*).

The world came into being by thy hand,
According as thou hast made them.
When thou hast risen, they live, (Psalm 104:30)
When thou settest they die.
Thou art lifetime thy own self, (Psalm 104:29)
For one lives (only) through thee.

Eyes are (fixed) on beauty until thou settest.
All work is laid aside when thou settest in the west.
(But) when (thou) risest (again),
(Everything is) made to flourish for the king...
Since thou didst found the earth
And raise up for thy son,

Who came forth from thy body:
The king of Upper and Lower Egypt, …Ahk-en-Aton, …and the Chief Wife of the King…Nefert-iti, living and youthful forever and ever.

PSALM 104 (KING JAMES VERSION)

Grammatical guide emphasis omitted

Note two things: the Hebrew Lunar Calendar and the fact that the Greek word translated for LORD in these passages was ADONI, possibly, even, ATON-I.

Bless the LORD. O my soul. O LORD my God, thou art very great; thou art clothed with honour and majesty.

2. Who coverest thyself with light as with a garment: who stretchest out the heavens like a curtain:
3. Who layeth the beams of his chambers in the waters: who maketh the clouds his chariot: who walketh upon the wings of the wind:
4. Who maketh his angels spirits; his ministers a flaming fire:
5. Who laid the foundations of the earth, that it should be removed forever,
6. Thou coverdest it with the deep as with a garment: the waters stood above the mountains.
7. At thy rebuke they fled; at the voice of thy thunder they hasted away.
8. They go up by the mountains; they go down by the valleys, which run among the hills.
9. Thou hast set a bound that they may not pass over; that they turn not again to cover the earth.
10. He sendeth the springs into the valleys, which run among the hills.
11. They give drink to every beast of the field: the wild asses quench their thirst.

12. By them shall the fowls of the heaven have their habitation, which sing among the branches.
13. He watereth the hills from his chambers: the earth is satisfied with the fruit of his works.
14. He causeth the grass to grow for the cattle, and the herb for the service of man: that he may bring forth food out of the earth;
15. And wine that maketh glad the heart of man, and oil to make his face to shine, and bread which strengtheneth a man's heart.
16. The trees of the LORD are full of sap; the cedars of Lebanon, which he hath planted;
17. Where the birds make their nests: as for the stork, the fir trees are her house.
18. The high hills are a refuge for the wild goats; and the rocks for the conies.
19. He appointed the moon for seasons: the sun knoweth his going down.
20. Thou makest darkness, and it is night: Wherein all the beasts of the forest do creep forth.
21. The young lions roar after their prey, and seek their meat from God.
22. The sun ariseth, they gather themselves together, and they lay them down in their dens.
23. Man goeth forth unto his work and to his labour until evening.
24. O LORD, how manifold are thy works! in wisdom hast thou made them all: the earth is full of thy riches.
25. So is this great and wide sea, wherein are things creeping innumerable, both small and great beasts.
26. There go the ships: there is that great leviathan, whom thou hast made to play therein.
27. These wait all upon thee; that thou mayest give them their meat in due season.
28. That thou givest them they gather: thou openest thy hand, they are filled with good.

29. Thou hidest thy face, they are troubled: thou takest away their breath, they die, and return to their dust.
30. Thou sendest forth thy spirit, they are created: and thou renewest the face of the earth.
31. The glory of the LORD shall endure forever: The LORD shall rejoice in his works.
32. He looketh on the earth and it trembleth: he toucheth the hills and they smoke.
33. I will sing unto the LORD as long as I live: I will sing my praise to my God while I have being.
34. My meditation of him shall be sweet: I will be glad in the LORD.
35. Let the sinners be consumed out of the earth, and let the wicked be no more. Bless the LORD, O my soul. Praise ye the LORD.

Text Notes

1. Hesiod, *Works and Days*, "The Five Ages" 129-245
2. "An Eruption Resembling That of Variola in the Skin of a Mummy of the Twentieth Dynasty (1200-1100 BC) "by M. Armand Ruffer and A. R. Ferguson, the *Journal of Pathological Bacteriology*, 15: 1, 1911. (This article is reprinted in *Diseases in Antiquity*, published by Charles C. Thomas Publisher, Springfield, Illinois, 1967.)
3. *Mycenaean Pottery II, Chronology*, by Arne Furumark, Skrifter Utgivna av Svenska Institute I Athen, 1972, page 115.
4. *Indians of New Spain*, by Motolinia, trans by Elizabeth A. Foster, Greenwood Press, Westport, Conn., 1977
5. "Minoan Painting and Egypt; the Case of Tell el-Dab'a," by Lyvia Morgan. Begins page 29 in: *Egypt, the Aegean and the Levant; Interconnections in the Second Millennium BC*, British Museum Press, London, 1995.
6. *Egypt, Canaan, and Israel in Ancient Times*, by Donald B. Redford, Princeton Univ Press, 1992, see chapter on the Hyksos.
7. From *Canaanites and Their Land*, by Niels Peter Lemche (Univ of Copenhagen), Sheffield Academic Press, 1991.
8. *JPS Torah Commentary to Jewish Publication Society Translation*, by Baruch A. Levine, edited by Nahum M. Saran, Jewish Publication Society, Philadelphia & NY, 1989, pgs 75 to 85—note: pages go "backwards" to follow the Hebrew.

9. citing an article in *Palestine Exploration Quarterly*, volume 104: 1972, pages 139-146, "Joshua 10:12-14 and the Solar Eclipse of 30 September 1131 BC," by J. F. A. Sawyer.
10. *Greek and Latin Authors on Jews and Judaism*, edited by Menahem Stern, Israel Academy of Sciences, 1976.
11. *The Tigris Expedition*, by Thor Heyerdahl, Doubleday & Co, NYC, 1981.
12. *Tin in Antiquity*, by R. D. Penhallurick, Institute for Metals Press, London, 1986.
13. unpublished TM 75 G 1860) Ebla tablet (from *The Hebrew Bible and Its Modern Interpreters*, by Douglas A. Knight and Gene M. Tucker)—.
14. *Genesis 12-36, Commentary*, Augsburg Publishing House, Minneapolis, translated by John J. Scullion, 1985.
15. *Arabia Before Muhammad*, by DeLacy O'Leary, London, Kegan Paul, 1927, pg 66.
16. "Mystery of the Mummies" symposium at the University of Pennsylvania Museum, Spring 1996, under dir of Dr. Victor H. Mair. also: Dr. Han Kangxin, Chinese Academy of Social Sciences, Beijing.
17. *Oedipus and Akhnaton*, by Emanuel Velikovsky, Doubleday, New York, 1960.
18. *The Coming of the Age of Iron*, edited by James D. Muhly and Theodore A. Wertime, Yale Univ Press, 1980.
19. "Near Eastern alloying and some textual evidence for the early use of arsenical copper," by E. R. Eaton and Hugh McKerrell, *World Archeology*, Volume 8, #2, (October) 1976, pgs 169-189, note especially from page 182 on.
20. *Black Athena, Volume II, The Afro-Asian Roots of Classical Civilization, the Archaeological and Documentary Evidence*, by Martin Bernal, Rutgers Univ Press, 1991, pgs 418-423.

21. *The Origin and History of Irish Place Names, Third Edition*, by P. W. Joyce, London, Kegan Paul, 1871—with many subsequent printings
22. *The Bronze Age in Barbarian Europe*, by Jacques Briard and translated by Mary Turton, Routledge & Kegan Paul, London and Boston, 1979, pg 182.
23. *Celtic Civilization and Its Heritage*, by Jan Filip, Academia Press, Prague, 1977, pg 19.
24. *The Ancient Near East; An Anthology of Texts and Pictures*, edited by James B. Pritchard, Princeton University Press, 1958, Pgs 226-230.

Index

Aanen, 42
brother of Tiya*****
Aaron, 41–42, 49–53, 56–57, 59
On35–36, 40–42, 45–52, 54–57
sun temple at On, 42, 101
Aaron, 41–42, 49–53, 56–57, 59
Aanen, 42
Aanen?, 42
brother, 36, 41–42, 51–52, 100–101, 136–137, 140–142, 144, 149
immunity to smallpox, 41
immunity?, 41–42, 50, 53, 61–62
Abraham, 27, 35, 55, 82, 105, 111, 113–118, 120–121
Maaibre, 27, 111
Naharin (Haran), 85
Achaean, 5, 21, 48, 127
Mycenaean, 10, 29, 48, 128, 140–141, 146, 168, 182, 186–187, 189, 192, 194, 200, 208, 212
Achaeans, 159, 168
Ahhiyawa, 168
Achan, 62, 65
smallpox–infected garment, 65
Aegean Sea, 29
Aegyptos, 136, 149–150, 154–155
Hikaptah, 104

Aeschylus, 4, 130, 133, 148, 155
Suppliants, 150–151, 153–155
Agade, 36–37
Akkad, 36–37
Agamemnon, 12, 134, 147, 158
Agenor, 149
Ahmose, 25, 29, 84, 88, 98, 150
Avaris, 26, 29–32, 54–55, 76, 79, 86, 88, 103–104, 150, 152
Hyksos, 13, 25–32, 35, 48, 54–55, 76, 79, 83–84, 86, 88–89, 94, 96, 99, 104–105, 108, 111, 116–118, 120–121, 128, 130, 135, 143, 145, 148, 150–154, 167, 231
Ahmose–si–abina, 30
El–Kab (near Aswan)*****
Ahmoses, 38
Ai, 61–65
name meaning a ruin, 65
Ai (city ruin)*****
Ai (ruined city)*****
Ai (ruins of city)*****
Joshua, 13, 55–57, 61–67, 154, 232
AIDS, 12, 22, 75
Ain Hawarah, 47
Ain Kadis, 48–49, 54, 58
Akhet–Aten, 25, 100, 102, 144–145, 168, 220
capital city, 25, 30, 79, 86, 99–100, 134, 144–145, 168, 176, 220, 222
Greek Street, 169
"New Thebes", 144, 168
Akhnaten, 0, 24–25, 31, 74, 87, 99–102, 123–124, 133, 137, 139–144, 146–147, 159–161, 168, 193, 200, 202, 220–223
Akhet–Aten (Horizon of the Aten)*****
Amon–Re, 24, 86–88, 98–101, 110, 114–116, 142–143, 202

Index • 239

Aten, 24–25, 31, 42, 87–88, 98–102, 121, 132, 139, 142–143, 160, 168, 201–202, 206, 220–222
   Aten heresy, 24, 31
   Aten prayers, 31
   Beloved of the Sun Disk, 99
   grandson of Joseph?*****
   part–Mitanni, 193
   pharaoh Ay, 24, 101, 136–137, 140, 142, 144, 148, 168
   proto–Hebrew religion*****
   proto–monotheism, 24, 133, 137, 202, 226
   Psalm, 99, 201, 221, 223–227
   Smenkhakhare, 100, 140–142, 144, 147
   Tel el–Amarna, 100
   The Hymn to the Aten, 99
   Tiya, 31, 42, 87, 95–99, 101, 133, 137, 139, 142, 144, 222
   Tutankhamon, 24, 101, 140, 142–143, 206
   Wide Legs, 139
   "monotheism", 98–99, 200, 203
Akhnaten (Amenhotep IV)*****
Akkad (Agade)*****
Alexander, 134, 145, 157
   Hittite name, 145, 157
Alps, 173
   mummified ancient man0*****
Alvarez, Walter*****
Amalek, 47–48
   Amyklai, 48
   Amyklar, 48
   Numbers 24:20, 47
   Sea Peoples, 21–23, 48, 133, 148, 151, 181
Amalekites, 56, 58
Amarna, 35, 100–102, 111, 143–144, 193, 202–203

Akhet–Aten, 25, 100, 102, 144–145, 168, 220
Amazon, 140
de Orellana, 140
Greek mythology, 140
amber, 169, 180, 191
Amenhotep I, 84
Amenhotep II, 85, 94
Mitanni, 82–86, 93–94, 97, 100–101, 105–106, 108–110, 114, 120–121, 128, 133, 138, 144, 146–147, 151, 155, 159–160, 168, 176–177, 183, 192–194, 220
Amenhotep III, 0, 31, 42, 87, 94–98, 110, 121, 123, 133, 137–140, 142, 144, 147
Yuya, 31, 42, 86–87, 94–99, 105, 110–112, 120, 133, 135–137, 142–144, 161
Akhnaten, 0, 24–25, 31, 74, 87, 99–102, 123–124, 133, 137, 139–144, 146–147, 159–161, 168, 193, 200, 202, 220–223
Egyptian artists, 94, 98
King Laius, 145
Tiya, 31, 42, 87, 95–99, 101, 133, 137, 139, 142, 144, 222
Yuya, 31, 42, 86–87, 94–99, 105, 110–112, 120, 133, 135–137, 142–144, 161
Yuya (Joseph?)*****
"marriage", 86, 96, 109, 121, 133, 144–145, 147, 155, 160
Amenhotep IV, 0, 24, 31, 87, 96–98, 124, 132, 137
Tiya, 31, 42, 87, 95–99, 101, 133, 137, 139, 142, 144, 222
Amenmesse, 103
Amerindian, 50, 138
Amman, Jordan, 59
Ammon, 60, 64
Amon, 24–25, 86, 94, 99, 103, 132, 134–135, 140, 142, 144
Amon–Re, 24, 86–88, 98–101, 110, 114–116, 142–143, 202
Mamre, or Mambre, 114

Amorite, 60
Amorites, 59–60
Anatolia, 82, 116, 146, 194, 200, 205
Ankhsenpaaten, 142
Antigone, 141–143
Meritaten, 141–143
Anubis, 156
Anyang, 107, 176, 207
both copper and tin, 176, 208, 211
Shang, 5, 73, 107, 176, 207, 210
Apis, 154, 156
Aqaba, 40, 58
Arabia, 40, 54, 58, 122, 232
Ares, 130
Argo, 128, 146
Argonauts*****
Argos, 65, 131–132, 149–151, 154–155
temple of Hera, 150
Aristophanes*****
Arundel Marbles, 20
Cromwell, 21, 100
John Selden, 21
Aryan invasion, 81–84, 107, 163, 193
Mitanni, 82–86, 93–94, 97, 100–101, 105–106, 108–110, 114, 120–121, 128, 133, 138, 144, 146–147, 151, 155, 159–160, 168, 176–177, 183, 192–194, 220
proto–Jewish peoples, 81
Asenath, 136
Asimov, Isaac*****
Asimov's Guide to the Bible, 116
Assyrian, 7, 21, 100, 168
OldAswan*****

Aten, 24–25, 31, 42, 87–88, 98–102, 121, 132, 139, 142–143, 160, 168, 201–202, 206, 220–222
  name was Shu, 160, 221
  proto–monotheists, 25
  Aten heresy, 24, 31
  Aten prayers, 31
  Biblical Psalms, 31, 99
  Aten–worship, 87, 168
  "monotheistic", 24, 87
  Atenists, 25, 88, 200, 202, 221
  Atreus, 146–147
  Avaris, 26, 29–32, 54–55, 76, 79, 86, 88, 103–104, 150, 152
  built 7 years after Hebron*****
  fell, 3–4, 12, 26, 37, 43, 58, 72, 84, 86, 137, 147, 161, 174, 194, 204
  Hwt Waret, 29, 150
  Pi–Rameses, 32, 46–47
  Rhind Mathematical Papyrus, 29
  Tel–Ed–Dab'a, 29
  volcanic island of Thera, 29, 80, 83, 107, 193
  Avaris (siege of)*****
  Ahmose–si–abina, 30
  Ay, 24, 101, 136–137, 140, 142–144, 148, 168
  Creon, 130, 140, 143–144, 148
  Ay (pharaoh)*****
  Aten religion, 101
  last "Amarna" pharaoh, 101
  Tiya's brother*****
  Aztec, 10, 50, 74
  Aztec language, 50
  leprosy, smallpox*****
  Azupirani, 36
  Baal–zephon, 47

Babylonian, 7, 21, 36, 171
OldBabylonish garment*****
Bedouin tribes, 49
Berdan, Francis F.*****
The Aztecs, 11
Bernal, Martin*****
Black Athena, 28, 67, 79, 116, 150, 168, 185, 232
Dan, 11, 147, 149–151, 153, 159–160, 179, 181–182, 192
Bible, 0, 6, 13, 35, 37–39, 41, 43, 45, 47–49, 51, 53–57, 59, 61, 63, 65, 67, 105, 116, 146, 159, 185, 201, 221, 232
smallpox epidemic, 10, 13, 20, 23, 27, 35, 40, 46, 48, 52–56, 58, 61, 63, 68, 72–77, 104, 111, 154, 160–161, 189, 199–201, 203, 205, 207, 209–211, 213, 215, 221
Biers, William R.*****
"The Dark Ages"Bilhah*****
Bitter Lakes, 47
Black Sea, 0, 128, 146, 178–179, 182, 194–195
Boiotia, 130–131
Boling, Robert G.,*****
Anchor Bible Series book, 63
Anchor Bible Series, Joshua*****
Book of Joshua, 65–66
Book of Joshua, 6:24, 65
Borlase, William Copeland*****
Naenia Cornubai, 188
brass, 183–184
bronze 6–10, 52, 54, 56, 58, 68, 72, 74, 116, 118–122, 127–130, 136, 138, 140, 142 163, 167–195220, 222, 224, 226, 228, 232–233
zinc and copper, 183–184
Brittany, 169, 176
bronze, 0, 4, 6–10, 12, 17–18, 20, 22, 24–26, 28, 30, 36, 38, 40, 42, 44–46, 48, 50, 52, 54, 56, 58, 60, 62, 64, 66, 68, 72, 74, 76–78, 80, 82,

100, 102, 104, 106–110, 112 132–134, 136, 138, 140, 142, 144, 146, 158, 160, 204–214, 218, 220, 222, 224, 226, 228, 232–233
  arsenic–copper, 26, 82, 173
  brass, 183–184
  tin–copper, 26, 82, 108, 173, 183
  bronze age, 12, 18, 20, 22, 24, 26, 28, 30, 36, 38, 44–46, 48, 50, 52, 54, 56, 74, 94, 96, 98, 100, 102, 104, 127–130, 144, 146, 148, 150, 152, 218, 220, 222, 224, 226, 228,
  bronze alloy, 26, 167, 205
  arsenic, 108, 167, 172
  tin, 0, 6, 68, 90, 106–110, 114, 119–122, 128, 147, 157–161, 163–164, 167–189, 191–195, 199, 201, 203–211, 213, 215, 219–220, 232
  bronze weapons*****
  Budge, Ernest Alfred Thompson Wallis (Sir)*****
  Babylonian Life and History*****
  "The Legend of the Birth of Sargon of Agade", 36
  Byblos, 132
  Byzantine empire, 146
  Cadmus (Kadmos)*****
  Cadmeia, 134
  Cairo, 30, 42
  Caleb, 55–57
  plague, 44, 56–57, 62, 73–74, 189–190
  Caleb, the son of Jephuneh, 57
  Canaan, 0, 13, 20, 27–31, 35, 40, 52–56, 58, 60–61, 63–67, 81–83, 85–86, 88, 95, 101, 103, 105–106, 110, 114–115, 117, 127–132, 134, 143, 146, 148–149, 151, 155–156, 160–161, 181, 187, 200, 213, 231
  catastrophe circa 1100 BC*****
  colonial, 5, 35, 38, 40, 60, 63–64, 83, 86, 88, 95, 109–110, 114, 117, 146, 149, 161, 186–187
  come back infected with smallpox, 53

Egyptian colony, 54, 160
Kahnanah in Egyptian, 35
Kahnanah in Egyptian itself, 35
Ki–na–ah–num in Mari, 35
Ki–na–hi in Amarna letters?*****
Ki–na–hi in the Egyptian?, 35
Kinahhu in Hurrian*****
too strong to take, 55
within Imperial Egyptian, 35
"spies" sent out, 52
Canaanite, 5, 10, 26–27, 55, 61, 67, 83–86, 99, 103, 110, 113, 117, 121, 128–130, 132, 134, 143, 145, 154, 159, 177
Minoan–Mycenaean–Mediterranean*****
Canaanite–Minoan*****
Canaanites, 26, 56, 58, 63–64, 67, 84, 160–161, 186, 231
Caphtor*****
Egyptian "Keftiu," Crete*****
Carter, Howard*****
Tutankhamon's tomb*****
Carthage, 67
founded, 48, 55, 67, 86, 130
Carthaginian, 67
Carthagenians*****
as Canaanites*****
catastrophe, 0, 3–13, 17–27, 29–31, 53, 60, 71–73, 77–78, 89, 121, 127, 129, 147, 149, 155, 159–160, 167, 172–175, 183, 188, 190–191, 200–201, 204–206, 208, 211–212, 215, 221
Celtic EmpireChinaChinese*****
Haniron casting*****
Chrysippus, 147
Cleveland Museum of Art (brochure)*****
Cockburn, Aidan and Eve*****

Mummies, Disease, and Ancient Cultures*****
Colchis, 128
Columbus, 29, 209
Conquest, The, 11
Constantinople*****
Sultan Mohammed II, 29
Coptic, 134, 141, 213
Cornwall, 158, 168–169, 171, 176, 180, 182, 185, 187–189, 192–193
Cortez, 10
cremation, 13
Creon, 130, 140, 143–144, 148
Ay (pharaoh)*****
means Ruler, 140
Crete, 0, 78–80, 83, 161, 169, 177
Pseira, 78, 169
cubit, 80
Cyclopes, 68
Cyprus, 36, 48, 177
Dan, 11, 147, 149–151, 153, 159–160, 179, 181–182, 192
"Don" found in a Yorkshire*****
Danuna, 181
D3–in, 181
Da Danaan, 181, 192
Danaan, 5, 147, 159, 181, 192
Danaos, 149, 151–154, 181, 192
Danites, 181
Danube, 169–171, 178–182, 191–192, 194
Dene, 181
Denyen?, 151, 181
Dnieper, 181
Tanaya, 181

Tin3y, 181
Ukraine Don, 181
Danaan, 5, 147, 159, 181, 192
Danaos, 149, 151–154, 181, 192
Danaus, 147, 155, 159
Danube, 169–171, 178–182, 191–192, 194
Danube (Danau, Danuvius)*****
Dardanelles, 158, 178–179
Dardanoi, 157
Egyptian records, 83, 149, 157
Dead Sea, 58–59
deben, 119–120
a weight of copper, 119
Delta, 0, 20–22, 25, 29, 31–32, 41–43, 45–46, 79, 84, 103, 150, 173
DeMille, Cicil B.*****
desert of Paran, 52
dm, 106–109, 171–172, 183, 185, 192, 219
tin, 0, 6, 68, 90, 106–110, 114, 119–122, 128, 147, 157–161, 163–164, 167–189, 191–195, 199, 201, 203–211, 213, 215, 219–220, 232
Dorian, 208
drdny, 157, 178
Egyptian dn–or–dm–word, 178
Eaton and McKerrell, 172
dm means tin, 171
Eaton, Ethel R.*****
Ebla tablet, 113, 232
Genesis, 13, 24, 26, 31, 35, 68, 95, 110–119, 135, 153, 232
eclipse, 66, 232
eclipse, 1131 BC, 66
invasion of Canaan by Joshua, 66
Edom,, 0, 48, 58–59, 63, 69

Gulf of Aqaba, 40, 58
Midian, 0, 40, 42, 47, 53, 58, 69
quarantine, 52, 54, 56, 58–59, 64
Egypt, 4–5, 13, 17–19, 21–31, 35–37, 40, 42, 46, 48–49, 51, 54, 60, 63, 66, 109–110, 112–118, 120–123, 131–132, 134–136, 138, 142–147, 149–153, 155–161, 167–169, 190–192, 194, 200, 202, 225, 227, 231
Amenhotep IV (Akhnaten)*****
Aten heresy, 24, 31
Exodus, 0, 13, 20, 24–25, 36, 38, 41–42, 44–45, 51, 53–54, 66–68, 75–76, 87, 111–113, 130, 154, 185, 200, 203
heretical religions, 24
Hyksos, 13, 25–32, 35, 48, 54–55, 76, 79, 83–84, 86, 88–89, 94, 96, 99, 104–105, 108, 111, 116–118, 120–121, 128, 130, 135, 143, 145, 148, 150–154, 167, 231
Imperial, 5, 7, 13, 21, 24–25, 29, 31, 35, 40, 46, 54, 67, 89, 93–95, 97–98, 104–105, 109, 113–114, 122, 131, 158–159, 161, 167–170, 176, 179–180, 182, 186, 193, 202, 207, 212–213
Karnak, 18, 103, 215
Luxor, 18, 103, 212
Memphis, Hikaptah, 104
plagues, 42–45, 73–74
Taawy, 105, 150
Egyptian, 0, 5, 13, 17–20, 23–31, 35–43, 46–47, 49–51, 53–55, 60–65, 68–69, 72, 74–76, 79–80, 82–89, 93–110, 112–119, 121, 129–137, 140, 142–143, 145–161, 167, 169–171, 174, 178, 180–187, 192–193, 201–202, 212, 217–221
army, 10, 17, 28, 46–47, 63, 83–85, 116, 134, 140, 144, 156–157
pharaohs, 18–21, 23, 27, 29, 38, 79, 84, 88, 95, 101, 103–104, 110, 118, 120, 142, 148–150, 152, 155, 161, 194, 215
Egyptian (monetary unit)*****
deben, 119–120

Egyptian army, 17, 28, 46, 63, 85, 156
unleavened bread, 46
Egyptian cubits, 80
Egyptian Delta, 31, 79
Egyptian Empire, 13, 18, 38, 62–63, 88, 93–94, 100, 104, 106, 115, 132–133, 135, 153, 167, 174, 219
Egyptian mummy, 74
eighteenth dynasty female, 74
Egyptian Thebes, 132, 134–135, 137, 143, 145
Greek Thebes, 129–132, 134, 137, 143–145, 148
Eilat–Aqaba, 40
El Niño, 75
chaos–caused stress, 75
el–Marah, 47
Eleazar, 59
electrum*****
Elim, 47
Wadi Gharandel, 47
Epaphos, 152–154
pharaoh Apophis, 152
Ephron, 115
epidemic, 10, 13, 20, 22–23, 27, 35, 40–41, 45–46, 48–49, 51–65, 67–68, 72–77, 104, 111, 154, 160–161, 189–191, 199–203, 205, 207, 209–213, 215, 221
Equatorial Africa, 43
Nile flooding, 42, 80, 218
Eratosthenes, 147
Ericson, Leif*****
Erzgebirge, 168, 178, 183, 185, 188, 191, 193
"Ore Mountains", 183
Eteocles, 130, 140–141, 143, 147
Eteoclus, 141

Etewoklewes, 141
name means True Fame (or, Just Glory)*****
Smenkhakhare and Tutankhamon*****
Etham, 47
Euphrates, 36, 82, 84, 109, 146, 151
Euripides, 129–131, 133, 138, 143
Suppliant Women, The1*****
The Phoenician Women, 129, 143, 161
Eusebius, 116
Exodus, 0, 13, 20, 24–25, 36, 38, 41–42, 44–45, 51, 53–54, 66–68, 75–76, 87, 111–113, 130, 154, 185, 200, 203
  climate–change caused nine "plagues", 44
  dermatitis breaking out into boils*****
  El Niño–type climate change., 45
  smallpox, 9–13, 20, 22–23, 25, 27, 35, 40–42, 44, 46, 48–65, 68, 72–77, 104, 111–112, 133, 138, 154, 160–161, 189–190, 199–201, 203, 205, 207, 209–211, 213–215, 221
  smallpox epidemic, 10, 13, 20, 23, 27, 35, 40, 46, 48, 52–56, 58, 61, 63, 68, 72–77, 104, 111, 154, 160–161, 189, 199–201, 203, 205, 207, 209–211, 213, 215, 221
  fall of Troy, 21, 128, 132–133, 147–148
  Filip, Jan*****
  Celtic Civilization and Its Heritage, 191, 233
  Florentine Codex, 11, 76
  Foster, Elizabeth*****
  Freud, Sigmund*****
  from the north foothills of the Tien Shan mountains in, 176
  Furumark, Arne*****
  "catastrophe zone", 10
  Gaza, 84, 86
  Genesis, 13, 24, 26, 31, 35, 68, 95, 110–119, 135, 153, 232

century, 4–5, 8–11, 13, 17–19, 21, 24–29, 45, 52, 67, 74–75, 79, 84–86, 89, 94, 96, 104, 108, 117, 120, 134–135, 144, 149–151, 158, 181, 183, 188, 191
   Genesis, 13, 24, 26, 31, 35, 68, 95, 110–119, 135, 153, 232
   Genesis 33:19, 119
   kesita, 119–120
   Genesis 46:31, 95
   Gibeon, 62–63, 66
   eclipse, 1131 BC, 66
   solar eclipse on September 30, 1131 BC, 66
   Gilgamesh, 111
   Gla, 21, 65
   Goetze, Albrecht*****
   Goshen, 0, 25, 30, 32, 42, 106, 172
   gsm, 25, 30, 106, 172
   Goshen (gsm)*****
   Faqus (modern city)*****
   not far from Avaris, 30
   Grant, Robert M.*****
   Eusebius as Church Historian*****
   Greece, 0, 8, 23, 65, 68, 84, 88, 116, 120, 128–129, 131–132, 143, 146, 150–152, 154, 157, 160, 168, 177–178, 180, 187, 192, 194, 200–201, 208, 212, 221
   75 percent drop in population, 23
   GreekAchaean*****
   dramaticGreek fortresses*****
   Gla, 21, 65
   Mycenae, 21, 65, 68, 127, 147, 158, 180, 191
   Tiryns, 21, 65, 68
   Greek myth, 127, 151
   Greek Thebes, 129–132, 134, 137, 143–145, 148
   Egyptian Thebes, 132, 134–135, 137, 143, 145

Thebes in Egypt, 131
Gulf of Aqaba, 40, 58
Hakeptah, 150
Residence of the spirit (ka) of Ptah*****
Hallstatt CultureHamor*****
Hannibal, 67, 113
title shofet, 67
Haran, 82, 85–86, 93, 95, 97, 99–101, 103, 105, 107–109, 111, 113–115, 117, 119–121, 144, 146, 155, 192
Hathor, 40, 47, 151, 153, 184, 218
Hat Hor, House of Horus, means wife*****
Timna, 40
Hatshepsut, 86, 93, 96, 212
Hatshepsut, "Queen"*****
Hatti (Hittite)*****
Hebrew, 5, 24, 39, 42, 47, 60, 89, 105, 111, 117, 119, 150, 153, 159, 161, 201, 213, 227, 231–232
ibri or apiru, 24
Hebrew alphabet, 39
Moses, 4, 12, 20, 24–25, 35–42, 44, 46–61, 66, 76, 112–113, 118, 130, 135, 137, 161, 200–202, 204, 221
Hebrews, 20, 25, 54, 60, 67, 215
ibri, apiru, etc., 54
Hebron, 54–55, 115
patriarchs and their wives*****
Helen, 145, 157, 220
Heliopolis, 0, 30, 162, 185
On or Anu, 30
Hera, 131, 150–151
Hera, temple of*****
Argos, 65, 131–132, 149–151, 154–155
Heshbon, 60

smallpox, 9–13, 20, 22–23, 25, 27, 35, 40–42, 44, 46, 48–65, 68, 72–77, 104, 111–112, 133, 138, 154, 160–161, 189–190, 199–201, 203, 205, 207, 209–211, 213–215, 221

Hesiod, 4, 6–8, 68, 180, 200

"The Five Ages"Heyerdahl , Thor*****

HittiteHittite Empire*****

smallpox epidemic, 10, 13, 20, 23, 27, 35, 40, 46, 48, 52–56, 58, 61, 63, 68, 72–77, 104, 111, 154, 160–161, 189, 199–201, 203, 205, 207, 209–211, 213, 215, 221

Hivites, 35

hka–ha–swt, 26–27, 35

Homer, 4–8, 62, 67–68, 127–128, 138–139, 148, 157, 159–160, 168, 180, 191–192, 194, 200

Horemheb, 24, 87, 101–103, 133, 144–145

"return to normalcy", 202

Horites, 105, 108, 192

Horus, 47, 153, 184–186, 219

Hyksos, 13, 25–32, 35, 48, 54–55, 76, 79, 83–84, 86, 88–89, 94, 96, 99, 104–105, 108, 111, 116–118, 120–121, 128, 130, 135, 143, 145, 148, 150–154, 167, 231

Avaris, 26, 29–32, 54–55, 76, 79, 86, 88, 103–104, 150, 152

bronze alloy, 26, 167, 205

Canaanite, 5, 10, 26–27, 55, 61, 67, 83–86, 99, 103, 110, 113, 117, 121, 128–130, 132, 134, 143, 145, 154, 159, 177

century, 4–5, 8–11, 13, 17–19, 21, 24–29, 45, 52, 67, 74–75, 79, 84–86, 89, 94, 96, 104, 108, 117, 120, 134–135, 144, 149–151, 158, 181, 183, 188, 191

Hivites?, 35

hka–ha–swt, 26–27, 35

Manetho, 26–28, 75–76

People Under Foreign Rulers, 26, 79

suppliant*****

Hyksos pharaohs, 27, 29, 118, 120, 152
Egyptian political collapse*****
Fifteenth Dynasty, 28
Merwosere Ya'cob–el, 27
Hyksos–Minoan–Canaanite, 83, 152
Hymn to the Aten, 99, 201, 222
Ice Age, 8, 50
Iliad, 48, 65, 158, 177, 180, 194
mysterious epidemic, 65
Imperial Egypt, 13, 21, 24–25, 35, 46, 54, 93, 97, 105, 113–114, 161, 168–169, 176, 179, 186, 202, 212
Imperial Egyptian, 35, 46, 95, 104, 131, 169–170, 180, 182
Indian Wars, 63
Indo–European word, 171
Io, 131–132, 151–154, 156
lament ioioioio*****
Thebans, 132
Ioleus, 65
Ioleus (Thessaly)*****
Iphis, 141
Iraq, 61
Ireland, 159, 181–182, 189–190
Iron, 0, 8–9, 77, 119–120, 146, 158, 173–175, 190–191, 194, 200, 204–214, 232
higher temperatures.*****
Tutankhamon, two daggers, 206
iron casting, 211
Chinese, 8, 73, 107, 176–177, 207, 210–211, 232
Isaac, 55, 82, 115–118, 120–121
sack–carried?*****
Israelites, 46–47
Sea of Reeds, 47

Index • 255

Jacob, 27–28, 35, 55, 82, 95, 118–121, 128, 152
Merwosere Ya'cob–el, 27
Mr–wsr–re Ya'kob–har, 152
multi–national corporate head*****
Jason, 128, 146
Jenner, Edward*****
Jephuneh, 57
Jericho, 61–65
Achan, 62, 65
Ai, 61–65
capture and burning, 65
Egyptian Empire, 13, 18, 38, 62–63, 88, 93–94, 100, 104, 106, 115, 132–133, 135, 153, 167, 174, 219
forces immune*****
Smallpox–infected?, 65
viciousness, 62
Jericho and Ai, 61, 63–64
ancient ruins, 61
fled plague–ridden cities to, 64
Jethro, 40–41
JewishJewish Publication Society*****
Jocasta, 123, 139, 143–144
Nefertiti, 0, 99–100, 115, 123, 138–139, 144, 146, 160, 193, 222, 227
Epicasta by Homer, 139
John Selden, 21
Jordan (Kingdom of)*****
Jordan (River)*****
Jordan River, 60–62
Joshua, 13, 55–57, 61–67, 154, 232
Joseph-, 31, 35, 42, 86–87, 93, 95–97, 99, 101, 103, 105, 107, 109–113, 115, 117, 119–121, 133, 135–137, 141–143, 159, 161

governor, 95, 135
Yuya, 31, 42, 86–87, 94–99, 105, 110–112, 120, 133, 135–137, 142–144, 161
Joseph (Mary's husband)*****
Josephus, 75–76
Manetho quote*****
Joshua, 13, 55–57, 61–67, 154, 232
Anchor Bible Series book, 63
Egyptian Empire, 13, 18, 38, 62–63, 88, 93–94, 100, 104, 106, 115, 132–133, 135, 153, 167, 174, 219
Egyptian–trained military officer?, 64
former Egyptian military man?, 61
plague, 44, 56–57, 62, 73–74, 189–190
solar eclipse on September 30, 1131 BC, 66
Joshua, the son of Nun, 57
Joyce, P.W.*****
The Origin and History of Irish Place Names1*****
Kadesh, 18, 48–49, 54, 61, 93, 103, 134, 148, 156–159, 192, 194
Ain Kadis, 48–49, 54, 58
Kadesh Barnea, 48–49, 54, 61
Kadmea, 130
Kadmeans, 132
Kadmos, 128–131, 143, 145–146, 148
Cadmeia, 134
founder of Thebes, 146
Nikmed, 128
Karnak, 18, 103, 215
kastira, 120, 171
Kazakhstan, 82
kesita, 119–120
Aryan word, 120
Greek word, 120, 129, 227

Kinahhu*****
King James version, 58, 119, 221, 227
Kingdom of Jordan, 63
Kurds, 61
Laius, 123, 140, 145, 147
Lake Menzaleh, 47
Lake Sirbonis, 47
Lake Timsah, 47
land of milk and honey, 54
late bronze age, 0, 22, 26, 78, 82, 106, 108–109, 119, 121–122, 129, 133, 155, 167, 169, 171–175, 177–183, 185, 187–191, 193, 202, 205, 209–210
  tin–bronze age, 109, 120, 167, 171, 173, 176–177, 187, 190–191, 193
  tin–copper, 26, 82, 108, 173, 183
Leah, 55
Lebanon, 84, 228
Lembke, Janet*****
Suppliants, 150–151, 153–155
leprosy, 11, 41, 49–50, 57, 75
  Hansen's disease, 57
smallpox, 9–13, 20, 22–23, 25, 27, 35, 40–42, 44, 46, 48–65, 68, 72–77, 104, 111–112, 133, 138, 154, 160–161, 189–190, 199–201, 203, 205, 207, 209–211, 213–215, 221
Levant, 48, 182, 231
Levine, 57, 231
  Commentary to JPS translation*****
Levine, Baruch A.*****
Leviticus-, 54–57
Leviticus, 54–57
  tsara 'at, 55, 57
Luxor, 18, 103, 212

Lydia, 146
Machpelah, 55, 115
Magna Carta, 133
Main River, 169–170
Mambre, 114
Manetho, 26–28, 75–76
Josephus quote*****
Shepherd Kings, 26
Marah, 47
Marco Polo, 180, 210
Mary, 0, 42, 141, 233
Merit, 141–142
McKerrell, Hugh*****
Medea, 146
Medenet Habu, 21, 192
Medes (Medoi)*****
Mediterranean, 13, 28, 30, 36, 47–48, 65, 79–80, 132, 154, 179, 181, 187–188
Memphis (Hikaptah)*****
Aegyptos, 136, 149–150, 154–155
Merenptah, 103
Merit, 141–142
Mary, 0, 42, 141, 233
Merit–Amen, 49–50
Meritaten, 141–143
Antigone, 141–143
daughter of Akhnaten and Nefertiti*****
means "Beloved of the Aten", 142
Merneptah, 19–20, 148, 215
Mesopotamia, 0, 5, 37, 72, 81–82, 173, 176, 193
Mesopotamian*****
Mexicans, 11, 65

Mexico, 10–11, 22–23, 50, 74–75
Conquest, The, 11
post–Conquest, 23, 63, 65
smallpox, 9–13, 20, 22–23, 25, 27, 35, 40–42, 44, 46, 48–65, 68, 72–77, 104, 111–112, 133, 138, 154, 160–161, 189–190, 199–201, 203, 205, 207, 209–211, 213–215, 221
Middle East, 13, 114, 117
Midian, 0, 40, 42, 47, 53, 58, 69
Timna, 40
Migdol, 47
military chariots, 19, 47, 172
Minoan, 26, 29, 79–80, 83–84, 161, 212, 231
Minoan–Mycenaean–Canaanite, 48
Miriam, 49–53
Ain Kadis, 48–49, 54, 58
death, 9–10, 20, 22–25, 49, 53, 65, 104, 112, 133, 144, 168, 173, 206, 223
drying blisters, 50
late stage of smallpox, 51
leprous, white as snow, 49
Merit–Amen, "Beloved of Amen", 49
Moses's sister*****
tabernacle, 49
Mitanni, 82–86, 93–94, 97, 100–101, 105–106, 108–110, 114, 120–121, 128, 133, 138, 144, 146–147, 151, 155, 159–160, 168, 176–177, 183, 192–194, 220
Amenhotep II, 85, 94
capital of Washukani*****
Dan?, 11, 147, 149–151, 153, 159–160, 179, 181–182, 192
Naharin (Haran)*****
Nhryn, also called Hurru, 105
play on words, 108, 150

Mizraim, 105, 118
Taawy, "The Two Lands", 150
Moab, 0, 59–60, 64, 69
near Amman, Jordan*****
Mohammed II (Turkish Sultan)*****
Morgan, Livia*****
Hyksos palace, 26
Moses, 4, 12, 20, 24–25, 35–42, 44, 46–61, 66, 76, 112–113, 118, 130, 135, 137, 161, 200–202, 204, 221
Midian, 0, 40, 42, 47, 53, 58, 69
Sargon I, 36–37
Tuthmosis, 0, 31, 38–39, 84–87, 94, 96, 109–110, 117, 133, 135, 144, 147–148, 160
Ahmoses, 38
Akhnaton's hymns, 38
cultural Egyptian, 37
died, 3, 9–11, 18, 23, 37, 49, 52, 56–59, 61, 65, 94, 97, 101, 104, 115–116, 133, 138–140, 142, 144, 174, 189, 194, 200, 203
Egyptian New Kingdom period, 35
Egyptian royal family, 37, 40
Exodus, Leviticus, and Numbers*****
extradition clause, 40
Hebrew alphabet, 39
immunity to smallpox, 41
infected with cowpox?, 40–41
legend, 36, 128, 130, 133–135, 143, 147, 189
means fashioned or created by, 38
name, 10, 24–25, 27–29, 31, 35, 38–39, 42, 48–49, 62, 64–65, 82–83, 86–87, 94–97, 99–101, 103–104, 107–110, 114–118, 120–121, 127–128, 130–132, 134, 136–137, 139–142, 145–146, 149–152, 155, 157–158, 160, 170, 181–183, 185–186, 192, 196, 213, 218–222
plagues, 42–45, 73–74

Rameses, 0, 5, 9–10, 12, 18–21, 23, 25, 31–32, 38–39, 47–48, 73, 85, 88, 103–104, 112, 133–134, 145, 148, 150–151, 155–159, 181, 196, 215
Sargon of Agade, 36
smallpox, 9–13, 20, 22–23, 25, 27, 35, 40–42, 44, 46, 48–65, 68, 72–77, 104, 111–112, 133, 138, 154, 160–161, 189–190, 199–201, 203, 205, 207, 209–211, 213–215, 221
son of, 38, 57, 87, 94, 114, 130, 141, 146–148, 153, 222
story of the birth, 36
the Egyptian, 5, 13, 18, 23–24, 26, 28, 30–31, 35–38, 40, 43, 46–47, 62–63, 72, 75–76, 79, 83–86, 93, 96–97, 99–100, 102, 105–108, 110, 116, 118, 132–135, 145, 147, 150, 152–153, 156, 170, 174, 180, 183–185, 218–220
Torah, 39, 56, 231
Tuthmosis, 0, 31, 38–39, 84–87, 94, 96, 109–110, 117, 133, 135, 144, 147–148, 160
Moses story, 37, 40
Sargon story, 37
Motolinia, 10–11, 50, 65, 74
History of the Indians of New Spain, 10
pen name of Fray Torobio, 10
smallpox appearing like leprosy*****
Mount Ararat, 80
Mtn, 82, 108
Muhly, James D.5*****
The Coming of the Age of Iron, 232
Mursilis, 73–74
Mutemwiya, 87, 94, 115, 133, 144, 160
Naharin (Haran), Mitanni (from)*****
daughter of the Mitanni king Tushratta, 109
Tuthmosis IV, 31, 86–87, 94, 96, 109–110, 133, 135, 144, 147, 160
Muwatallis, 159

Mycenae, 21, 65, 68, 127, 147, 158, 180, 191
burned, 13, 57, 65, 155
Cyclopes, 68
Mycenaean, 10, 29, 48, 128, 140–141, 146, 168, 182, 186–187, 189, 192, 194, 200, 208, 212
  Achaean, 5, 21, 48, 127
Mycobacterium leprae*****
mysterious malignant skin disease, 55
Naharin (Haran)*****
Nahuat, 50
Nahum 3:8, 25, 134
  Thebes as No, 134
Nefertiti, 0, 99–100, 115, 123, 138–139, 144, 146, 160, 193, 222, 227
  Amenhotep IV's chief wife, 97
  Beautiful One Who Has Come, 97
  decline and fall5*****
  Jocasta, 123, 139, 143–144
  mother–in–law Tiya, 97
  wife of Amenhotep III, 137
neo–catastrophism*****
New Canaan, 63
New Canaan, Connecticut, 63
New Kingdom, 5, 13, 17–19, 25, 29, 31, 35, 38, 49, 72, 83, 86, 88–89, 98, 104–105, 112, 114, 116–117, 122, 131–133, 135–136, 144, 149–150, 153, 159, 167, 176–177, 181, 186, 190–191, 200, 202, 204
  New Kingdom Egyptian, 5, 13, 18–19, 83, 88, 98, 104–105, 114, 132–133, 136, 153, 167, 181, 202
  New Kingdom Egyptian Empire, 13, 18, 88, 104, 132–133, 167
New Testament, 42, 142
New World, 22, 29, 50, 201, 209
Nikmed, 128

Kadmos, 128–131, 143, 145–146, 148
Nile, 0, 18, 20–22, 25, 29–30, 32, 41–43, 45–46, 77–78, 80–81, 84, 103, 150, 178, 215, 218, 225
Nile Delta, 0, 20–22, 25, 29, 32, 41–42, 45–46, 84, 103, 150
Pi–Rameses, 32, 46–47
Nile flooding, 42, 80, 218
El Niño, 75
No Amon, 25, 99, 132, 134–135
(Niwt Imn), the City of Amon*****
Thebes, 0, 25, 29, 65, 79, 86, 94, 99–100, 103, 128–135, 137, 139–141, 143–146, 148, 158, 163, 168
Thebes (Egypt)*****
Noah, 80
North Sea, 0, 169, 195
Numbers, 43, 47–50, 52–55, 57–58, 77, 80, 155, 157, 180, 189, 210, 213–214
Numbers (Book of)*****
Numbers 12, 50, 52–53
Numbers 13, 54
Numbers 14, 53, 57–58
Numbers 14:37, 53, 55, 57–58
Numbers 20, 49, 53
Numbers Book of)*****
Nun, 57
Nuremberg, 170–171, 178–179, 182, 195
portages near, 178–179
Odyssey, 48
Sea Peoples, 21–23, 48, 133, 148, 151, 181
Oedipus, 124, 130, 137, 139–140, 143, 145, 147, 159, 161, 232
fat feet, 139
fat legs, 139
Oedipus the King, 145

Old Testament Deity, 56
Old World, 0, 3, 5, 8, 10–12, 19, 50, 63, 174, 201, 209
On, 0, 4, 7–9, 11–12, 17, 21–24, 26, 29–31, 35–36, 40–42, 45–52, 54–57, 59–62, 66, 68, 72–76, 78–79, 81–83, 85, 89, 93–102, 104–111, 113–115, 117–119, 121–122, 128, 130–142, 144–146, 149–151, 153–162, 168–170, 172–179, 181–183, 185–189, 191–194, 196, 199, 203–209, 211–212, 214–215, 218–219, 221–224, 226, 229, 231–232
   Mary, 0, 42, 141, 233
Orchomenus, 65
Orellana, Francisco de*****
Osarseph, 75–76
Osman, Ahmed*****
Stranger in the Valley of the Kings, 30
Oxford, 20
Arundel Marbles, 20
Ozero Issyk Kul, 106
OzymandiasO'Leary, DeLacy*****
Arabia Before Muhammad, 232
Palestine, 84
Paran, 52, 54
passover, 44, 46
patriarchs, 121
Pax Britannica*****
Pelasgus, 151
Pelops, 146–147
Penhallurick, R.D.*****
Tin in Antiquity, 106, 175, 178, 232
Pentheus, 148
Tuth–mosis, 0, 31, 38–39, 84–87, 94, 96, 109–110, 117, 133, 135, 144, 147–148, 160
Persia, 81, 106
Persianpharaoh*****

Great House, 105, 152–153
pre–catastrophe pharaohs, 18–19
Phoenician Women, The,*****
Amarna period, 102, 111, 143–144, 193, 202–203
Hyksos Egypt, 83, 105, 143, 145
New Kingdom Empire, 72, 88, 117, 144
Pi–hahiroth, 47
pr Hthr, 47
Pi–Rameses, 32, 46–47
Avaris, 26, 29–32, 54–55, 76, 79, 86, 88, 103–104, 150, 152
plague, 44, 56–57, 62, 73–74, 189–190
Caleb and Joshua, 56–57
Caleb and Joshua survived?*****
Plague Prayer of Mursilis, 73
plagues, 42–45, 73–74
frogs, 43
hail, 43, 45
locust, 43
Nile flooding, 42, 80, 218
Polynices, 140–141, 147
in Greek, "Belligerent"*****
Tutankhamon and Smenkhakhare*****
population, 3, 8–13, 23, 26, 43, 46, 50, 56, 58, 60, 64, 72, 75, 77–78, 86–88, 122, 129, 138, 147, 157, 159, 167, 169, 172–176, 182, 188, 191, 200–201, 204, 208–209, 211–214
declinePort Said*****
Potiphar (Potiperah)*****
pir–di–per–re, he whom Re gives, 136
pr Hthr, 47
Psalm, 99, 201, 221, 223–227
Pseira, 78, 169
Pylos, 65, 141

burned, 13, 57, 65, 155
pyramids, 0, 5, 11, 14, 18, 68, 71, 97, 138
fictions to explain, 68
Queen Elizabeth I, 93
Rache*****
Rahab, 62
Rameses, 33*****
  Moses, 4, 12, 20, 24–25, 35–42, 44, 46–61, 66, 76, 112–113, 118, 130, 135, 137, 161, 200–202, 204, 221
  name, 10, 24–25, 27–29, 31, 35, 38–39, 42, 48–49, 62, 64–65, 82–83, 86–87, 94–97, 99–101, 103–104, 107–110, 114–118, 120–121, 127–128, 130–132, 134, 136–137, 139–142, 145–146, 149–152, 155, 157–158, 160, 170, 181–183, 185–186, 192, 196, 213, 218–222
  Ra–moses, 38
  Rameses I, 145
  Rameses II, 0, 5, 18–20, 31–32, 85, 88, 103, 134, 148, 150, 155–159, 196
    400th anniversary of the founding of Avaris, 31
    Avaris, 26, 29–32, 54–55, 76, 79, 86, 88, 103–104, 150, 152
    Kadesh (Syria)*****
    Memnon, 158
    peace treaty, 19, 40, 103, 134, 158–159, 168
    Pi–Rameses, 32, 46–47
    treaty with Hittites*****
  Rameses III, 12, 19–21, 23, 48, 104, 133, 148, 151, 181
    assassination attempt, 23
    death, 9–10, 20, 22–25, 49, 53, 65, 104, 112, 133, 144, 168, 173, 206, 223
    died circa 1153 BC, 23
    grandson Rameses V, 23
    Medenet Habu, 21, 192
    Sea Peoples, 21–23, 48, 133, 148, 151, 181

Sea Peoples defeated*****
smallpox, death from*****
Rameses IV, 18, 71*****
Rameses V, 0, 9–10, 19–20, 23, 25, 73, 104, 112, 133, 215
mummified smallpox vesicles, 9
mummy, 9, 73–75, 88, 94, 142, 206, 231
smallpox, 9–13, 20, 22–23, 25, 27, 35, 40–42, 44, 46, 48–65, 68, 72–77, 104, 111–112, 133, 138, 154, 160–161, 189–190, 199–201, 203, 205, 207, 209–211, 213–215, 221
smallpox epidemic, 10, 13, 20, 23, 27, 35, 40, 46, 48, 52–56, 58, 61, 63, 68, 72–77, 104, 111, 154, 160–161, 189, 199–201, 203, 205, 207, 209–211, 213, 215, 221
Rameses V, 0, 9–10, 19–20, 23, 25, 73, 104, 112, 133, 215
Rameses XI, 104
Re, 7, 9, 24–25, 27, 38, 48, 55, 66, 68, 77, 82, 86–87, 89, 100, 102–103, 116, 136, 140, 147, 153, 161, 171, 173–174, 178, 180, 189, 204, 206, 213, 219, 222–223, 231
Rebecca, 55
Red Sea, 47
Sea of Reeds, 47
Redford, Donald B.*****
Egypt, Canaan, and Israel in Ancient Times, 27–28, 231
Hyksos, 13, 25–32, 35, 48, 54–55, 76, 79, 83–84, 86, 88–89, 94, 96, 99, 104–105, 108, 111, 116–118, 120–121, 128, 130, 135, 143, 145, 148, 150–154, 167, 231
Regensburg, 170
Rephidim, 47–48
mouth of a river?, 48
Rhind Mathematical Papyrus, 29
Rhine, 169, 179–180, 182
Rhine–Main, 170, 179
RomanRome*****

Rothenberg, 40
Rothenberg, Dr.*****
Ruffer, M.A. (Sir)*****
"An Eruption Resembling That of Variola in the Skin…, 9, 231
Sanskrit*****
saphahat, 57
Sarah, 55, 115–118
Sargon I, 36–37
Moses, 4, 12, 20, 24–25, 35–42, 44, 46–61, 66, 76, 112–113, 118, 130, 135, 137, 161, 200–202, 204, 221
Sharru–kin, 36
Sargon story, 37
Moses story, 37, 40
scarabs*****
Sea of Reeds, 47
Red Sea, 47
Sea Peoples, 21–23, 48, 133, 148, 151, 181
Levant, 48, 182, 231
Odyssey, 48
smallpox epidemic, 10, 13, 20, 23, 27, 35, 40, 46, 48, 52–56, 58, 61, 63, 68, 72–77, 104, 111, 154, 160–161, 189, 199–201, 203, 205, 207, 209–211, 213, 215, 221
Septimus Severus, 116
Sesostris II, 35
Genesis, 13, 24, 26, 31, 35, 68, 95, 110–119, 135, 153, 232
Seth, 19, 149
Seti, 19–21, 88, 103, 145, 148–149, 194
Canaanite Baal or El, 145
Seti II, 19–21, 148
Seven Against Thebes, 141, 145
Egyptian Eighteenth Dynasty, 145
Severin, Tim*****

Odyssey, 48
The Ulysses Voyage, 177
The Voyage of the Argo, 128, 146
"story map", 177
se'et, 57
local inflammation, boil, mole*****
Shang, 5, 73, 107, 176, 207, 210
bronze–age, 0, 4–6, 21, 68, 71, 73, 75, 77–79, 81, 83–85, 87, 89, 104, 106–107, 109–110, 119–122, 127, 129, 131–132, 134, 141, 147, 149–151, 156–158, 161, 167, 169–172, 174–180, 183–184, 186, 188, 191, 200–203, 208, 210, 219
  capital city of Anyang, 176
  Shang Dynasty, 5, 73, 176, 210
Shechem, 35
Sesostris II, 35
skmm, 35
Shelley, Percy ByssheShiloh*****
Shistocerca gregaria locust, 43
shofet (judge)*****
Sihon, 60
Sile, 30
Tjaru, 30
Sinai, 0, 20, 24–25, 30, 40, 45–46, 48–49, 54, 58, 63, 69, 95, 111, 212
  sixth century BCskmm*****
  smallpox, 9–13, 20, 22–23, 25, 27, 35, 40–42, 44, 46, 48–65, 68, 72–77, 104, 111–112, 133, 138, 154, 160–161, 189–190, 199–201, 203, 205, 207, 209–211, 213–215, 221
  500 vials stored, 214
  AIDS, ebola, 75
  airborne sneezes, 12

catastrophe, 0, 3–13, 17–27, 29–31, 53, 60, 71–73, 77–78, 89, 121, 127, 129, 147, 149, 155, 159–160, 167, 172–175, 183, 188, 190–191, 200–201, 204–206, 208, 211–212, 215, 221

epidemic, 10, 13, 20, 22–23, 27, 35, 40–41, 45–46, 48–49, 51–65, 67–68, 72–77, 104, 111, 154, 160–161, 189–191, 199–203, 205, 207, 209–213, 215, 221

leprosy, 11, 41, 49–50, 57, 75
looked like lepers*****
vesicles, 9, 51

smallpox epidemic, 10, 13, 20, 23, 27, 35, 40, 46, 48, 52–56, 58, 61, 63, 68, 72–77, 104, 111, 154, 160–161, 189, 199–201, 203, 205, 207, 209–211, 213, 215, 221

Smenkhakhare, 100, 140–142, 144, 147
solar eclipse, 66, 232
Book of Joshua?, 65–66
September 30, 1131 BC, 66
Sophocles, 4, 129–130, 133, 138
Sothic cycle, 103
Spartoi, 130
Thebes, 0, 25, 29, 65, 79, 86, 94, 99–100, 103, 128–135, 137, 139–141, 143–146, 148, 158, 163, 168
sphinx, 0, 97, 161, 163
Spring Equinox, 44, 151
Succoth, 47
Tjeku, 47
Succoth (Tjeku)*****
Suez, 30, 47
Supiliuliulimas, 193
Suppiluliumas, 159
Suppliant Women, The*****
Suppliants, 150–151, 153–155
Taawy, 105, 150

Two Lands, 105, 118, 150, 222–223
tabernacle, 49
Tadzhikastan, Khirghizistan*****
Tambora, 107
Tantalus, 146
Tarwy (Taawy)*****
Mizraim, 105, 118
Tauri (Crimea)*****
Tel–el–Ajjul, 84
Thaneni, 117
The Bitter Lakes, 47
The Bronze Age in Barbarian Europe, 190, 233
The Coming of the Age of Iron, 232
The Phoenician Women, 129, 143, 161
The Two Lands, 150, 222–223
Thebai, 130
Theban dramas, 137, 142, 156–157
Egyptian history, 13, 18, 29, 82, 105, 156, 158, 193, 202
Theban god, 24
Thebe (nymph)*****
Thebes, 0, 25, 29, 65, 79, 86, 94, 99–100, 103, 128–135, 137, 139–141, 143–146, 148, 158, 163, 168
  Akhet–Aten, 25, 100, 102, 144–145, 168, 220
  Amon, 24–25, 86, 94, 99, 103, 132, 134–135, 140, 142, 144
  burned, 13, 57, 65, 155
  Epigoni, 145, 147, 158
  Hellenistic name, 25
  No Amon, 25, 99, 132, 134–135
  No in Nahum 3:8, 25
  Nut Amen, 25
  Spartoi or "sown men", 130
  Thebes (Greek)*****

Kadmos, 128–131, 143, 145–146, 148
Thebes in Egypt, 131
Greek Thebes, 129–132, 134, 137, 143–145, 148
Nahum 3:8, 25, 134
No–Amon, 131
T-'pe, or T–Apit, 134
Thebes of Greece*****
Thera, 29, 79–81, 83, 107, 154, 193
Aryan invasion, 81–84, 107, 163, 193
Calisto, 154
Hyksos invasion, 83
Thera (Santorini)*****
"flood" of Noah?, 80
Thoth, 38, 148, 156
Tien Shan (Tyan Shan)*****
Tigris, 36, 78, 82, 109, 146, 232
Timna, 40
Hathor, 40, 47, 151, 153, 184, 218
Midian, 0, 40, 42, 47, 53, 58, 69
north of modern Eilat–Aqaba, 40
  tin, 0, 6, 68, 90, 106–110, 114, 119–122, 128, 147, 157–161, 163–164, 167–189, 191–195, 199, 201, 203–211, 213, 215, 219–220, 232
Kyrgyzstan, 176
Aryan invasion, 81–84, 107, 163, 193
Babylonian kassitira, 171
Bukhara, 176
dm, 106–109, 171–172, 183, 185, 192, 219
Egyptian word, dm, 171
Greek kassiteros, 171
Indo–European word, 171
kastira, 120, 171

Mitanni, 82–86, 93–94, 97, 100–101, 105–106, 108–110, 114, 120–121, 128, 133, 138, 144, 146–147, 151, 155, 159–160, 168, 176–177, 183, 192–194, 220

New Kingdom Egypt, 49, 89, 105, 112, 116–117, 122, 131, 159, 167, 176, 190–191, 200

petroleum, 109, 120, 167, 169, 171, 173, 175, 177, 179, 181, 183, 185, 187, 189, 191, 193

Shang, 5, 73, 107, 176, 207, 210

Thailand, 176

Tien Shan, 106–109, 122, 168, 176, 182, 192

tin–bronze age, 109, 120, 167, 171, 173, 176–177, 187, 190–191, 193

  vital to bronze–age, 68

  tin ingots, 106, 167, 179

  tin ore, 0, 106, 109, 122, 163–164, 167–168, 170–171, 174, 179, 182–184, 186, 188, 191, 193, 205

tin–bronze age, 109, 120, 167, 171, 173, 176–177, 187, 190–191, 193

Hyksos, 13, 25–32, 35, 48, 54–55, 76, 79, 83–84, 86, 88–89, 94, 96, 99, 104–105, 108, 111, 116–118, 120–121, 128, 130, 135, 143, 145, 148, 150–154, 167, 231

Late Bronze Age, 0, 22, 26, 78, 82, 106, 108–109, 119, 121–122, 129, 133, 155, 167, 169, 171–175, 177–183, 185, 187–191, 193, 202, 205, 209–210

tin–trade, 159, 171

Troy, 4, 21, 62, 65, 105, 128, 132–134, 145, 147–148, 157–159, 192, 194

Tiryns, 21, 65, 68

Cyclopes, 68

Tiya, 31, 42, 87, 95–99, 101, 133, 137, 139, 142, 144, 222

Akhnaten, 0, 24–25, 31, 74, 87, 99–102, 123–124, 133, 137, 139–144, 146–147, 159–161, 168, 193, 200, 202, 220–223

Amenhotep III, 0, 31, 42, 87, 94–98, 110, 121, 123, 133, 137–140, 142, 144, 147

Amenhotep IV, 0, 24, 31, 87, 96–98, 124, 132, 137

Joseph, 31, 35, 42, 86–87, 93, 95–97, 99, 101, 103, 105, 107, 109–113, 115, 117, 119–121, 133, 135–137, 141–143, 159, 161

pharaoh's "house" (meaning wife)*****

Yuya, 31, 42, 86–87, 94–99, 105, 110–112, 120, 133, 135–137, 142–144, 161

Tjeku, 47

Tjeku, 47

Tokugawa*****

bakufu, 64

Torah, 39, 56, 231

English translation, 56

Trojan War, 0, 20–21, 65–67, 145, 147, 157–158, 220

pestilence, 65

sixty to seventy years before Jericho?*****

Troy, 4, 21, 62, 65, 105, 128, 132–134, 145, 147–148, 157–159, 192, 194

fall of, 1194 BC*****

fall of, June 5, 1209 BC*****

mysterious "plague", 62

strategic tin–trade strangle hold, 159

tsara 'at, 55, 57

described, 35, 41, 43, 45, 57, 131

Leviticus, 54–57

like smallpox, 57, 74, 76

mysterious malignant skin disease, 55

Tsara–at's progress, 57

Tumulus Culture, 5, 172, 190–191

Urnfielders to become the Celts*****

Turkey, 61, 146

Tutankhamon, 24, 101, 140, 142–143, 206
Kheperu Neb–Re, 143
Tutankhaten, 101, 142
Tuthmosis, 0, 31, 38–39, 84–87, 94, 96, 109–110, 117, 133, 135, 144, 147–148, 160
created by the god Thoth, 38
Moses, 4, 12, 20, 24–25, 35–42, 44, 46–61, 66, 76, 112–113, 118, 130, 135, 137, 161, 200–202, 204, 221
name, 10, 24–25, 27–29, 31, 35, 38–39, 42, 48–49, 62, 64–65, 82–83, 86–87, 94–97, 99–101, 103–104, 107–110, 114–118, 120–121, 127–128, 130–132, 134, 136–137, 139–142, 145–146, 149–152, 155, 157–158, 160, 170, 181–183, 185–186, 192, 196, 213, 218–222
Tuthmosis I, 84
Tuthmosis III, 84–85, 94, 117
battle, 18–19, 21, 47, 66, 84–85, 93, 103, 131, 148, 156–159, 192, 194
Hatshepsut, 86, 93, 96, 212
Rameses II, 0, 5, 18–20, 31–32, 85, 88, 103, 134, 148, 150, 155–159, 196
war, 0, 3, 12, 18–21, 58, 65–67, 74, 76, 83, 85, 93–94, 112–113, 116–117, 130–134, 144–145, 147, 156–158, 168, 174, 194, 203, 205, 218, 220
Tuthmosis IV, 31, 86–87, 94, 96, 109–110, 133, 135, 144, 147, 160
Mutemwiya, 87, 94, 115, 133, 144, 160
Yuya (Joseph?)*****
Two Lands, 105, 118, 150, 222–223
Tyre, 129, 132, 149
Ugarit, 65, 74, 128–129, 132, 155, 177
Ugarit (Ekeret)*****
burned, 13, 57, 65, 155
Ulysses, 21, 177
unparalleled, 3–5, 7, 9, 11, 13, 107, 147

catastropheUr*****
Urnfield Culture, 5, 190–192
Uzbekistan, 82, 106
Vancouver's Expo '86, 40
variola, 0, 9, 11, 22, 74–75, 188, 215, 231
variola virus, 11, 22, 74–75, 188, 215
active on clothing, 22
breath or a sneeze, 22
Velikovsky, 137, 140–141, 232
Oedipus and Akhnaton, 137, 232
Velikovsky, Immanuel*****
vizier, 30
Wadi Amarah, 47
Marah, 47
Wadi Gharandel, 47
Elim, 47
Warren Commission, 23
Washukani*****
Wertime, Theodore A.5*****
West Bank, 61
Westerman, Claus*****
Genesis 12–36, Commentary*****
Wilderness of Etham, 47
Suez Canal, 47
Wilderness of Paran, 54
Wilderness of Zin, 54
Williams, Matthew*****
Wood, Michael*****
"Parian Chronicle Marble", 20
World Archeology, 171, 232
Eaton and McKerrell article in*****
Worlds in Collision, 137

Yuya, 31, 42, 86–87, 94–99, 105, 110–112, 120, 133, 135–137, 142–144, 161

Amenhotep III, 0, 31, 42, 87, 94–98, 110, 121, 123, 133, 137–140, 142, 144, 147

Egyptian prime minister, 95, 133, 136, 143, 149

family of Akhmim, 105

Hyksos ancestors?*****

Joseph, 31, 35, 42, 86–87, 93, 95–97, 99, 101, 103, 105, 107, 109–113, 115, 117, 119–121, 133, 135–137, 141–143, 159, 161

Meritaten, 141–143

Tiya, 31, 42, 87, 95–99, 101, 133, 137, 139, 142, 144, 222

Tuthmosis IV, 31, 86–87, 94, 96, 109–110, 133, 135, 144, 147, 160

Zethos, 134

Zeus, 131, 151, 153, 221

zinc, 183–184

Zipporah, 40–41

cowpox, 40–41, 50, 214

"Caucasian" mummies, 122

"neo–Hyksos", 89, 93, 95–99, 101–103, 105, 107, 109, 111, 113, 115, 117, 119, 121, 133, 142–145, 147, 154–155

Theban saga, 145–146

"neo–Hyksos", 89, 93, 95–99, 101–103, 105, 107, 109, 111, 113, 115, 117, 119, 121, 133, 142–145, 147, 154–155

Phoenician Women, The*****

"re", 7, 9, 24–25, 27, 38, 48, 55, 66, 68, 77, 82, 86–87, 89, 100, 102–103, 116, 136, 140, 147, 153, 161, 171, 173–174, 178, 180, 189, 204, 206, 213, 219, 222–223, 231

means "mouth" in Egyptian*****

"The Dark Ages,", 8, 67, 89, 94, 127, 129, 131, 133, 135, 137, 139, 141, 143, 145, 147, 149, 151, 153, 155, 157, 159, 161

The Archeology of Greece"The Five Ages"*****

CPSIA information can be obtained at www.ICGtesting.com
Printed in the USA
LVOW050050250812

295891LV00003B/87/A